SPACE FOR DANCE

An Architectural Design Guide
by Leslie Armstrong, A.I.A.
and
Roger Morgan

Edited by Mike Lipske

1984

AUTHORS' ACKNOWLEDGMENTS

The authors wish to acknowledge with thanks Rhoda Grauer and Ellen Pierce, the former director and assistant director, respectively, of the Dance Program at the National Endowment for the Arts, for initiating the project; David White of Dance Theatre Workshop, for introducing us to the Endowment; Alan Buchsbaum and Stephen Tilly of Design Coalition, Jonathan Butler, James Rogers and Charles Baskett of Butler Rogers Baskett, for their support, and lighting designer Beverly Emmons, for her counsel during the preparation of the book; and finally Charles Zucker, the project director, and Marcia Sartwell, the project editor, for seeing us through from beginning to end.

This book was commissioned by the Design Arts Program and the Dance Program of the National Endowment for the Arts.

Francis S. M. Hodsoll, Chairman
National Endowment for the Arts

Michael Pittas, Director
Design Arts Program

Nigel Redden, Director
Dance Program

Project Director: Charles Zucker
    Assistant Director, Design Arts Program

Editorial Director: Marcia Sartwell

Designer: Anthony Russell

Illustrators: Viorel Popescu
            Gill Anderson

Editorial Assistants: David Richardson
                       Martin Vinik
                       Tibor Kerekes

Design Assistants: Mark Ulrich
                   Christopher Burg

Research Assistants: Gina Barnett
                      C. M. Priester

Copyright © 1984 by the Publishing Center for Cultural Resources.
All rights reserved.

Library of Congress
Cataloging in Publication Data

Armstrong, Leslie, 1940-
  Space for dance.

  Bibliography: p.
  Includes index.
  1. Theaters — United States — Construction. 2. Dancing — Stage-setting and scenery. I. Morgan, Roger, 1938- II. Lipske, Mike. III. Title.
NA6830.A85 1984   725'.822   84-4919

CONTENTS

1 Chapter One 8
Dancers and Dance Places
A quick look at the interdependence of space and dance, and at various theatre forms and sizes.

2 Chapter Two 14
Planning and Building
How — and by whom — a dance theatre is designed and built; guidelines for renovating alternate spaces.

3 Chapter Three 28
On Stage
Design criteria for stages of fully equipped proscenium theatres and for smaller alternate spaces.

4 Chapter Four 48
Spaces for the Public
Design criteria for audience spaces, from the entrance, through the lobby, and into the house.

5 Chapter Five 58
Backstage Spaces for Performers
Requirements for dressing rooms, toilets and showers, rehearsal spaces, and other backstage areas.

Chapter Six 72
Support Spaces for Crew and Staff
Criteria for an efficient backstage area, with spaces for theatre technicians, crew, and administrators.

6

Chapter Seven 84
Technical Equipment
Stage-rigging, lighting, and sound systems in proscenium theatres and alternate spaces.

7

8

Chapter Eight 100
Case Studies: Proscenium Theatres
From Salt Lake City to Syracuse, a look at seven theatres of various styles that meet the needs of dance.

Chapter Nine 138
Case Studies: Alternate Spaces
"Found" spaces for dance, from a So Ho sweatshop to a Mission district warehouse.

9

Appendix A 150
Critical Facts on Proscenium Theatres
Detailed information on design and construction, on lighting and sound systems, and on backstage areas.

Appendix B 160
Barrier-Free Access to Dance
Access, with dignity, from the parking lot to backstage.

Appendix C 166
A Planning Workbook
How to take stock of resources, plan a feasibility study, and organize a building program.

Glossary 172

Bibliography 182

Index 186

Photo Credits 191

Dance has come of age in America. The superstardom of Rudolph Nureyev and Mikhail Baryshnikov, the television broadcasts of live performances, the development of college and university circuits for touring companies—all attest that dance is no longer the preserve of the cognoscenti. So do the numbers: According to a Louis Harris poll, thirty-eight million Americans watched at least one live dance performance in 1980.

But if the house that dance draws has grown, the number of good homes for dance lags behind. While America's large opera houses work well for dance, usually only the biggest companies can afford to play them. For the most part, dancers perform in spaces designed for musicians, actors, or even basketball players, and endure the cramped, rock-hard stages of concert halls and movie palaces, or high-school and college auditoriums and gymnasiums.

Good performance spaces for dance are scarce because, until recently, they were thought unnecessary. A generation ago, a "dance buff" was considered an elitist. Not many Americans cared to be so characterized, or cared for the art form in question. Since dance had such a small audience, many performing arts facilities were planned and built with little consideration for its needs, because dance companies were not perceived as major potential users of those spaces. Further, information on the requirements of dance—and how to fulfill them—could not be found in most design guides or technical tracts on the performing arts.

Space for Dance has been written to redress this lack of information. What builders need, and what has so often been lacking when theatres are constructed, are persons able to define the art of dance and its needs for architects, and designers able to translate those requirements into buildings that work for performers and patrons.

Toward this end, the authors have conducted dozens of interviews with dancers, choreographers, company managers, theatre consultants, lighting designers, acousticians, musicians, critics, architects, planners, and performing-arts facility directors. From these interviews have come guidelines for matters as broad as deciding whether to renovate an old theatre or build a new one, and as specific as the location of electrical outlets for sound systems.

Space for Dance speaks to two groups of readers. For dancers, choreographers, and company managers who hope to build their own space for dance, or who will help guide their cities or towns in the construction of theatres suitable for dance, it offers a manual of design and building processes. For other prospective builders of dance spaces—local governments, community groups, or individual sponsors, and their planners and architects—it offers an introduction to the world of dance, with suggestions on how the demands of dance can best be realized in bricks and mortar.

Space for Dance aims high. Sponsored by the Design Arts and Dance Programs of the National Endowment for the Arts, jointly researched and written by an architect and a theatre-design consultant, the book is meant to narrow the gap between our growing national demand for dance performances and the inadequate number of dance performance spaces. But the book is also a plea—that all those new, renovated, or restored theatres qualify as genuinely superb spaces for dance. That premise—that America can build not just more dance theatres but can build great ones—is the challenge implicit in this book.

Michael J. Pittas, Director
Design Arts Program
February 1984

DANCERS AND DANCE PLACES

1

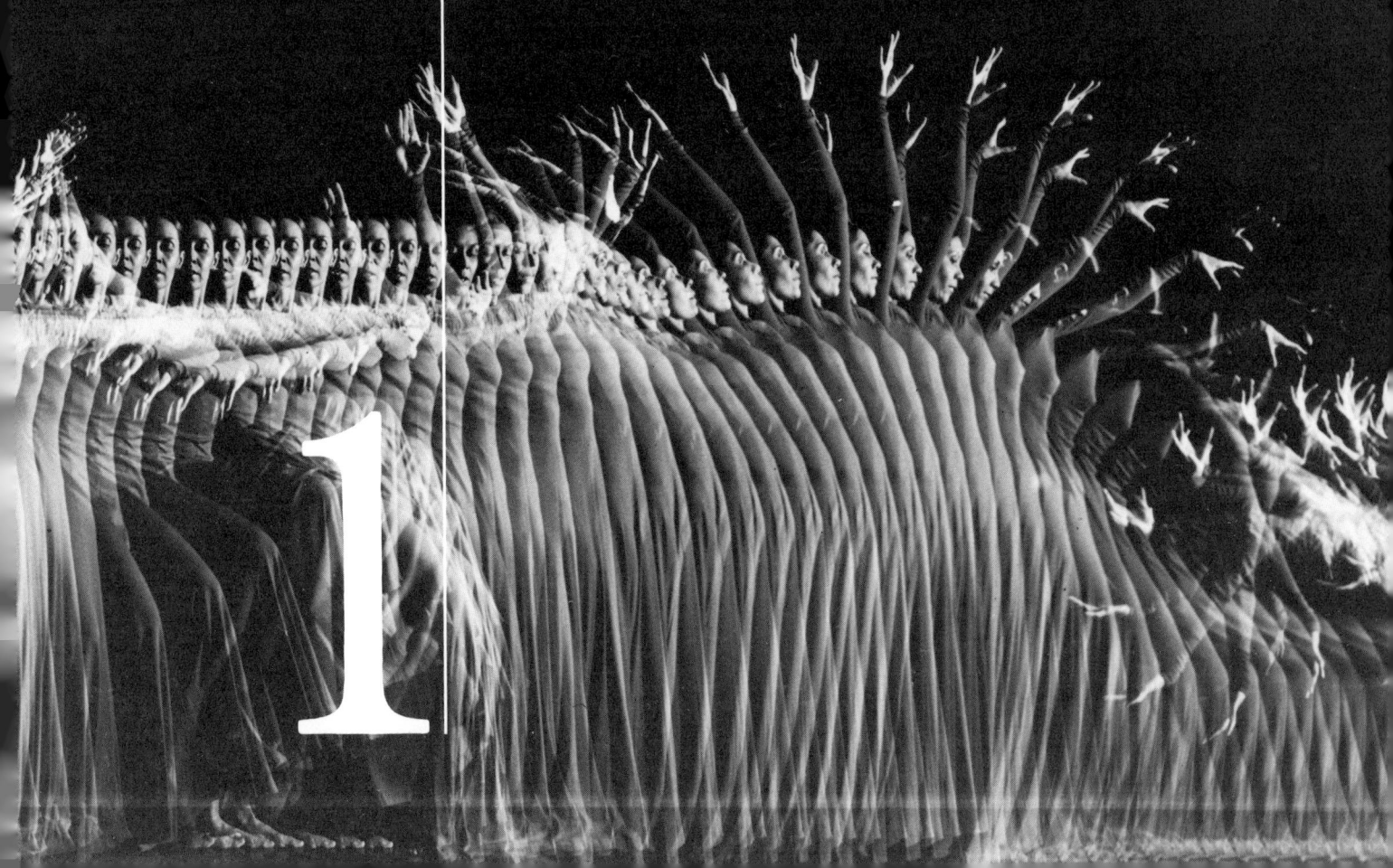

"Space," said choreographer George Balanchine, "is everything." A symphony can be enjoyed live or on record, a play can be seen or read, but dance emerges through the single medium of space. Without space, dance does not exist.

The human body brings space to life and dance into being. And the choreographic placement of dancers' bodies describes the volume within which dance is performed. Choreography itself consists of a changing series of images built upon combinations of the human body. For that reason, the empty space between dancers is as critical as the space each occupies. Because the body—choreography's building block—is almost uniform in size, nearly all choreographers want basically the same size performing area, even if their expressive styles are as different as toe shoes and sneakers. Compressing or expanding dancers' spacing alters the pictures imagined by the choreographer, and thus the dance itself.

Sufficient space, consistently sized, is so critical that many companies establish minimum standards for stages where they will perform, and refuse bookings when the performance area is inadequate.

Dance may be performed by a solo artist or a troupe of one hundred. It may be accompanied by music—live or recorded—or presented in silence. The dancers may wear tutus or blue jeans. There are dance traditions but no dance laws. Nor is there a single ready-made pattern for the theatre that will fit every dance company. Yet, fortunately for theatre planners and builders, virtually all dance companies—small or large, post-modern or classical—demand the same things of the space they work in:

1. Dancers need a large, open performance area. Many dance companies cite a performing area 45 feet wide by 40 feet deep by 16 feet high as a minimum. Beyond the basic stage seen by the audience, dancers require space to enter, to exit, and to circulate. In tighter quarters, companies are hard-pressed to perform works as originally choreographed and rehearsed.

2. Dancers require a multilayered, "sprung" stage floor, to prevent damage to their feet, legs, and hips. The floor must also have a smooth, nonslip surface.

3. The dancers' work space must be draft-free and kept at a constant temperature between seventy-five and eighty degrees Fahrenheit. If the air temperature falls, overheated dancers may develop muscle cramps and spasms.

4. In performance, a dance company needs good stage lighting and masking, proper acoustics, and—in the absence of musicians—a top-notch sound system.

5. Backstage design is nearly as important to dancers as the planning that goes into the performance area. From morning class or technical rehearsal to the end of the evening performance, dancers spend more hours in the theatre than do actors, musicians, or singers. Thus, they make greater demands on dressing rooms, restrooms, and other backstage support spaces.

Before describing how these demands can be met in the variety of theatre forms used by dance companies, it is useful to take a closer look at those theatre forms and at how they affect dance.

THEATRE FORMS

Although there is no one correct style of theatre for dance, the most commonly used forms are proscenium and end-stage theatres. In the proscenium theatre, the audience sits on one side of a raised performing area, viewing the dancers from a single vantage point. The proscenium arch frames the stage, separating spectators

> "Dance, a faculty of motion, feeds on space.... Dancers move essentially on the stage floor, but the audience is far less aware of the floor than of the comparatively large space in height, mostly in back of the stage and to the left and right of it, against which the movement is visually inscribed.... The stage space, when left without movement, is essentially perceived by the audience in two dimensions. It is the movement of the dancers that reveals to them the presence of the third dimension."
> Rouben Ter Arutunian, scenic designer
> *In Search of Design*

Opposite: Dancer Carmen De Lavalade. Choreography consists of a changing series of images built upon combinations of the human body.

Choreography's basic building block: the dimensions of the dancer's body.

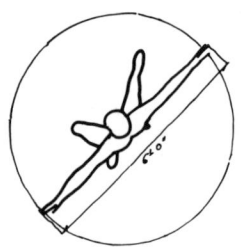

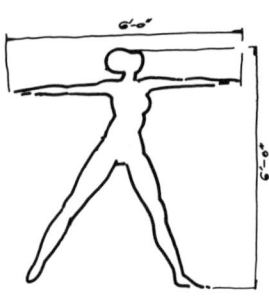

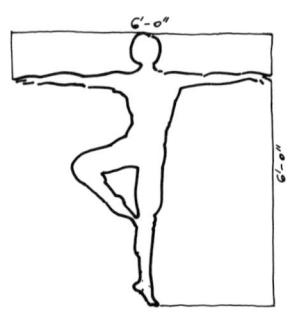

The choreographic placement of the dancers' bodies defines the space within which dance is performed.

physically and psychologically from performers. Above the stage is a stagehouse, where stage lighting and scenery hang out of view of the audience.

Spectators in a theatre with an end stage also sit opposite a raised platform, but there is no stagehouse to conceal technical equipment. Nor is there a proscenium arch to frame the stage: dancers and audience occupy the same volume, and the atmosphere is more intimate.

Each format, proscenium or end stage, allows the choreographer maximum control over what the audience sees. Proscenium and end stages are also popular because they are prevalent. To find new audiences for their work, most dance companies tour, if not nationally then regionally. Thus, much of the company repertoire will have been created to fit the proscenium and end stages usually awaiting dancers on the road.

In a theatre with a thrust stage, the audience sits on stepped risers around three sides of a raised platform. As with end stages, lights and other equipment are in full view, and performers and spectators share the same space. However, most thrust stages do not work well with dance. The performance area is usually small, and access to the stage is limited by the audience's presence on three sides. At some thrust theatres, performers can approach the front of the stage through tunnels or "vomitories" that run beneath the steeply sloped audience area. Those tunnels, narrow and with scant headroom, slow down dancers who must move quickly to and from the stage or from one side to the other. An arena stage, entirely surrounded by the audience, offers even fewer points of access than a thrust stage.

Both stage styles complicate choreography. When spectators watch from three sides of a thrust stage or surround an arena, the choreographer must consider how the dancers look from many angles and cannot present the single powerful image allowed by a proscenium or end stage with its one vantage point.

Another theatre form is the alternate, or "found" space. These theatres often consist of one large room, a "loft" space, in which a company will rehearse, hold classes, choreograph, and present their work to the public. Seating is often on cushions, folding chairs, or the floor. Many of these alternate spaces are carved out of old warehouses or constructed in renovated school buildings, churches, or community rooms. They offer space, lower rent, and limited seating for interested audiences.

THEATRE SIZES

The number of seats in a dance theatre does not determine the size of the performing area. But seating capacity—thus potential audience size—does alter the sense of space in and around dance. A three-thousand-seat theatre offers a different ambiance from one that seats three hundred persons. That difference in atmosphere affects performers and their audience.

Most of America's older opera houses, as well as performing-arts civic centers built in the 1960s and 1970s, seat from fifteen hundred to thirty-five hundred patrons. Few of these large theatres were designed specifically for dance. But they usually have ample stage space and—in the case of older theatres—may possess twice the charm of more modern, better-equipped houses.

Some dance authorities say theatres seating more than five hundred persons have a negative effect on expressivity, and that the idiom of certain companies has changed when they began touring in very large houses. Fearing that subtlety cannot be read from the back rows, dancers may exaggerate their movements. However, only a handful of dance companies can even afford to tour the large and extra-large proscenium theatre circuit. American Ballet Theatre, the Joffrey Ballet, and others design their work for these spaces. But because these companies need large audiences to defray massive production and touring costs, they are also often locked into playing just the super theatres.

For many dance companies, big has never been best, and a medium-size theatre with five hundred to a thousand seats, or an even smaller space with fewer seats and with exposed lights and rigging, may be chosen over a huge proscenium theatre with full stagehouse.

A dance company that is well-regarded but that lacks the following of, say, the Joffrey Ballet is more likely to sell all the seats if it performs in a medium-size theatre. However, while medium-size theatres were built, and still stand, in almost every American city, few at present are suitable for dance. Although many of these old vaudeville houses have been renovated and are being used by performing artists, most of the renovators failed to consider the needs of dance; they thus barred the door on otherwise fine theatres for dancers.

Some choreographers prefer creating works for small or alternate spaces. Merce Cunningham is one such innovator in nonproscenium choreography, and his concepts have shaped much of today's modern and post-modern dance. Carolyn Brown, former dean of dance at the State University of New York's Purchase campus, danced with Cunningham for twenty-two years. She believes "a choreographer will create for proscenium only if there is nothing else to create for," and says that if more nontraditional spaces were available, choreographers would make more dances to fit them.

On the other hand, says lighting designer Beverly Emmons, "the more unique a space, the more unique the work will have to be that's made for it." Emmons feels that dealing with nontraditional space can be complicated and that the artist may need more time, thus more money, to create for that space.

Whether nontraditional spaces make choreography more complicated or simply more challenging—or both—many dancers, choreographers, and dance companies cherish these spaces. And alternate spaces nurture and produce much of America's best new choreography. Thus, while *Space for Dance* focuses on larger, more traditional theatres for which precise guidelines can be drawn up, the book also offers general, flexible guidelines for planning, building, and equipping smaller theatres. The ingenuity required by these spaces cannot be prescribed, and the exact specifications for renovating a particular loft, factory, or other "found" space must be developed by the dance company and architect designing the alternate space.

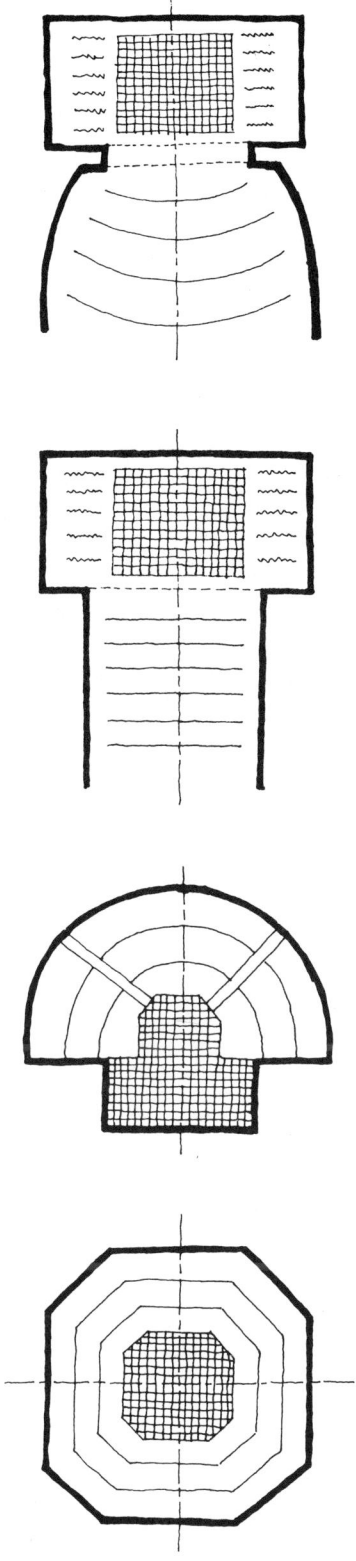

Basic Theatre Forms
Proscenium
End stage
Thrust or apron
Arena

Performance spaces reflect the diversity of dance in the twentieth century: At the New York State Theatre in Lincoln Center, above, the New York City Ballet produces Coppelia; the Dance Theatre of Harlem, far left, performs in New York's Solomon R. Guggenheim Museum; and at the Jacob's Pillow Dance Festival, left, students dance against a backdrop of the Massachusetts woods.

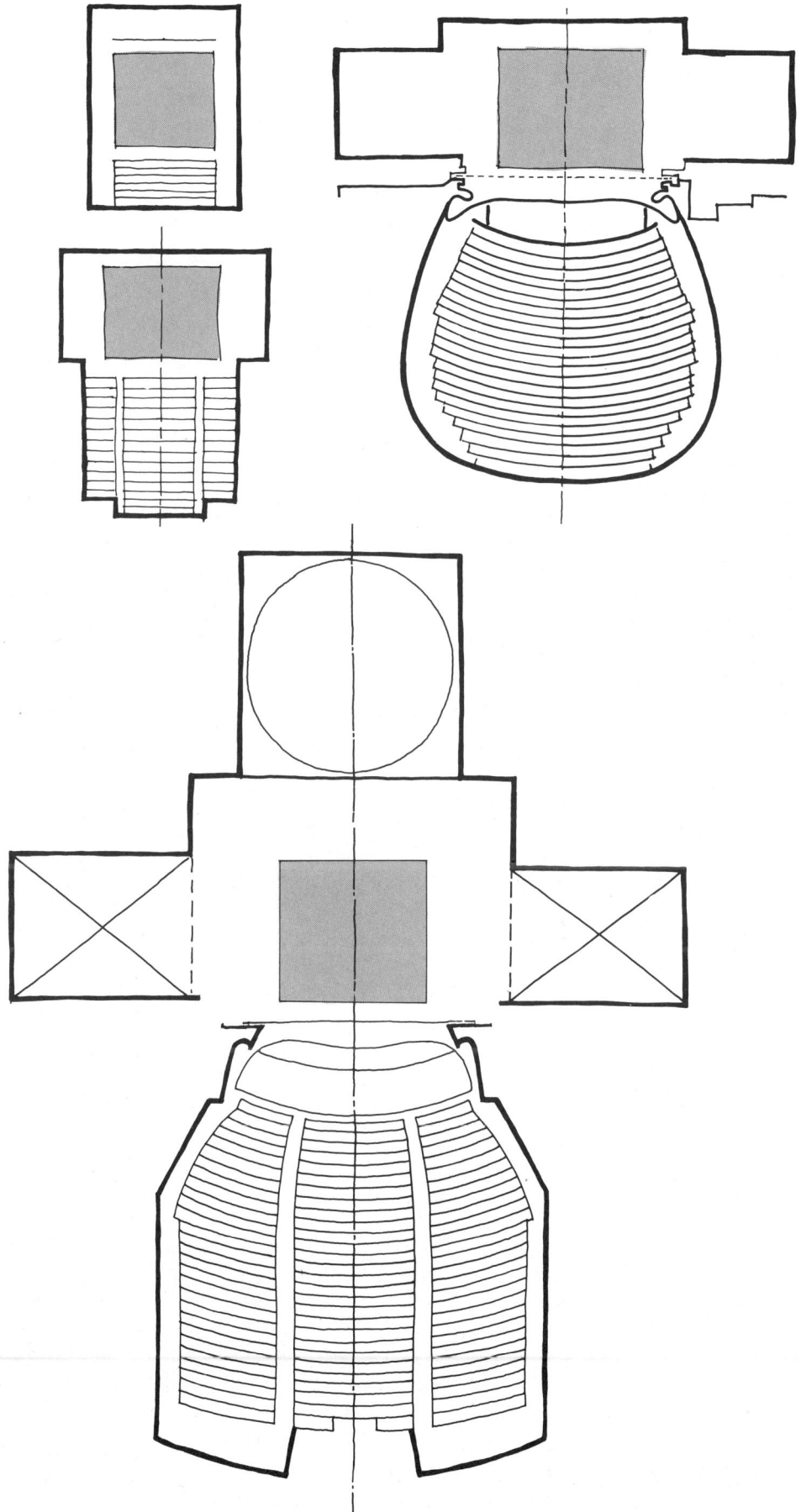

The sizes, seating capacities and overall ambiance of these four New York City theatres differ greatly, as do the companies who play them, yet the dimensions of the performing areas are virtually identical.

Bessie Schonberg Theatre
Home of Dance Theatre Workshop
Capacity: ± 150

Joyce Theater
Home of the Feld Ballet
Capacity: 474

New York State Theatre
Home of the New York State City Ballet
Capacity: 2,729

Metropolitan Opera House
Home of the American Ballet Theatre
Capacity: 3,788

PLANNING AND BUILDING

2

"A good dance theatre is just a good theatre with special attention to the stage-floor construction—and a good laundry," says Joseph Golden, executive director of the highly regarded Civic Center of Onondaga County in Syracuse, New York.

Dance houses are no more complicated or expensive to build than other theatres. In fact, theatres designed solely for dance can be less complex and costly because the emphasis is on unobstructed space rather than stagecraft. In this chapter, the general steps in planning, designing, and building a dance theatre are outlined, and the jobs of the experts are discussed.

DEFINING THE CLIENT

The choreographer, producer, government official, or arts patron considering the need for a new space for dance seldom works alone. In theatre-building projects, "the client" tends to be an assemblage of like-minded souls organized into a building committee. Often this collective client serves two masters.

First, the client is the authorized representative of the people and organizations that will eventually pay to build the theatre. Second, the client speaks for the group, or groups, that will use the space. Even when a dance company builds its own home, separate arms of the organization are likely to fulfill distinct client roles. Dance requirements, however, will be defined by the choreographer or artistic director, working with management, as part of the client committee.

(For a checklist of questions that will help a building committee define its overall purpose, see Appendix C, "Take Stock of What You've Got.")

THE PLANNING/FEASIBILITY STUDY

Early in the planning process the client calls in consultants to help determine the feasibility of his ideas. The first and most important consultant to be retained by the client is either an arts-planning expert or a theatre-design expert with skill in planning and designing for dance. In the early stages of planning a large, multipurpose facility, both are essential. For less complicated, single-use facilities, the skills of a theatre-design consultant may be enough. In either case, the consultant must understand more than just the physical and technical requirements of dance. He must also be an expert in facilities management, including such fundamentals as building-maintenance and theatre-production costs. The theatre-design consultant ensures that the plans developed by the architect serve the needs of performing artists and their audiences. The architect (who is next to be selected and whose qualifications are discussed later in this chapter), with the help of structural and mechanical engineers, shapes those needs into a cohesive statement of space, form, texture, and light.

Another helpful expert, important during early planning is the cost consultant. Working from preliminary sketches and gross square-foot requirements, the cost consultant makes rough construction cost estimates, or "take-offs."

Of major importance in considering project feasibility is the selection of a site for new construction or of a building for renovation.

"The theatre is an event for the people who go," says William Hammond, executive director of the Alvin Ailey American Dance Theater. "The more you make that event easy and accessible, the more they are going to want to go."

While the artists appearing on stage are a theatre's biggest drawing card, the attractiveness and location of the house can also determine its success or failure as a

Aaron Davis Hall
City College of the City of New York
Completed in 1979
Seating capacity of Theatre A: 750
Seating capacity of Theatre B: ± 300
Principal users:
Leonard Davis Center for the Performing Arts
Principals of the design team:
Architect: Abraham Geller and Associates
Theatre design consultant: Jean Rosenthal and Associates

Above: Lobby
Theatre A

Opposite: Aaron Davis Hall at night.

New York State Theatre prior to the redesign of the proscenium.

business. Choosing the best site—whether for a new theatre or a renovated one—is critically important.

"Funkiness," says dancer and dance consultant Elizabeth Martin, "has panache for large numbers of people only in sophisticated cities." At regional theatres, she says, "proximity to shopping complexes, restaurants, and galleries, plus safe public transportation and plentiful parking, can radically affect audience development." Martin further advises that "if teaching goes on in the same facility as performance—not an unusual way for a resident dance company to sustain itself and its facility—it must be safe and accessible for daytime classes for children and for evening classes of young men and women."

Dancers' needs must also be considered during site selection. Convenient shops and restaurants, and perhaps a nearby park, offer a respite from their backstage cloister. A clause from the basic contract of the American Guild of Musical Artists, the dancers' union, formally acknowledges that dancers merit more from life than sprung floors:

> AGMA (e) **Transportation to Places of Performance or Rehearsal**
> The employer agrees that in the event that the artist while on tour only shall be required to perform or rehearse in any town at a place further than one half (1/2) mile from a central point near which the majority of the artists shall be quartered (to be mutually agreed upon by the artists and the employer), then bus or similar transportation to and from such place shall be provided for all artists by the employer at its own expense. If the artist is scheduled for rehearsal outside the theatre of performance, the employer will grant the artist sufficient time to allow the artist travel time to reach the theatre of performance in addition to the time requirements of subparagraph 22(f). In the event of inclement weather, or if the route between the hotel and the theatre is deemed to be unsafe, after consultation between the AGMA representative and the employer, a bus shall be available to artists one half (1/2) hour after curtain time to provide transportation to the hotel. Similarly, if there are no eating accommodations available, the employer shall make provision to transport the artists to a restaurant.

Renovating an existing structure, rather than building from the ground up, can stretch the theatre-construction budget. (Renovation or rehabilitation can also be a tonic for a neighborhood drifting toward decrepitude.) Even when a full-blown renovation will cost as much as a new theatre, the end product may possess those two attributes so often absent from contemporary buildings—quality and charm. As one critic of dance, and of dance spaces, says, "A revamped movie house is far superior to an economical tin shack. Revamped theatres in all stages of workability and completion are more congenial. You can forgive their shortcomings."

However, before embarking on a renovation project, cast a cold eye on the object of your affection. Be sure local zoning regulations and building codes will permit a theatre on the site, and carefully evaluate the building's exterior condition (including front and rear facades, roof, windows, fire escapes, and nearby sidewalks, sideyards, and alleys), interior condition (including column spacing, potential stage size, floor-to-floor heights, passenger and freight lifts, and construction of floors, walls, ceilings, and fire stairs), and mechanical systems (heating-and-cooling, electrical, and plumbing equipment, and sprinklers and other emergency systems).

(For a step-by-step summary of the process, see Appendix C, "The Three Components of a Feasibility Study.")

THE BUILDING PROGRAM

In architecture and theatre planning, the building program is a statement of the client's needs and intentions, usually presented as a list of the spaces to be included in a facility, and their functions, sizes, and relationships to each other. A detailed building program also includes technical equipment and furnishings that will go in each space.

A building program can be prepared by an architect, a theatre-design consultant, or a specialized building-program consultant. In any case, the consultant begins to develop a dance company's building program by interviewing the artistic director and the manager, or by preparing a questionnaire that they can answer. (Several of the performing arts references cited in the Bibliography include sample questionnaires). Generally, the artistic director is most concerned with performance and rehearsal spaces. Thus, when crafting a building program, the consultant should also interview the technical director and production manager, for they know best how the company's dancers and technicians use other theatre spaces. The consultant should interview dancers, as well as set, costume, and lighting designers.

If the client is not a dance organization, or if a collective client does not include a dance group, the design consultant must take special care when drafting the building program. Almost invariably, when the needs of dance are not accommodated early, the resulting theatre can prove barely adequate or entirely unsuitable for dance performances.

In general, a performing-arts facility's building program must identify the specific needs for:
- the stage
- support spaces for performers
- spaces for the audience
- support spaces for technicians, crew, and artistic and administrative staff.

While developing a program for these four areas, the client should keep certain points in mind. The first is a matter of attitude: go for the best. As any theatre builder reviews cost estimates, the temptation arises to scale down plans here and there. But begin with too many compromises, and one ends with a theatre that serves no purpose well.

At the same time, the client must carefully consider the costs of operating and maintaining the performing-arts facility. Maintenance, and its price, can be affected by the client's choices of interior and exterior finishes, by the locations of entrances, and by the plans for moving materials and people through the theatre.

Equal thought should go into the design of heating-ventilating-cooling systems and to the cost of operating them. In any new building, the cost of buying and installing mechanical systems (which also include plumbing, electrical, and safety equipment) can account for thirty-five to forty-five percent of the total construction expense. In a new performing arts facility, those mechanical costs may climb even higher.

The client should also become familiar with applicable building codes. Theatres generally fall under the heading of "places of assembly." The codes specify requirements for public places, such as:
- allowable building materials and finishes, based on their ability to retard fire
- permissible seating configurations, including distances between seats and rows
- minimum dimensions for aisles and cross-aisles
- number and size of exits
- minimum dimensions for exit corridors, stairs, lobbies, and exit lights and signs
- emergency lighting and power systems

Building codes may also specify design rules for backstage areas and lighting and control booths, and may include criteria for access by handicapped persons. (For guidelines on rendering theatres barrier-free, see Appendix C.)

Finally, the client should consider plans for future expansion to include spaces and equipment that might have to be sacrificed to honor the current construction budget.

While the building program is in process, the client, theatre-design consultant,

Zellerbach Hall
University of California at Berkeley
Completed in 1968
Seating capacity of the auditorium: 2,015
Seating capacity of the playhouse: 500 to 700
Principal users:
Auditorium: Committee for Arts Lecturers
Playhouse: Department of Dramatic Arts
Principals of the design team:
Architects: Vernon DeMars and Donald Hardison
Theatre design consultants: Paul Landry, Ben Schlanger

Main facade

PROGRAM AND SQUARE FOOTAGE ANALYSIS

Space Name	Sq. Footage Suggested 19 Sept 75	Sq. Footage	Remarks
Front of House			
Box Office	100	100	located at street level
Outer Lobby	—	A.R.	
Lobby	A.R.	A.R.	not incl. corridors of galleries = 2985 sq.ft.
Coat Room	250	110	
Public WC's reg. for handicapped & for children	A.R. " "	A.R. " "	
Custodian	20	25	
Lounges, phones	A.R.	A.R.	
Bar/Concessions	"	"	can be part of inner and outer lobbies
Program/Concession Storage	"	"	
House Manager's office	100	60	
Theatre			
Orchestra Seating	6400	5185	Planned for 800 now cap. = 700 + 35 or so in observation gallery
Gallery Seating	—	315	
Orchestra pit	500	500	35-40 musicians 10 sq.ft./person 50 sq.ft./timpani and piano
Trap Room	—	A.R.	10 traps 4 ft. sq. net sq.ft. = 160
Stage incl. wings	2,500	2,770	prosc. opening 40'-0". SL wing = 12'-0" wide, SR wing = 32'-0" grid for full fly tower 65'-0" above deck, for modified fly tower @ 35'-0" above deck
Back Stage			
Receiving	A.R.	A.R	net = 45 sq.ft.
Scene/Prop Shop	1850	770	there is insufficient room in building for such large shops given program requirements of other user groups
Costume Shop/Wardrobe	250	275	
Laundry	100	45	
Dimmer Racks	150	150	to be included in sound lock or trunk storage at orchestra pit level below
Electrician's Workshop & Storage	250	250	to be carved out of mech room under highest part of lobby

Space Name	Sq. Footage Suggested 19 Sept 75	Sq. Footage	Remarks
Tech Dir. & Designer	200	120	
Manager's Office	—	75	
Admin. Office	—	75	
Clerical	—	160	
Rehearsal Room	1200	730	a room as large as originally programmed was not considered necessary
Orchestra Trunk Room	A.R.	510	
Music Library	80	205	
Instrument Storage	200	225	
General Storage	300	300	to be carved from mech. rooms as design is refined
Star Dressing Rooms	150	100	cap. 1-4 persons each w/private shower & WC
"	150	100	"
"	150	100	cap. 1-3 persons
Chorus Dr. Room	450	315	cap. 15 persons, 2 lavatories
"	450	315	"
Chorus WC's Showers	A.R.	A.R.	net sq. footage = 165 each
Green Room w/kitchenette	350	575	can double as reception rm. or member's club
Off Stage Waiting	—	150	for actors etc. only
Crews WC & Lockers	A.R.	A.R.	net sq. footage = 35
Janitor's Closets	A.R.	A.R.	net sq. footage 20 each
Back of House			
Projection & Follow Spot	200	215	
Lighting Control	120	105	stage manager to be back stage
Sound Control/Recording	120	210	
Projectionist's WC	A.R.	A.R.	net sq. footage = 25 sq. ft.
Catwalks (12)	A.R.	A.R.	
Mechanical	A.R.	A.R.	
Total Net Sq. Footage	16,690*	15,240	

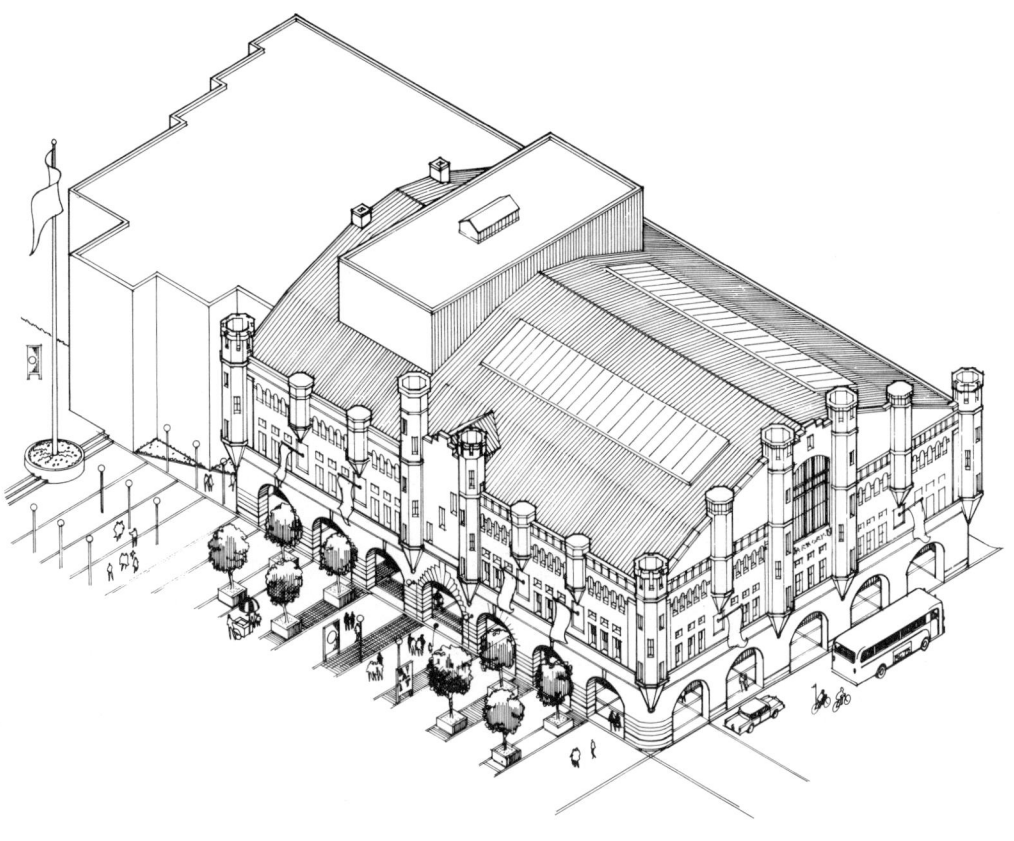

Schematic design drawings explore the physical and economic feasibility of converting the Blues Armory in Richmond to a multi-use performing-arts facility.
Plan for orchestra level (third floor)

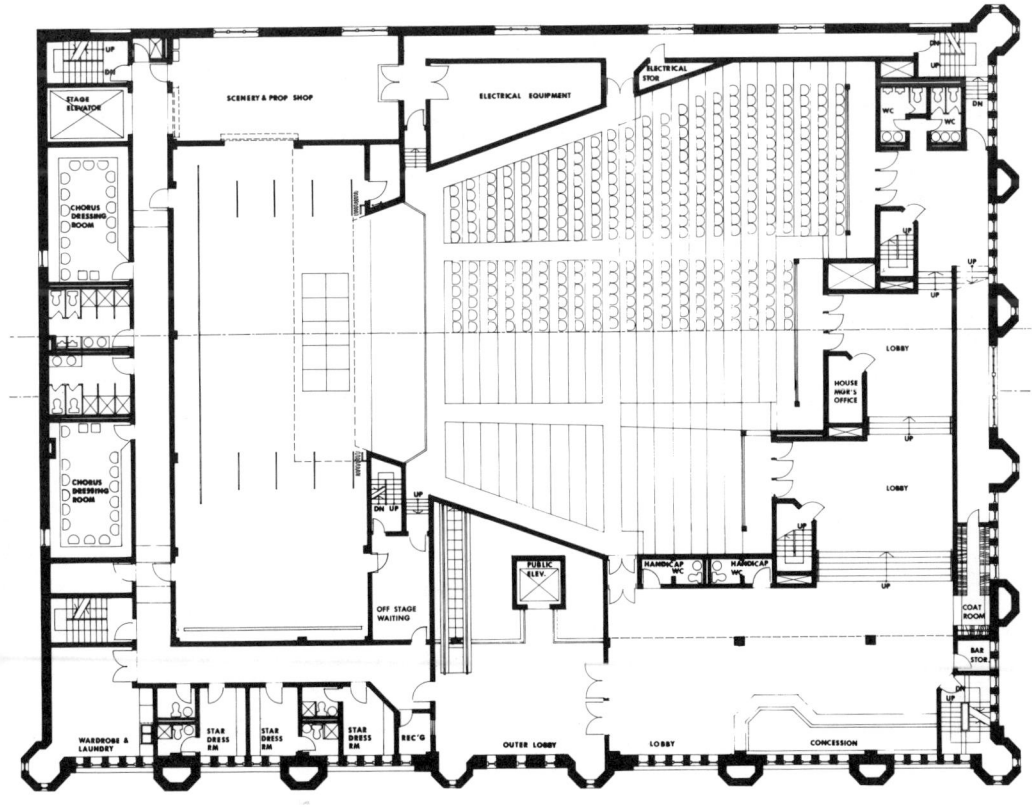

Opposite:
A sample building program for a multi-use performing-arts facility, prepared by Armstrong/Childs, architects, and Roger Morgan Studio, Inc., theatre-design consultants, in collaboration with member groups of the Federated Arts Council of Richmond, Virginia.

New York State Theatre, Lincoln Center
New York, N.Y.
Completed in 1964
Seating capacity: 2,729
Principal users:
New York City Ballet
New York City Opera
Principals of the design team:
Architects: Philip Johnson Associates
Theatre design consultants: Ronald Bates, Donald Oenslager, Walter Unruh

The San Francisco War Memorial and Performing Arts Center includes the San Francisco Opera House, right, where the San Francisco Ballet performs.

and a consulting architect must formally test how well the building program will fit a particular site or building, and at what cost. At a minimum, the preliminary study will consist of basic diagrammatic plans and sections, one or two interior and exterior sketches or renderings, brief written reports from the architect and other consultants, and a preliminary cost estimate.

(See Appendix C, "Organizing Your Building Program," for a checklist of items that a building committee is responsible for during this preliminary phase.)

THE DESIGN TEAM

For many architects, designing a theatre is an enticing prospect, plus a stiff challenge. "The architect is expected to design a building people want to go to, not one they have to go to," says lighting designer and theatre consultant Gilbert Hemsley. "To be successful, he must put more time, effort, and creative energy into a theatre building than any other project his firm might handle."

The architect who helped with the feasibility study does not necessarily follow through on the theatre's design. If the architect has the professional qualifications, however, he could be included in a list of architects (local or nationally known practitioners with experience in designing for the performing arts) who will be considered. The client's selection committee should narrow the field to ten or fifteen architects, who will be asked for more extensive examples of their work. From three to five final contenders should be invited to the site for separate interviews, after which the committee can make its ultimate selection.

Even on projects where use of government funds requires that architects submit competitive bids, the architect's fee should not be the sole cause for final selection. The quality of the architect's past work and how that work bears on the project at hand; references from previous clients regarding the architect's competence, integrity, and accessibility throughout a project; and the potential client's subjective measure of the man or woman being considered should be assessed along with any price tag.

Between the end of the feasibility study and the beginning of actual design work, most theatre-building projects enter a state of limbo, and members of the original design team may move on to other work. Now that an architect has been hired, if a new theatre-design consultant must also be brought in, "a member of the building committee should personally visit and talk to the theatre personnel who deal with that consultant's work on a daily basis," says Gilbert Hemsley. "Beware of architects who furnish the consultant as a package deal," he warns. "In the end, the client—not the architect—has to live with the theatre."

PREPARATION OF DRAWINGS AND SPECIFICATIONS FOR BID

The architectural work that precedes actual construction occurs in three stages—schematic design, design development, and the construction-documents phase.

During schematic design, the architect analyzes the building program and proposes alternate schemes, and sometimes study models, for programmatic elements, circulation patterns, exterior mass, fenestration, materials, and structural and mechanical systems. Ultimately, one scheme will be approved by the owner. (In contractual language, the client is now the "owner," whether he rents or has purchased the building site.)

In design development, the architect makes more detailed drawings of the chosen scheme's exterior appearance and major interior spaces, and prepares preliminary drawings for structural, mechanical, and electrical systems and for construction materials and finishes—all subject to the owner's review and approval. At this time, the architect also determines probable costs for the building project, by having the job estimated by an outside consultant or general contractor, or by persuading the owner

San Francisco Ballet Building
San Francisco, California
Completed in 1983
Sole User: San Francisco Ballet
Architect: Willis Associates, Inc.

Company member Eda Holmes and student Antonio Sousa, bottom photo, rehearse in the new studios.

Workers lay out the stage and construct proscenium boxes for Wilmington's Grand Opera House. At bottom, the ceiling cove has been broken to allow optimum location of control-room windows.

to hire a construction manager. Unlike the general contractor, the construction manager does not bid for his role. He is retained as part of the design team. He usually knows his way around the materials marketplace better than either the owner or the architect, and can advise — impartially — on the most economical approach to construction methods and scheduling.

During the construction-documents phase, the architect, with help from engineers and other consultants, prepares the working drawings and technical specifications that will guide the theatre's builders. The drawings show every aspect of the building and how its parts connect. The written specifications for all work and materials are categorized by construction trade. In addition to setting forth standards of quality, approval processes for each building material and product, and procedures for constructing the building's component parts, the specifications also include "General Conditions" relating to insurances and bonds, and an invitation to bid and bid submittal form if the project is to be competitively bid. If a construction manager is on board, he prepares bid packages for interested subcontractors.

When public funds are involved, anyone may bid so long as he can meet the general conditions set forth in the architect's specifications. Otherwise, construction documents are sent to invited bidders. The architect and consulting engineers answer bidders' questions about the project and issue clarification drawings and addenda to the construction documents as warranted.

Bids are usually due at the architect's or owner's offices at a specific time on a specific day. On large projects, they arrive in duplicate or triplicate on a bid form included in the "Invitation to Bid" section of the architect's specifications, and they are submitted in sealed envelopes. To assure builders that their bids are not being leaked to competitors, the envelopes are opened at a time designated in the architect's specifications. Typically, the owner is allowed a week to determine that the lowest bid is reliable. The winning bidder is then formally announced. If the winning bid is more than the owner can afford, drawings and specifications are revised to reduce the scope of work. Only then is the actual contract drawn up.

The American Institute of Architects provides the following summary of the responsibilities of architect and owner throughout construction:

> During construction, the Architect by onsite observations endeavors to guard the owner against defects and deficiencies in the work of the Contractor, but the Architect does not supervise construction. The Contractor, not the Architect, is solely responsible for construction means, methods, techniques, sequences, and procedures, and for safety precautions and programs in connection with the work. The Architect likewise is not responsible for the Contractor' failure to carry out the work in accordance with the contract documents, but he does have a responsibility to notify the Owner of any such failure or unsatisfactory performance about which he becomes aware.
> On larger or more complex projects, the Architect, if required and authorized by the Owner, will assign a full-time project representative to maintain liaison with the Contractor and to conduct extensive onsite observations. The Architect receives additional compensation for this service.
> The Architect's Basic Services are concluded when a final certificate for payment is issued to the Owner. However, when the construction phase is exceeded or extended more than thirty days beyond the completion date specified in the contract for construction, the Architect is entitled to compensation for services beyond the thirtieth day on the basis of actual time required.

The construction phase — when the theatre slowly rises from the building site or an old structure is gradually remade into a new performing space for dance — will be measured in minute details, seemingly endless paperwork, and daily crises. Cost overruns, one after another, can be counted on. The owner without a construction manager will be wise to assign a full-time clerk-of-the-works to monitor progress. Meanwhile, the owner takes the long view, dreams of the theatre's inaugural season, and signs the checks.

The San Francisco Ballet Building under construction.

For a chart summarizing the design process and the responsibilities of key persons, see Appendix C, "Products and Decisions for Design Implementation."

BUILDING SMALLER FACILITIES AND ALTERNATE SPACES

Creators of small showcase theatres and alternate spaces for dance tend to be young, dedicated, and inexperienced in matters involving construction or the building trades. Dancers or choreographers, they have already devoted years to honing their art, not to planning and building spaces for dance. Suddenly, they are drafted into a consortium of artists rehabilitating a downtown warehouse, or appointed to a building committee at the college where they teach. Yet despite the difficulties, these smaller theatres are built—and often very well.

The following scaled-down, theatre-construction primer is offered with the aim of encouraging even better alternate spaces for dance, and in the belief that well-managed building projects will lead to better dance.

BASIC DECISIONS

Almost invariably, the lean construction budget of the client developing an alternate space precludes building a theatre from the ground up. Thus the client's first choice is whether to buy or rent the structure to be renovated. Eldon Elder's *Will It Make a Theatre?* (published by the Off-Off Broadway Alliance, and excellent reading for anyone planning an alternate space) argues strongly against ownership:

> ... the newly established theatre should rent everything during the first phase. This keeps initial investment to a minimum, keeps the company flexible with options open for change and unfettered by property should they want to move or expand after two or three seasons. The extreme of this point of view is summed up by one theatre consultant who advises, "A young, new, not-for-profit theatre should start by renting everything, including the toilets." An additional reason for renting is that many grants will allow rentals, but will not support purchases for capital improvements.

One of New York's first alternate spaces, The Kitchen Center for Video, Music, Dance and Performance is regularly booked for dance despite the closely spaced columns.

Andy deGroat and Dancers perform at The Kitchen.

However, tenancy holds its perils. Dancers and other performing artists have poured their life savings into renovating run-down properties, only to fall prey to landlords who see their real estate has appreciated. A landlord may try to evict a dance group in order to rent a revitalized loft at a higher price. By refusing to maintain the building, or by withholding heat or hot water, the owner may leave the dancers little choice but to move on.

After the difficult decision to rent or buy, comes the question of where to build. Access to public transportation and parking tend to be less important for alternate spaces than for major performing arts facilities. The success of New York's off-off Broadway theatres, and of performance lofts in the warehouse districts of both Manhattan and San Francisco suggests that some urban audiences will go anywhere for quality. There is even an advantage to building in run-down neighborhoods on the far side of town: traffic sounds and noisy neighbors will rarely be a problem during performance hours, which means the expense of acoustically isolating a raw loft or manufacturing space can be lessened.

PROFESSIONAL HELP

Before renting or buying *any* potential alternate space, the client should have a professional engineer thoroughly inspect the building. *Will It Make a Theatre?* warns:

> Initial reactions are notoriously deceptive and nowhere is this truer than when looking at old buildings. They are romantic, intriguing, full of "possibilities." The imagination commences to work overtime to weave fantasies. Your emotional response on first encounter with a building is important, but ultimately the condition behind the facade will be more important. So take a closer look at the condition of any building in which you are seriously interested, and check it for what signifies trouble.

Elder's book provides an exterior and interior checklist for prospective theatres, the essence of which follows:

EXTERIOR

1. Look for cracked or sagging masonry, a clue to the degree of settling that has occurred and to the building's overall stability.
2. Note roof damage, or chipped or scaling plaster in the ceiling below the roof, either of which can indicate leaks.
3. Check stoops, entrances, and doors with an eye to future access by performers, patrons (including the handicapped), and equipment. Check fire escapes for rust or the need for repair.
4. Thoroughly examine the rear of the building for possible building-code violations, and for the potential for better ventilation and other improvements.

INTERIOR

5. Examine the basement for evidence of poor drainage and past flooding.
6. Measure the spacing of structural columns and load-bearing walls, and locate major heating, plumbing, and electrical risers as well as roof drains to be sure a proper performance space for dance can be carved out.
7. Study the dimensions, locations, materials, and the condition of stairs and corridors for their suitability for theatre circulation, and for whether they meet the safety standards in local building codes. Also gauge the condition and load capacity of elevators and their accessibility to handicapped patrons.
8. Check floors for sagging and warping and for their ability to support the potential live load; this is the weight floors are permitted to carry in addition to any dead load.
9. Examine walls and ceilings for leaks and—for purposes of sound isolation—determine the type of material and number of layers between your space and the neighbors.
10. Look for dry rot or corrosion in window frames and sashes; misalignment or failure to close properly means future heat loss, water damage, and noise.
11. Check the age and efficiency of heating, ventilating, and air conditioning systems, and their noise levels when operating.
12. Look for rust and leaks in plumbing risers and fixtures and in the building's sprinkler system.
13. Check the building's electrical service—whether it is AC or DC, and whether the amperage and voltage available in your space can accept power demands imposed by stage lighting and air conditioning. Review the age and condition of wiring, the fuse or panel box, and electrical meters.
14. Determine the effectiveness of fire-prevention and any other emergency systems in the building.
15. Finally, consider the building's overall security, noting possible means of unauthorized entry, such as skylights, trap doors, and shared stairs and corridors.

After a rigorous inspection of the building, the engineer or an architect (who can be hired on a consulting basis and paid by the hour) should check with local authorities to determine whether the space is in violation of local zoning regulations or building codes. The architect or engineer will then be able to provide a *rough* estimate of what it will cost to remove any code violations and to renovate the space. If the price is right, the dance group should hire a lawyer experienced in real estate or landlord/tenant law to negotiate the documents of sale or lease.

Most spaces affordable to emerging dance companies or choreographers have problems that must be corrected before occupancy. At the least, safety violations will

59 Wooster Street, New York—home of The Kitchen.

have to be removed, or the certificate of occupancy amended. This demands the expertise of a professional engineer who knows the local codes and how to prepare and file plans and applications with governing authorities. If the space must be thoroughly redesigned, and even when the work will be done in phases, a good architect should be paid to prepare comprehensive drawings and specifications for the total scope of renovation. Architectural drawings and specifications are a form of insurance. Called "contract documents" as well as "construction documents," they describe not just the design but also the quality of materials and workmanship that will be provided. If construction proves unsatisfactory, a set of drawings initialed by both parties—the contractor executing the work and the dance company paying for it—carries more weight than a letter of agreement or a verbal contract sealed with a handshake.

MASTER PLAN AND BUDGET

Before beginning any design or construction work, a theatre-building dance group should draft a detailed master plan. The plan describes the group's long-range intentions for both renovating and equipping the space. Even work clearly beyond the group's present means should be included in the master plan, so that a comprehensive budget can be drawn up. Preparing a budget may seem less pressing than raising the money to pay for construction. But the more comprehensive the budget, the easier it will be to win the confidence of a bank or other funding source.

In addition to the construction-cost estimate, the budget should include fees paid to architects and other consultants, plus an allowance (usually eight to ten percent of the construction cost) for the architect's and consultants' out-of-pocket expenses, such as blueprinting, telephone calls, travel, and the like. The budget must also allow for a contingency fund (fifteen to twenty-five percent of the construction cost) to correct errors or omissions in architectural drawings and hidden problems that become evident during demolition, and to accommodate anything from strikes to a sudden scarcity of building materials.

An even more comprehensive budget will include debt service on loans taken out for the project, rental of the building during renovation, legal fees, staff salaries, operating expenses for the company to rehearse elsewhere during construction, and start-up costs (including new furnishings and equipment) for the day the dance group moves into its new home.

Before drawing up the budget, prospective theatre builders should consider how much of the construction work will be done by themselves, and how much by tradesmen. If dancers will perform most of the labor, the builder/dance group must measure the quantities of materials—equivalent to the ingredients in a recipe—set forth in the construction drawings. (A method for doing this is described on pages 148-157 of Leslie Armstrong's *The Little House*, a design and construction manual for small-scale, single-family housing, published by Collier Macmillan, 1979.) Next, the builder should solicit competitive prices for the materials needed, as well as for any labor the dance group will not do. Specialized work, such as installing electrical wiring or building a rigging system, should never be attempted by amateurs. To do so is difficult, dangerous, and often illegal.

A dance group that wants to avoid doing all the sawing and hammering, but that lacks money to hire a general contractor, can still be its own contractor. That way, the group is spared an outside contractor's surcharge for overhead and profit—a savings that can be devoted to renovation.

However, after having construction drawings approved by the local authorities, the dancer or choreographer who puts on a contractor's cap will have to obtain the required building permits and take out property-damage insurance for the facility, workers-compensation insurance for the building crew, and public-liability insurance for everyone from trespassers to the theatre's first patrons. He may also have to arrange for temporary power, portable toilets, and adequate access for work trucks. The contractor also orders materials, schedules deliveries, arranges for the removal of debris and the storage of materials, and coordinates the comings and goings of the various subcontractors. In short, he gives up dance for the duration.

CONSTRUCTION

On small-scale renovation projects, the builder's architect should check subcontractors' references as well as actual work done by the firms. In addition, each subcontractor should be asked to submit a financial statement verifying that he or his company can sustain a loss should anything go awry during construction. Contracts should be written so that the client is obliged to pay only for materials already purchased and labor already completed.

Small subcontractors can have legitimate cash-flow problems. They may need a nominal advance at the beginning of the job, and may have to be paid every two weeks. But once the job is underway, the subcontractor must have sufficient personal cash or credit to pay for two weeks' worth of his crew's labor and for their materials.

Finally, to ensure that subcontractors, or the general contractor, see the job through, the client should deduct ten percent from each application for payment. When all work has been done to his satisfaction and the project has been officially "signed off"—and this sometimes happens months after an alternate space has opened—the client dips into his construction budget and releases the ransom money.

3 ON STAGE

An architect's drawing of an empty stagehouse suggests the fairground before the fair—a space vast and waiting. Confronted with plans for a rectangle stretching 100 feet wide and 60 deep, the individual or group paying to build the theatre may wonder why a few square yards cannot be sacrificed, why a back corner cannot accommodate a badly needed office or two. But what is not apparent to them is the mass of equipment and the number of crew members and performers that must not only fit, but fit with enough breathing space for efficiency and ease of movement.

Using imagination for a pencil, draw the space and shade in the performing area. On each side, add the wings with their layers of hanging backdrops. Arrange a rigging system along one wall, and overhead hang scenery for the next performances. Along the walls, stack scenery for the second half of the current performance. Haul in the stagelighting booms with their miles of cable, and add some warm-up barres and rosin boxes. Add quick-change booths and a work station for the stage manager. Behind the backdrops, allow room for the crossover, the corridor performers race through when moving from one side of the stage to the other. Finally, bring on the bodies: forty, fifty, or more performers, twenty to thirty stagehands, a stage manager, dressers, musicians, and everyone else who makes the performance happen. The space that once looked as if it had room to spare is now filled to capacity.

THE PERFORMING AREA

Once built, stage space can be made to appear smaller. Enlarging it is impossible. In a multipurpose theatre, the width and depth of the performing area must satisfy the needs of the user requiring the most room—usually a dance company.

The rear or upstage edge of the performing space is defined by the placement of the background, whether a cyclorama, a painted backdrop, a velour curtain, or a scrim. If a crossover corridor is not built into the stagehouse, upstage dimensions must include room for dancers passing behind the background. An additional 5 to 6 feet of upstage depth should also be allowed for proper lighting of the backdrop: when a dancer illuminated by stage lights or a followspot enters the stage at the farthest upstage entrance, light can be thrown past the dancer onto the backdrop—an unwanted effect; allowing extra upstage depth, beyond the actual performing area, helps prevent such lighting conflicts.

The downstage edge of the performing area is at the curtain line or at the performers' entrance point nearest the audience. The space projecting past the downstage line is called the apron. During the nineteenth century, the apron usually extended 15 or 20 feet beyond the curtain. Since then, theatre architecture has changed and aprons have receded toward the stage. Modern aprons amount to a lip just forward of the curtain, with or without footlights. Lately, some theatre directors have brought actors closer to the audience by extending the apron out into the orchestra, thus projecting the players far forward of the proscenium arch. But in houses designed for dance as well as theatre, such stage extensions must be removable. Because dancers almost always enter and exit at right angles to the center line of the stage, any extra space downstage of the curtain line is unusable; the empty space may create an esthetic gulf between audience and dancers.

However, since the principal dancers in ballet take their bows in front of the house curtain, they need a shallow apron to stand on. Its surface should be the same material as that of the stage (so both surfaces will blend when the curtain is up) and it should be roomy enough for bowing performers plus the curtain behind them (a curtain with full

In ballet, principal dancers generally take their bows on the apron in front of the house curtain.

Opposite: Footlights and side lighting illuminate Martha Graham on stage.

The proscenium stage—empty.

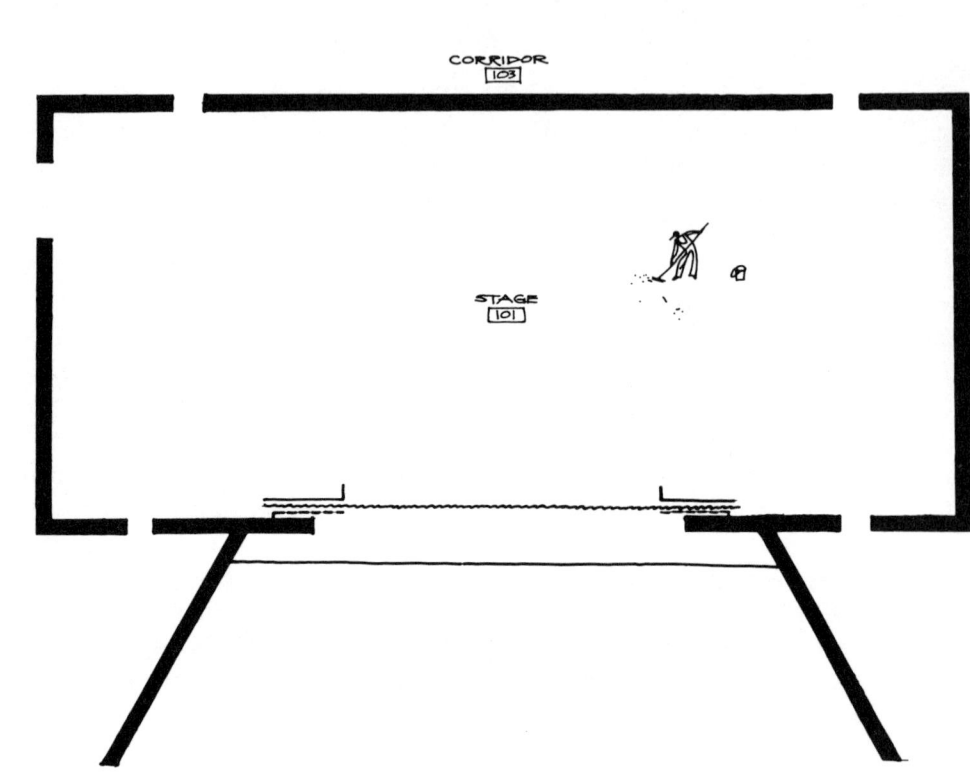

The same proscenium stage—in full operation.

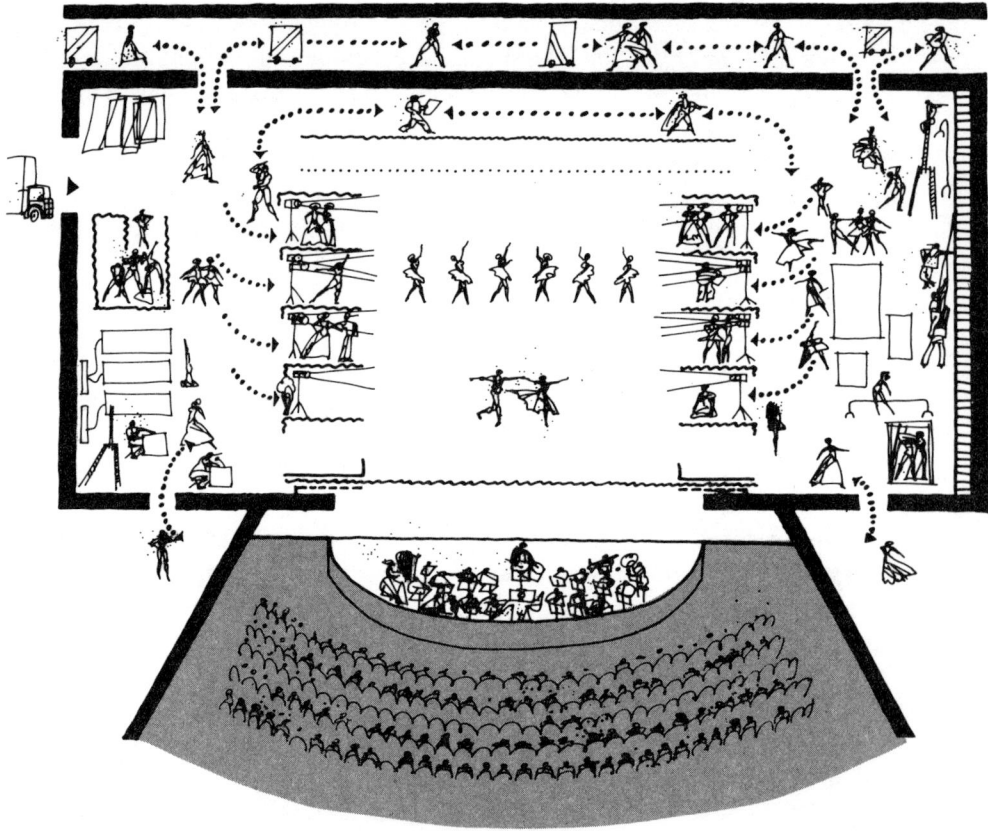

folds may occupy up to 18 inches of stage depth). Also, approximately 2 feet of downstage space or apron should be regarded as a dancer's safety zone. Without that extra margin between the downstage edge of the performing area and the actual edge of the stage, performing dancers risk tumbling into the orchestra pit; many dance companies mark off the space with tape on the stage floor.

DIMENSIONS FOR THE PERFORMING AREA

Asked what were the optimum dimensions for a dance stage, lighting designer and theatre consultant Gilbert Hemsley answered, "For ballet, large enough to do *The Nutcracker* with a corps de ballet of 60 and a 30-foot tree—and do it well!" *The Nutcracker* is the single best money maker for every major American ballet company. While each company stages its own version, most consider a performing area 45 feet wide by 40 feet deep the minimum necessary. Many prefer a space 60 feet wide.

But the dance stage must be wider than the actual performance space. A proper stage includes a minimum of 10 to 15 feet of wing space on each side. These are transition zones between the performing area and offstage. Performers preparing for an entrance need wing space in which to warm up, to catch their breath, or to concentrate on a difficult passage. An entrance can be ruined if the dancer, crowded into a tiny area, is bumped by another performer or a stagehand.

Exits, when a dancer runs or leaps into the wings, or departs the stage holding another dancer aloft, also require ample space. At one New York theatre, where wing space is almost nil, dancers are said to lean mattresses against the walls, and to station themselves in the wings to catch colleagues making fast exits. Dance is demanding, but leaping offstage into a mattress seems one demand too many.

The wing space is occupied by more than dancers entering and exiting. Lighting equipment mounted on vertical steel booms (known as torms, trees, or ladders) is positioned in the wings for side-lighting effects. Dancers expect to cope with booms; but where there is ample wing space, booms can be positioned to be less obstructive.

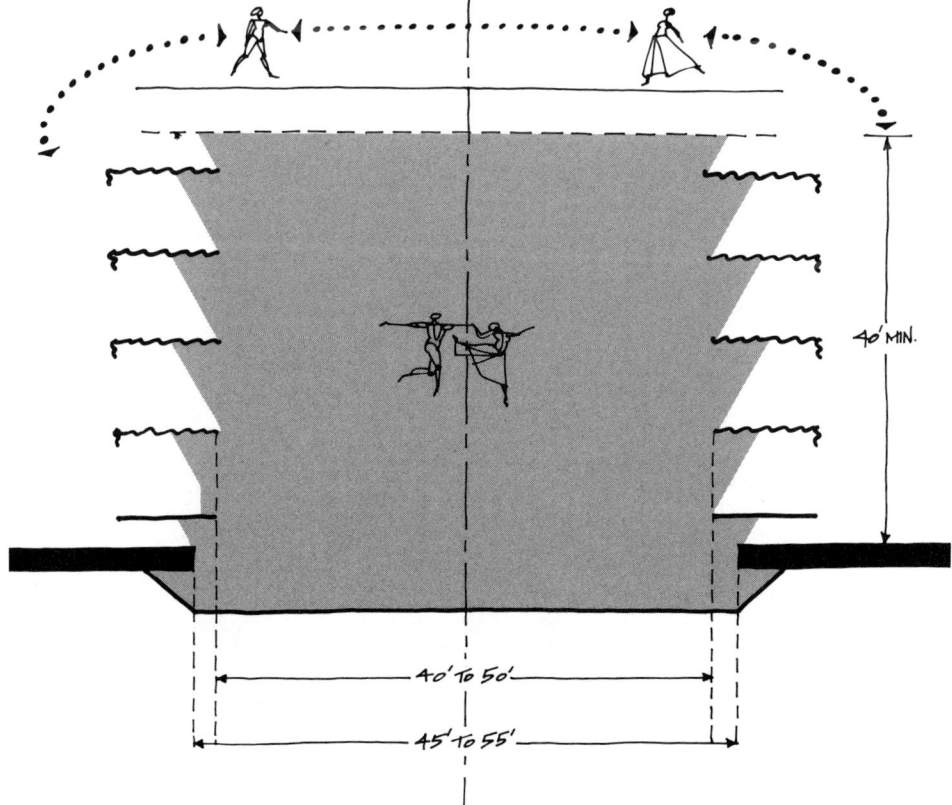

The floor plan of the performing area within a proscenium stagehouse shows the critical dimensions and principal components of stage drapery and masking used for dance.

31

Pressure points: A 110-pound dancer leaping in sneakers lands with a bearing pressure of 40 pounds per square inch distributed over the forward area of her sneaker sole.

A 110-pound modern dancer landing on the ball and five toes of her bare foot tolerates 130 pounds per square inch of bearing pressure.

A 110-pound ballet dancer on pointe withstands a bearing pressure of 360 pounds per square inch.

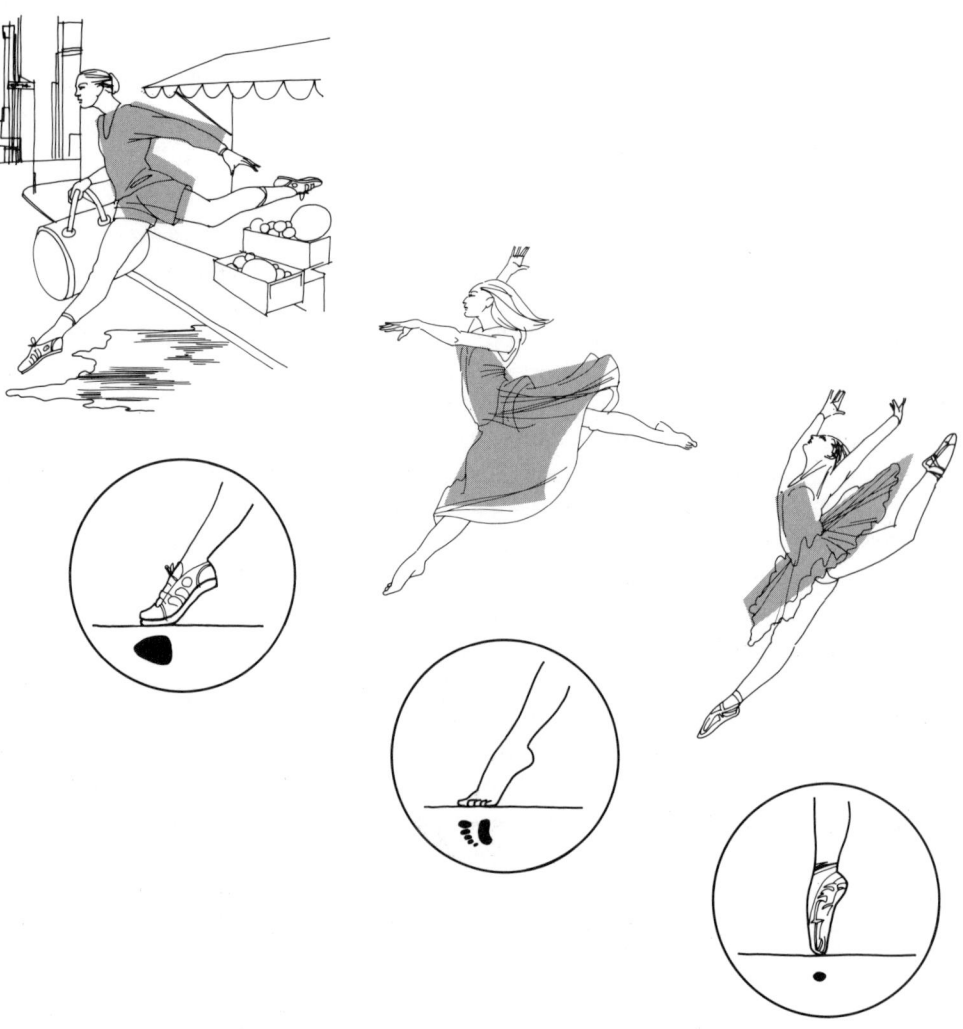

THE STAGE FLOOR

Audiences thrill at the sight of airborne dancers. Performers worry about the landing strip. Choreographers and dancers care more about the quality of the floors upon which they perform and rehearse than about any other part of the theatre. Stress caused by performing on hard, rigid, or uneven floors can damage a dancer's joints, tendons, muscles, and ligaments.

Because dancers frequently work barefoot or in thin slippers or shoes, the floor's surface is also important. A dance stage should be nonslippery and smooth. The floor must be well-maintained (a splinter or nail can incapacitate a dancer for weeks), and should be neither cold nor damp. It must be free of electrical receptacles, telephone or microphone outlets, sliding partition tracks, and other devices that might seem to render the performing area more flexible.

STAGE-FLOOR SUBSTRUCTURE

There is no one correct way to construct a floor for dance. Many versions of the "basket weave" floor have been built. Each relies on several layers of wood strips, with each new layer laid at a right angle to the one below it. The layers diffuse the impact of a dancer's step, transferring it from layer to layer and finally down to the supporting concrete slab or steel beams. Another style of substructure uses coiled springs set beneath wooden planks. Still other dance floors get additional bounce from neoprene or rubber pads.

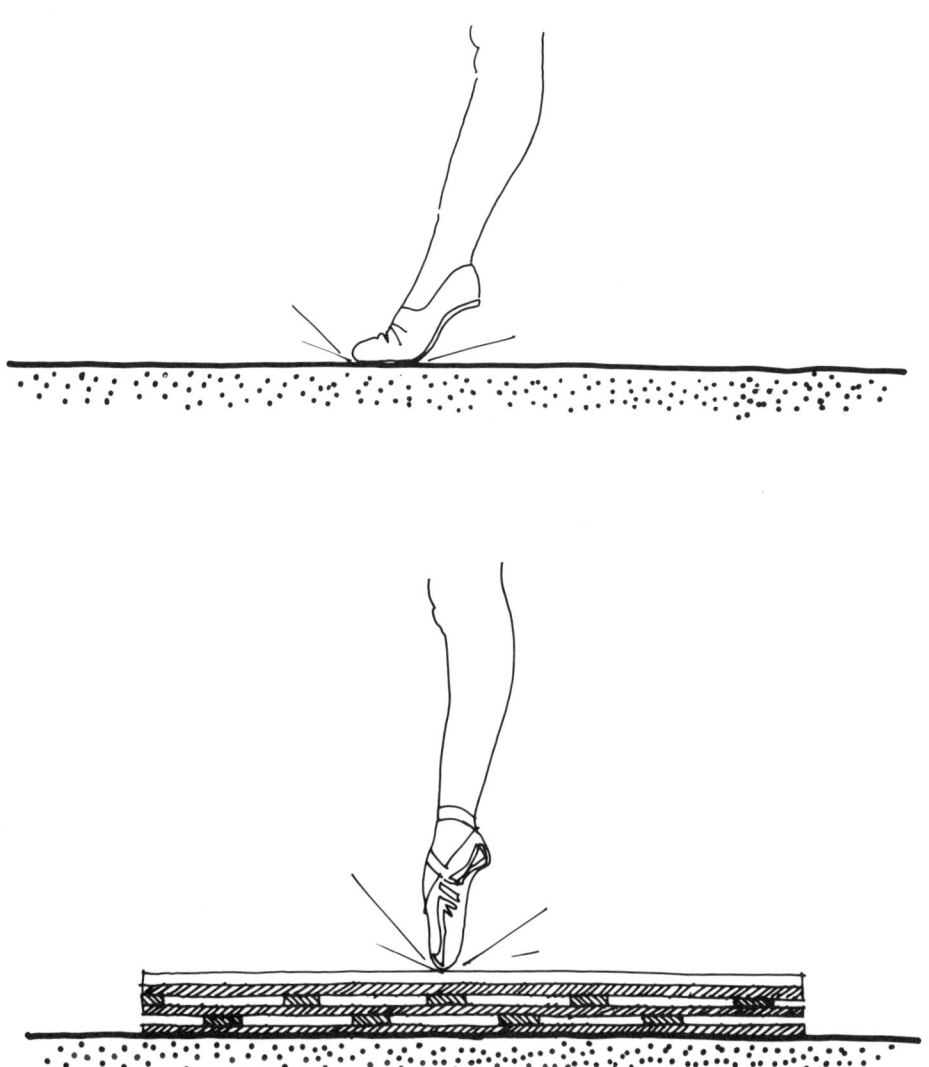

The 130-pound per square inch bearing pressure of the dancer in sneakers is cushioned in part by the resilient sole of her shoe. For dancers landing on toe shoes or barefoot, the higher pressure must be cushioned by resiliency in the construction of the sub-floor. (Calculations prepared in collaboration with Robert Silman, structural engineer.)

To ensure that floors for the San Francisco Ballet's new studios were properly resilient, project architect Charles Rueger conducted research on construction methods used by other major dance organizations. Rueger found that the National Ballet of Canada (NBC) and the National Ballet School use a finish floor of "battleship linoleum placed directly on top of two layers of half-inch plywood laid down with staggered joints." According to Rueger:

> This underlayment is supported by two layers of 3/8-inch thick 3 inch by 3 inch rubber pads (hollow core) spaced 16 inches on center laid directly on a concrete structural slab. The rubber pads were supplied by Northern Flooring of Toronto. The NBC installation is now 15 years old and reportedly has had no problems. Those who use these floors are pleased with the results.

Also according to Rueger:

> The School of American Ballet (SAB) and the Dance Building at the New York State University at Purchase (SUNY Purchase) utilize battleship linoleum over a 3/4 inch plywood underlayment, supported on flat-laid 2 x 4's spaced 16 inches on center. These 2 x 4's in turn are supported on 1-inch high, 1-inch diameter coil springs that are spaced 12 inches on center in staggered rows. The springs rest on wood blocking affixed directly to the concrete structural slab. Apparently the degree of resiliency can be adjusted by changing the on-center spacing of the springs. Both SAB and SUNY, the prime users of the floors, swear by them, but some outsiders are not so enthusiastic. Should this solution be utilized, we suggest that the degree of resiliency be determined through experimentation with the support spacing.

Methods for constructing resilient floors for dance:

Five-layer basketweave

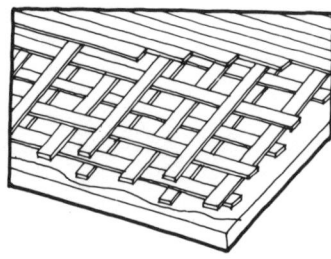 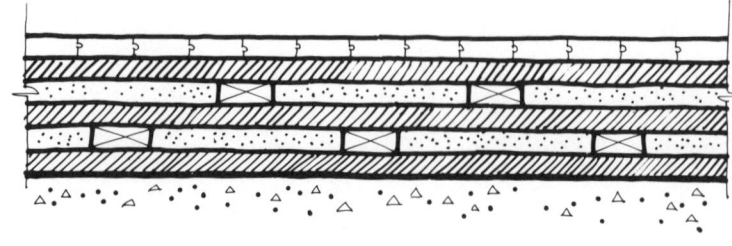

Three-layer basketweave

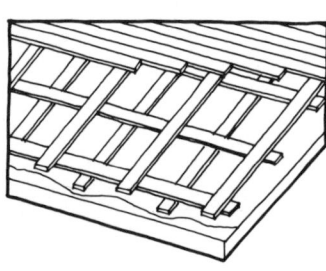 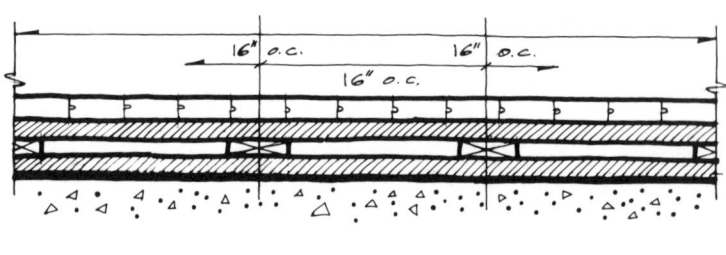

Resilient pad base

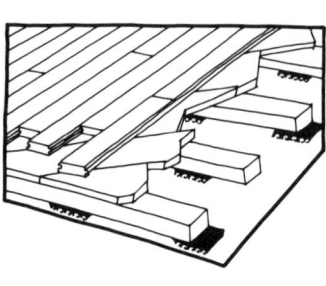 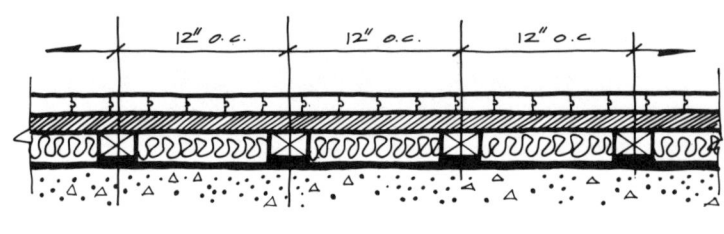

Spring box base

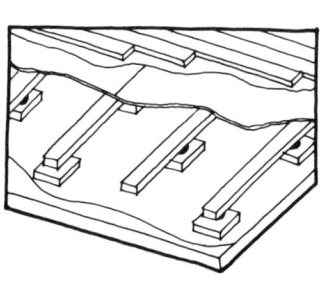 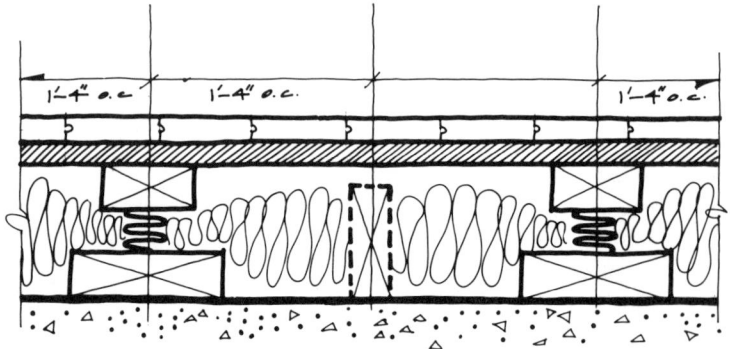

The stage and rehearsal floors at the Crouse-Hinds Concert Theatre, at the Civic Center of Onondaga County, Syracuse, New York, start with 1 x 4's laid flat atop resilient fiberglass blocks set 12 inches on center. These 1 x 4's are then bolted to the structural slab to put the fiberglass blocks in compression. Next comes a second layer of 1 x 4's perpendicular to the first, laid 18 inches on center (16 inches proved too stiff, 24 inches too bouncy). A third layer of 1 x 4's laid 18 inches on center (again, perpendicular to the layer immediately below) is covered with two layers of 5/8-inch plywood—at right angles to each other—topped off with 4 x 8-foot sheets of masonite.

For the restoration of the Grand Opera House in Wilmington, Delaware, architects on the project wanted a floor that would please the many touring companies expected to perform there. A poll of dancers revealed that the floor at the New York State Theater was a favorite. The original flooring contractor for the State Theater complemented the architects' research by revealing a few trade secrets. The stage floor built at Wilmington proved a hit with dancers; architectural specifications can be found at the end of this chapter.

Installing a resilient floor is relatively simple, until one comes to the edges. Enough space must be left between the flooring and walls to allow for expansion and contraction caused by changing temperature and humidity. A base molding (either a wood strip or steel angle) should be attached to the wall to permit the floor to move beneath it. The bottom of the molding should project enough to cover the gap between floor and wall.

With so many ways to construct resilient floors, and so many partisans of this method or that, the careful builder will poll principals of dance companies expected to use the stage. Mock-ups, sample floor panels measuring at least 8 feet by 8 feet, should also be built for dancers to test.

TRAPS

If the same stage will be used for dance and opera, there may be more than the usual number of arguments over floor design. Opera companies prefer stiff floors able to support heavy, rolling scenery wagons. Opera also relies on traps, removable or hinged sections in the stage floor. Unfortunately, trap doors and the rest of the stage are never uniformly resilient. As a general rule, stage floors designed principally for dance should not be fitted with traps.

SURFACE MATERIALS—FIXED AND PORTABLE

The best surface for most multi-use stage floors is wood, usually tongue-and-groove strips of pine or some other softwood. But the surface of many such stages is likely to be filled with holes from the nails and screws used to anchor scenery in operas and musicals. On these wooden stages, a smooth cover—usually black or gray linoleum or vinyl—must be taped to the floor before dance performances.

However, if the stage will be used solely for dance, the floor may be finished in wood or linoleum. If wood, maple or oak should be used, to prevent splintering, and the finish should be stain, not paint. A dark brown, dark gray, or black stain, uniform across the entire stage, is best. Lighter floors are highly reflective, making it almost impossible to avoid illuminating parts of the performing area meant to be dark. Some small dance companies prefer performing on light-colored floors and may choose a bright surface in a space designed for their exclusive use. But in a multipurpose theatre or one that will serve many dance companies, the floor color should be dark brown, dark gray, or black; companies that want a lighter shade can always lay down portable flooring.

A valuable guide to both portable and permanent dance flooring is *The Technical Production Handbook*, written by M. Kay Barrell, and published by Western States Arts Foundation. According to Barrell, various types of roll flooring can serve as a portable surface for dance:

> The first is battleship linoleum. It was manufactured by Armstrong Floors until 1974 (with its petroleum base, it was a casualty of the oil crisis). In the past, it was the only available portable floor, and has great nostalgic value for those performers who never had to move it themselves. It is very heavy and very brittle, and therefore does not travel well. And if it is unrolled at any temperature below 50 degrees, it tends to self destruct. It makes a fine permanent installation, however, because it wears well and has a very good surface, and if it only has to move within your building, it can last many years.

On tour, stagehands install the Cleveland Ballet's portable, three-layer basketweave dance floor.

After the demise of battleship linoleum, the standard touring floor for dance was a double-sided sheet vinyl known as "Marley," manufactured by a company of the same name in Great Britain. Marley, according to *The Technical Production Handbook*:

> . . . is very thin, light, and pliable. Cold does not affect it and it can be folded and creased without breaking. It's the ideal floor to tour with because it can adapt to shapes so easily and still hold up. But since it is so thin, it has no internal resilience and can be ripped up by protruding screws and nails.

Marley was no longer produced after 1978. The name, however, has come to be used for portable dance flooring in the same way "Kleenex" stands for paper tissues. Meanwhile, other manufacturers are offering comparable products; some of these portable floors are one hundred percent polyvinyl chloride and reversible; others are laminated to a foam backing or core for increased resiliency and sound absorption.

MAINTAINING A CONSTANT TEMPERATURE

A constant temperature between seventy-five and eighty degrees Fahrenheit is the rule in dance performance and rehearsal spaces. Yet drafts and noise from the heating and cooling equipment required to keep temperatures constant can annoy performers and audience alike. Ducts and registers should be large, so air travels through them slowly and silently, and they should be positioned so as not to blow air onto performers or stage draperies, causing the latter to flutter or billow.

Placing ducts high up on the upstage or back wall may complicate matters on stage: one duct protruding two feet downstage from the wall creates the same effect as if the entire wall had been moved two feet forward; a wide backdrop or cyclorama will have to be moved downstage, and performance space will shrink. To preserve space, ducts feeding air to the stage are best run along side walls of the stagehouse, beneath the galleries and catwalks of the rigging system.

OFFSTAGE

Offstage and backstage are often interchangeable terms, usually meaning any theatre production space out of view of the audience. However, this book uses offstage to refer to the area beyond the masking that creates the wings but within the stagehouse of a proscenium theatre. Backstage will be used for production spaces beyond the stagehouse.

During a dance performance, all is quiet offstage. But with the close of each piece, at the instant the curtain falls, the mood changes. Dancers collapse after a strenuous passage, or run to adjust an eyelash or a seam. Other performers warm up or change costumes while rushing stagehands change the set for the next piece. Crew, dancers, and managers thread their way through a jumble of props, rigging equipment, patch panels, switchgear, stage lights, effects projectors, road boxes, shipping crates, changing booths, costume racks, pianos, ladders, and scaffolding.

Plenty of space is needed to accommodate all this offstage equipment and activity.

By asking questions, the theatre designer can begin determining just how much space. How many dancers are in the largest company that will use the theatre? How many stagehands run the company's performances? Does the company use much built scenery, or does it prefer a backdrop and velour masking? Does it rely heavily on special effects or elaborate costumes? After querying potential users, if it is still unclear how much space is needed, the theatre designer should provide more rather than less. Offstage will always be filled.

OFFSTAGE AND BACKSTAGE CIRCULATION FOR PERFORMERS

During a performance, a dancer may exit stage left and, moments later and perhaps wearing a new costume, enter stage right. The crossover—a passageway behind the cyclorama or a separate corridor entirely behind the stage—allows dancers to travel the edge of a performing area without being seen by the audience. Crossovers should measure at least 5 feet wide. A separate crossover usually remains a dancers' domain, free of scenic elements or stage machinery. Crossovers within the stagehouse may be partly obstructed by scenery; thus low-level guide lights should illuminate the dancers' path. (Below-stage crossovers are another approach, but the stairs at each end can be dangerous for running dancers.)

Although the crossover floor should be resilient, extending a complicated basket weave subfloor offstage can be prohibitively expensive. On the other hand, raw concrete, even when covered by wood finish flooring, is unacceptable. At the least, offstage subflooring should be 3/4 inch plywood on a layer of wood sleepers (1 x 4's or 2 x 4's laid flat). Finish material, if not the same as the stage, should be nonslip cushioned tile or linoleum. Specifications for crossover, wing, and other offstage floors—surfaces not used for dance rehearsal or performance—are included in the Wilmington Opera House stage-floor specifications at the end of this chapter.

Floors on-and-offstage, in dressing rooms, and in other areas used by dancers, should never be waxed. Wax sticks to slippers, shoes, and bare feet. When transferred to the stage floor, it leaves slippery spots. Carpet on offstage and backstage floors is also inadvisable, since the rosin ballet dancers use on their slippers will cut it to shreds. Unwaxed, cushioned linoleum, or cushioned vinyl sheeting or tile, work best offstage.

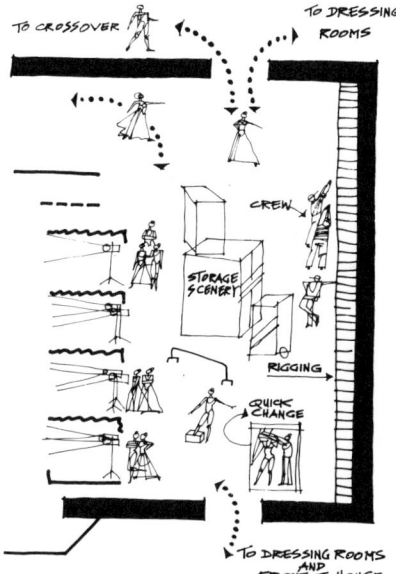

Offstage spaces in the stagehouse.

OFFSTAGE CIRCULATION FOR CREW AND CHOREOGRAPHERS

Stagehands need easy access to the stage and must be able to maneuver quickly through the offstage jungle. They also need access to the crew room backstage: some crew members will be needed in the stage area at all times during a performance, but most wait in the crew room until they are called for a scene shift. The crew also works in the space above the stage, where rigging and lighting systems are housed. In large stagehouses, a small two-person elevator should be installed to lift stagehands to the grid floor and counterweight-loading platforms. When an elevator is not called for, stairways are preferable to ladders. To save space, stairways should stand as close to the edges of the stagehouse as possible.

In theatres where original dance works are being developed, the choreographer makes frequent trips between stage and auditorium. An unobtrusive pass door on one or each side of the stage area, or a portable step unit, allows the choreographer to move easily back and forth between the seats at orchestra level and the stage.

THE PROSCENIUM

Successful theatres adapt easily to the demands of different users. Even a theatre designed exclusively for dance must satisfy the needs and preferences of a variety of

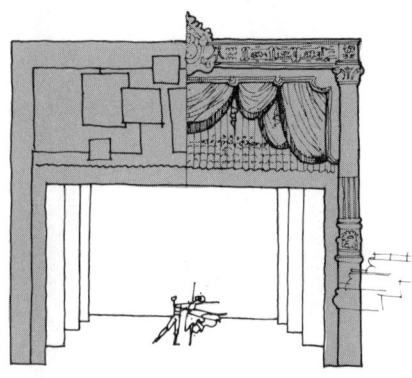

Before the show, the proscenium arch, with its decorative drapery, focuses the audience's attention. When the house lights dim and the curtain opens, the focus narrows to the smaller stage picture defined by stage masking.

choreographers and designers. The architect and theatre-design consultant for a space for dance should work closely with choreographers and scenic and lighting designers when determining the size and shape of the proscenium.

THE PROSCENIUM ARCH

The width of the proscenium arch is vitally important. Too narrow an arch will pinch the stage picture, and may encroach on the breadth required for choreography. If the arch is too wide, a dance company using the stage may be unable to fill the full width. However, since sightlines for the audience are usually calculated for the full opening, if the company installs temporary masking at the sides, the change will obstruct the view of patrons seated along the sides of the theatre.

The width of the proscenium arch is dictated fairly rigidly by the kinetic requirements of dance, but the height is more a matter of esthetic choice. A high proscenium arch creates a sense of grand scale. A low arch diminishes this scale and flattens the stage picture. Most choreographers seek the highest opening possible.

The upper reaches of the proscenium arch may be hung with permanent decorative draperies or a simple horizontal border. The border establishes the maximum height of the stage picture.

Scenic designers for dance customarily create a portal within the proscenium opening. The portal does the same work as a mat placed around a painting, providing a visual transition between the choreographer's stage picture and the architectural frame of the proscenium. Seats at far ends of those rows nearest the stage will have slightly restricted views of the portal, but at least part of the portal edge should be visible from every seat in the house. Also, if the top of the proscenium arch is curved, the spring line of the curve must start above the lowest point of the border, grand drape, or portal, so the top of the stage picture remains horizontal. The shape of the proscenium arch should not compete with stage scenery, and racy designs should be avoided. The top may be straight or curved, but the sides must always stand plumb.

THE PROSCENIUM STAGEHOUSE

In classic proscenium theatres, a stagehouse—from which scenery can be flown in and out—rises above the stage. "Flying" means scenery is raised (flown out) or lowered (flown in), and the lofty area above the stage, where scenery hangs out of sight of the audience, is called the "fly space."

The vertical distance needed to lift scenery beyond view of the audience dictates the height of the stagehouse. First, the architect must establish the "working height" of the stagehouse—the distance between the stage floor and the highest point to which rigging battens (pipes supporting scenery and lighting) may be flown. This elevation, in turn, determines the height of the structural steel grid built across the entire stagehouse. Some 7 to 10 feet beneath the theatre's roof structure, the grid floor supports—and provides access to—the pulleys and sheaves through which steel cables or hemp lines run to the rigging battens suspended below.

To determine the working height, also called grid height, the architect studies the production history of companies that will use the stage. The company with the greatest demand for production support space will set the grid height for the theatre. Managers of that company should tell the architect the distance between the stage floor and the bottom of the company's downstage masking borders and portal (the company should also provide the architect with its standard hanging plan).

This distance defines the height of the stage picture. To calculate working height, the architect multiples the height of the stage picture by 2.5. Thus, the clear space for flying and storing scenery should be no less than 2½ times the height from the stage floor to the bottom of the masking.

If the theatre will present opera, extra height may be needed in the stagehouse. Scenic elements used in opera tend to be taller than those for dance, so more height is needed to hide the scenery when it is flown out.

Cheating on grid height to save construction dollars is a false economy. When the grid is built too low, the crew will be forced to lower the top line of the masking borders to hide the bottoms of scenic pieces flown out. That, in turn, flattens the stage picture. Other remedies for inadequate height, such as raising the bottom of flown pieces with secondary battens, add costly time to each scene shift and may require extra stagehands.

For the architect, a dance company's hanging plan can be a guide to other details of stage dimensions. The drawings will give the width of standard drops, methods of dealing with side masking, and the typical playing depth (the distance from curtain line to first backdrop or cyclorama). They also show the maximum heights for floor-supported scenery, typical stage-lighting deployment, the total amount of scenery used by the company, and more. Such scenery and lighting requirements establish the scope of design problems that must be solved in the spaces above, behind, and beside the performing area.

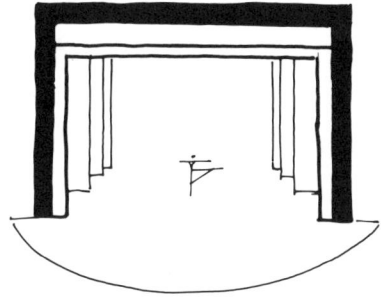

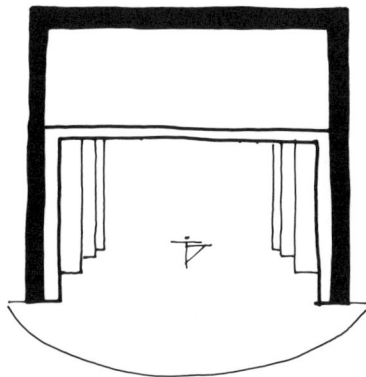

The proportions of the proscenium arch affect the stage picture. If the arch is too low, the picture appears flat. A properly proportioned arch, bottom picture, is nearly square.

MUSIC FOR DANCE

Many dance companies prefer performing to live music. However, only the largest companies can afford to travel with a full orchestra. Others may perform to live music at home, but tour with taped music. And still other companies prefer performing to taped music, at home and on the road.

SOUND SYSTEMS FOR RECORDED MUSIC

To satisfy all imaginable users, a dance theatre should be fitted with a high-fidelity sound system for playing recorded music. Large houses require specialized amplifiers and loudspeakers capable of wide range frequency response and capable of generating sound pressure equal to that produced by a symphony orchestra. Before deciding which system seems appropriate for a particular space, and for one's budget, seek the advice of a sound-systems specialist.

THE ORCHESTRA PIT

A large ballet company's orchestra pit may hold from sixty to ninety musicians. The minimum orchestra for a touring company may number forty players. The architect designing the pit should know not just how many musicians will use it, but also anything unusual about the house orchestra, such as its use of a particularly large number of bulky instruments. Some orchestra pits are designed so their size can be adjusted according to production needs—an advantage to management since space not needed for musicians can seat more patrons.

Musicians seldom agree on the appropriate height for an orchestra pit. Since the pit will be used by a variety of players, flexibility should be incorporated into the design. A sophisticated method for changing the height of the pit involves a lift that raises and lowers the floor forward of the stage apron. Temporary risers or adjustable platforms are an alternate, less expensive method.

The floor must be low enough that double-bass players can stand in the rear of the pit, often beneath the stage. However, if the pit is too low, seated musicians will have to crane their necks—and perhaps compromise their playing—to see the conductor (the conductor, in turn, needs a clear view of his players in the pit and of the dancers on stage). Figuring the head room at the rear of the pit at 6 feet 8 inches, the height of a standard door, is a good compromise. The minimum pit depth below the stage floor

The height of the stagehouse is dictated by the height of the stage picture demanded by the companies that will use the theatre.

The orchestra pit must permit the conductor to see every member of the orchestra as well as the performers on stage without interrupting the audience's sightlines.

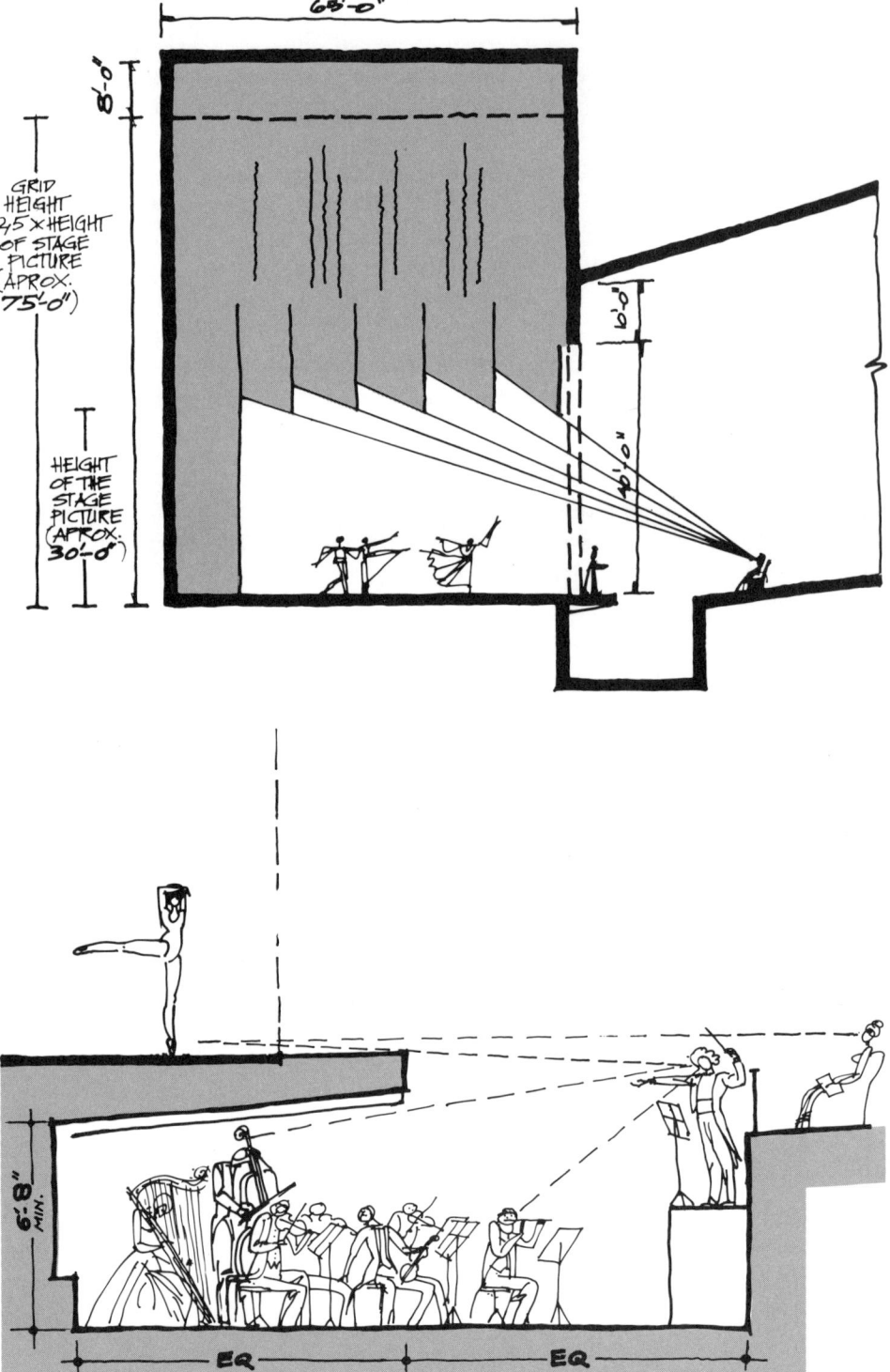

An adjustable orchestra pit has many advantages. When the floor is in its lowest position, it creates the traditional orchestra pit.

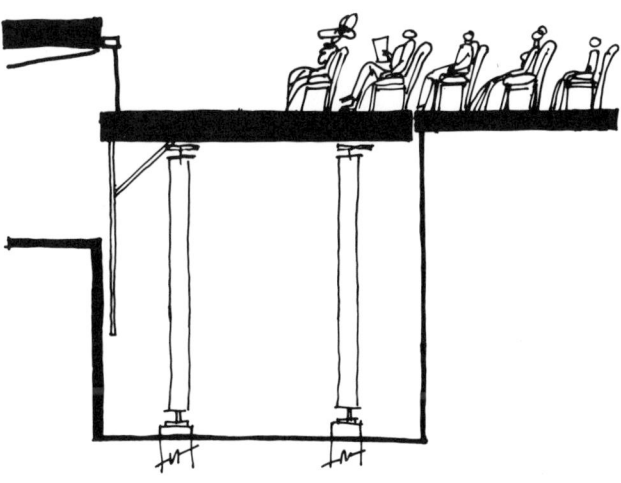

In the intermediate position, the pit floor acts as an extension of the audience-seating area.

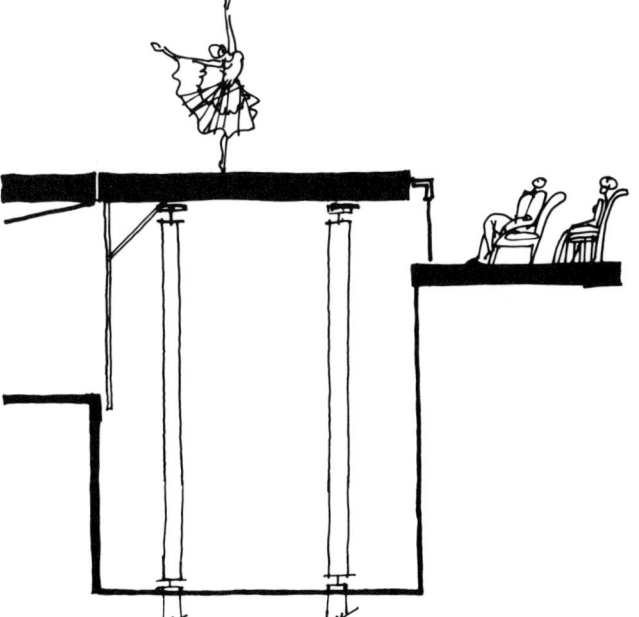

When fully raised, the pit floor provides an extension of the stage. If this is to be used for dance, the construction of the pit floor and sub-floor must be identical to the stage floor.

will then equal the head room plus the thickness of the overhanging stage floor.

The orchestra pit should be at least as wide as the proscenium opening. Proper depth can be determined by dividing the effective width of the pit into the total number of square feet required. A minimum factor of 15 square feet per musician should be used, with extra space allowed for stairs and passageways. Most musicians are happier, and play better, with even more room.

Orchestras usually prefer a pit that does not undercut the stage; an overhanging apron is physically and esthetically confining. On the other hand, a deep undercut creates a fuller sound, and the extra floor area can accommodate musicians and their belongings. The decision to bury or not to bury part of the orchestra beneath the stage turns on the question of how many choice seats for theatre patrons will be displaced by the pit.

At best, orchestra pits are cramped spaces, filled with chairs, music stands, instruments, and musicians. A large pit should allow players to enter from either side, to shorten if not eliminate the obstacle course.

Another consideration in planning the orchestra pit is the acoustical requirements of the space. Carpets can be laid on parts of the floor to dampen sections of the orchestra. Movable draperies can be used to absorb certain frequencies and thus "tune" the pit. The overhanging stage apron and the orchestra pit railing can also be acoustically treated. The pit railing may be designed to reflect the sound of the pit orchestra up onto the stage so performers can hear the music more clearly. In planning this space the advice of an acoustician is essential.

SUPPORT SPACES FOR THE PIT

Dance programs often include a variety of works, each of which may require different instrumentation. Thus the orchestra pit may have to be rearranged at each intermission: an adjacent storage room simplifies matters. Temperature and humidity in the storage room should be controlled to protect musical instruments.

Pianos are an often overlooked theatre-storage problem. Without extra piano-storage space offstage, the large instrument may claim valuable space within the stagehouse. Storing the piano beneath the stage often works well; that way, the piano can be rolled directly into the orchestra pit when needed.

Musicians need a lounge, toilets, lockers, and a dressing room. If the musicians leave the theatre for lunch or dinner, they need a safe place to put their instruments. A conductor's suite, if provided, should have a private toilet. The suite should also have room for a dressing area, a couch, a piano, and the conductor's guests.

The orchestra in a repertory theatre uses a staggering amount of music, and an orderly music library is essential. To determine how much space is needed, the architect should consult the orchestra librarian.

MINIMUM REQUIREMENTS FOR ALTERNATE SPACES

A performance space 45 feet wide by 40 deep may be ideal for dance, but the ideal is rarely at hand for most small companies. Whatever the width and depth of the performing area, the ceiling should stretch at least 16 feet above the stage floor. Higher is better: many dancers say low ceilings constrict performers and flatten choreography, and lighting designer Beverly Emmons adds that with less than 20 feet of height, proper lighting angles cannot be developed.

Newborn dance companies may have to compromise on space, but they should be stubborn perfectionists when it comes to the stage floor. Subfloor construction must be resilient, the surface smooth. Sometimes, floors in old loft buildings are already resilient enough for dance. Surfaces may need professional sanding, a new layer of

At the Mali Theatre in Leningrad, the stage scarcely overhangs the pit. Instead, the pit extends almost one-third of the way into the orchestra seating. This arrangement is preferred for opera and ballet because there is no stage-overhang to impede full orchestral sound.

oak or maple tongue-and-groove strips, or—the cheapest alternative—a covering of masonite or linoleum. If the existing wood floor is stiff, uneven, or damaged, a new dance floor will have to be designed and built atop the present surface. Methods for constructing a resilient substructure are described earlier in this chapter.

If the performing area will be used for rehearsal, one long wall should be fitted with mirrors and perhaps a barre (options for installing mirrors and barres are described in Chapter 5). A curtain must be provided to draw across the mirrors during performances.

ACOUSTICAL TREATMENTS

"Found" spaces for dance can come with built-in acoustical problems. Windows and skylights may need sealing, to block noise from the street or from adjacent spaces. Walls and ceilings may need insulating, or a separate, inner "skin" may have to be constructed—a costly affair. Such a skin usually consists of a floated floor (for example, many layers of wood atop resilient mounts), several sheets of drywall on staggered studs or resilient channels, and a multilayer drywall ceiling suspended on resilient hangers. Glass fiber or mineral wool is inserted in the spaces between the skin and the original structure. The skin must then be fully caulked to render it airtight. Finally, parallel walls can create a flutter effect. This can be countered by strategically placing sound-absorbing materials on ceilings and on upper parts of walls, per the direction of an acoustical consultant.

OFFSTAGE REQUIREMENTS

In a small showcase theatre or alternate space, offstage is often a catchall area containing the crossover, wings, warm-up room, prop, scenery, and costume stops, canteen, and general storeroom. For efficiency and security, separate lockable spaces should be available for each of these functions. At the least, lockable cabinets should be provided for valuable items. The door or doors between offstage and the performing area should be wide enough to accommodate moving scenery. During performances, offstage lighting levels must be kept low enough for dancers to enter and exit the performing area without admitting shafts of light to the stage.

HEATING AND VENTILATION

The skylights and windows that brighten lofts and other alternate spaces also admit drafts. Broken panes should be replaced and leaky sashes caulked. If drafts remain, windows and skylights can be covered with panels of clear plexiglass or lexan. The panels can be bolted to a wood frame, and the frame attached to window edges with wing nuts, for easy removal in summer and for cleaning. Some provision should be made for blacking out skylights. Otherwise, company lighting rehearsals and performances must await sunset.

Other problems arise in found spaces. An aging furnace may have to be supplemented by electric or gas-fired space heaters. Once windows are sealed, the space may be too stuffy; some form of ventilation system will be needed to supply fresh air to dancers and the audience. In many alternate spaces, heating and air-conditioning equipment roars so loudly that it has to be switched off during performances. Before signing a lease or making a down payment on a promising space for dance, have it inspected by a trustworthy heating and plumbing contractor. Some foundlings are best passed by.

STAGE AND REHEARSAL STUDIO FLOOR CONSTRUCTION

Adapted from the specifications for the Grand Opera House, Wilmington, Delaware, and the Brown University Performing Arts Complex, Providence, Rhode Island.

GENERAL

I. *Work Included:*

Furnish and install wood-flooring systems specified herein, including wood-support systems, subflooring, and other accessory items. Sand and finish wood flooring, both new and existing.

II. *Submittals* (samples, shop drawings, or other documentation provided by the contractor to the architect to show that materials purchased for installation are the same as specified in the contract):

Samples: 12 inch long pieces of strip-wood flooring.

III. *Applicable Standards:*

A. Finish maple flooring: according to standards of the Maple Flooring Manufacturers Association (MFMA).
B. Plywood: U.S. Product Standard P.S. 1-74.
C. Softwood (sleepers): U.S. Product Standard P.S. 20-70.

IV. *Storage and Acclimatization:*

A. Do not store finish flooring in the building until "wet" work has been completed and the building is dry. Store finish flooring in the building at least three days under similar conditions of humidity and ventilation to that in spaces receiving the wood flooring.
B. Maintain the following temperatures:
   1. In storage areas, 70 degrees Fahrenheit maximum, 50 degrees minimum.
   2. In areas of installation, three days prior to installation and during installation, 70 degrees Fahrenheit minimum.
C. If finish flooring is to be installed during high-humidity periods (from late spring to early fall), allow an acclimatization period of two to three weeks before sanding.
D. Delivered materials should be in manufacturer's original containers, cartons, or wrappings, with contents clearly labeled.

V. *Job Conditions:*

Verify conditions of existing spaces where new wood-flooring systems are to be installed, specifically the condition of existing floors, and the relationship of new wood-floor levels to other floors (primarily at doorways).

PRODUCTS

I. *Multi-use Stage Floor:*

A. Finish Flooring: 1¼ inch by 2¼ inch first grade edge grained yellow pine or Douglas fir.
B. Subflooring: 3/4 inch plywood, C-D grade.
C. Sleepers: 1 inch by 4 inch pine, Construction grade, kiln dried.
D. Insulation: Flexible glass fiber, 3 pounds per cubic foot density, 1½ inches thick in continuous rolls.
E. Vapor Barrier: W. R. Meadows "Sealtight" board, or approved equal, 1/8 inch.
F. Surface Finish:
   1. Sealer: Oleoresinous sealer of manufacturer approved by MFMA.
   2. Stain: To be selected by owner.

II. *Rehearsal Studio or Stage Floor Exclusively for Dance*
A. Finish Flooring: 33/32 inch by 2¼ inch first-grade hard maple, tongue-and-groove end-matched.
B. Sleepers, insulation, and vapor barrier: same as for multi-use stage floor.
C. Surface Finish:
   1. Oleoresinous sealer, of manufacturer approved by MFMA.
   2. Polyurethane varnish optional.

EXECUTION
I. *Preparation:*
Remove debris, mortar daubs, or spackle. Sweep "broom clean."
Check existing floors for level.

II. *Installation—Stage Floor*
A. Vapor Barrier: Place boards over entire area, with joints hand-tight and taped.
B. Sleepers: 3 layers 1 inch by 4 inches at 16 inches on center.
   1. First layer: Install at 90 degrees to the direction of finish flooring. Keep 1/2 inch from perimeter walls. Shim as required to maintain a tolerance level of 1/8 inch in 10 feet. Set in cold-applied asphalt mastic.
   2. Second Layer: Install at 90 degrees to first layer. Nail at each point of lap. Ends of sleepers should occur only over supports. Do not penetrate membrane.
   3. Third layer: Install at 90 degrees to second layer. Offset 8 inches from first layer. Nail at each point of lap. Ends of sleepers should occur only over supports.
C. Insulation: Install between second and third layers of sleepers. Lap ends at least 6 inches; butt tight to sides of sleepers.
D. Subflooring: Install plywood over sleepers, long dimension at right angles to top layer of sleepers, nailing to sleepers 8 inches on center using 8d helical or annular ring nails.
E. Strip Flooring:
   1. Lay first course with grooved edge alongside wall. Keep edge of flooring 1/2 inch away from wall.
   2. Nail first course with finishing nails and countersink. Toenail subsequent courses at an angle of 50 degrees where tongue meets shoulder. Nail at each point of bearing over sleeper, using 7d or 8d helical shank, finishing head nails.
   3. Face nail last course and countersink.
   4. Stagger end joints.
   5. Putty countersink holes with a material of the same hardness as the wood.
   6. Install edging (base molding) affixed to wall, not to flooring.

III. *Installation—Rehearsal Studio Floor*
Same as for multi-use stage floor, but no subflooring required.

IV. *Sanding*—(all wood-floor systems, new and existing):
A. Use power sander, the type of paper, and the number of cuts necessary to take down high spots and bring strips perfectly flush with each other.
B. Final sanding should be done with fine paper, leaving the floor velvet smooth and in such condition that no sanding marks will show through when finish is applied.

V. *Finishing*—(all wood-floor systems, new and existing) to commence immediately after sanding:
A. Vacuum thoroughly. Sweep surface with a naphtha-treated cloth or tack rag

under a hair brush.
- B. For floors to receive stain, apply one coat of stain. Allow to dry before applying second coat. Allow to dry thoroughly before sealing.
- C. Apply coat of sealer, thoroughly penetrating into wood. Work first against the grain, then smooth out with the grain. Avoid leaving puddles of sealer on the floor.
- D. After coat is thoroughly dry, steel wool. Vacuum and/or sweep with naphtha-treated cloths.
- E. For floors to receive varnish, apply one coat of satin varnish after steel wooling and vacuuming of sealer coat.

VI. *Protection:*

Allow 48 hours before any traffic is permitted on finished floor. Protect floor with non-staining reinforcing Kraft paper, with joints lapped and taped. Maintain protection until floor is to be used for intended purpose.

SPACES FOR THE PUBLIC

4

Most of us have suffered enough evenings in inconsiderate theatres, where our seats were set so far to one side that only half the stage was visible, where performers played peekaboo behind the head of the gentleman sitting in front of us, where leg room was nil, and where the better part of each intermission was spent shuffling up the crowded aisle to the lobby.

A few simple standards constitute the rights of every paying patron:
1. Each seat in the house must provide a full view of performers, wherever they may be on stage. Good sightlines are especially important in dance. Choreography, the shaping of space through body movement, suffers when its moving parts go unseen.
2. Seats should be comfortably wide, and rows spaced to spare the knees of long-legged theatre-goers.
3. Exits should be numerous and conveniently placed, to let the theatre empty quickly during intermissions and at the end of the program.
4. The lobby should be spacious and restrooms plentiful. Dance programs often consist of several short pieces, separated by as many as three or four intermissions. Thus audience members leave their seats more often and spend more time in the lobby or visiting restrooms than they might at plays or music concerts.
5. Handicapped persons need easy access to the house and all its facilities, including drinking fountains, restrooms, telephones, and concession stands.
6. Finally, a measure of humility is called for. The developers of a large, publicly funded performing arts complex may feel obliged to present their community with a palace, partly to justify the dollars spent building the facility. When that happens, architecture can upstage performers. Worse, an architectural showboat may cost so much that stage and backstage spaces must be scaled down. One job of the theatre-design consultant, who should be involved in the project from the start, is to protect the client from making such a mistake by keeping the needs of performers and stage crew in sharp focus during the planning process.

FROM THE OUTSIDE IN

For many Americans, an evening of dance, music, or theatre starts in a parking garage. Even in large cities, where mass transit or taxis are available, out-of-towners will drive to the theatre. The architect should give thought to the physical and psychological transition visitors will make as they pass from a dimly lit garage or outdoor parking lot into a glittering lobby crowded with patrons making their way to the performance.

At Lincoln Center in New York City, an extensive subterranean circulation system accommodates visitors arriving from the nearby subway, in taxis, and in cars that require on-site parking. At the lowest lobby levels of the Metropolitan Opera and Avery Fisher Hall, a wall of glass windows and doors gives onto a brightly lit internal street, where passengers disembark from limousines, cabs, and private cars. The area has been further enhanced by the recent addition of the Met's gift shop across the internal street. Those who wait while drivers park their cars need not endure an architectural purgatory of the sort found at most urban theatres with parking facilities.

THE BOX OFFICE

No two box offices function the same. Some box office managers insist that telephone orders be taken in the same space as window orders, so all tickets and ticket

Opposite: The main lobby of the New York State Theatre, Lincoln Center, New York.

racks will be in one place. Others want telephone orders taken separately to isolate the noise of ringing phones. Some managers prefer having mail and subscription orders processed in administrative offices, and not in the box office.

Although this small space is critical to the theatre's operations, it usually receives scant attention during the design process. The box office should be prominently located, but in a side or outer lobby separate from the main lobby. This makes for better security and reduces the need to light, heat, or cool the main lobby when the box office is open but the theatre is not. Despite differences in operating procedures, general requirements for most box offices are similar. The following case study suggests some box office basics.

During the restoration of the historic Grand Opera House in Wilmington, Delaware, the box office was built into an adjacent storefront. Because rental income from the storefront was important to the operation of the Opera House, the box office was designed to be little larger than a custodial closet. Several successful seasons later, the Opera House management is considering giving the entire storefront over to the box office.

Plans for a new box office at Wilmington call for a separate foyer, so lines can form without congesting the main lobby. The foyer offers barrier-free access from the street, as well as from the main and outer lobbies. Ticket rates and the theatre-seating plan are clearly visible to customers in line, an often overlooked service for patrons.

The box office windows are prefabricated and fitted with bulletproof laminated glass; vertical openings beside each window permit unamplified conversation between customers and ticket sellers, but are small enough to block a gun barrel. The ticket racks lining the wall to the rear of the windows are accessible to employees out front, but also convenient to the two telephone sales stations around the corner in the workroom. The workroom has two long counters for processing telephone orders, mail orders, and subscriptions. Because the box office is sometimes so busy that no one can leave for lunch, a small Pullman kitchen has been provided. Opposite the kitchen is a coat closet; beyond is a small restroom.

The box office manager's space is fitted with a desk, files, and a small conference table. But the most important item here is the small safe for box office receipts still on hand at the end of the day. A ship's ladder leads to a storage gallery ringing the entire box office, where records and unsold tickets are kept.

THE LOBBY

A well-designed theatre lobby should be ample yet not too large, and should feel a bit crowded even when a performance is not sold out. Too vast a lobby subdues the public; during intermissions, it may rob patrons of the excitement generated by the performance.

Theatre-goers enjoy seeing other members of the audience and being seen themselves. Balconies and grand stairs afford excellent opportunities for people-watching and should be included in the lobby design. Lighting should be bright, and acoustics such that when the lobby is full the crowd purrs but does not roar.

In facilities with more than one theatre, lobby space should be shared and tickets taken as near the entrance of each auditorium as possible. Entrances to each theatre must be clearly designated, and a system provided for paging audiences. Each entrance should also be designed to block sound and light, so intermissions in one theatre do not disrupt the performance in another.

A theatre should be kind to late-comers. At many concert halls and opera houses, tardy patrons cannot enter the auditorium until the end of the first piece or act. While the performance may be broadcast on closed-circuit monitors in the lobby, watching the first third of a dance program on television seems a stiff penalty for a late

The lobby at Zellerbach Hall in Berkeley, California, serves the main auditorium and a small experimental theatre.

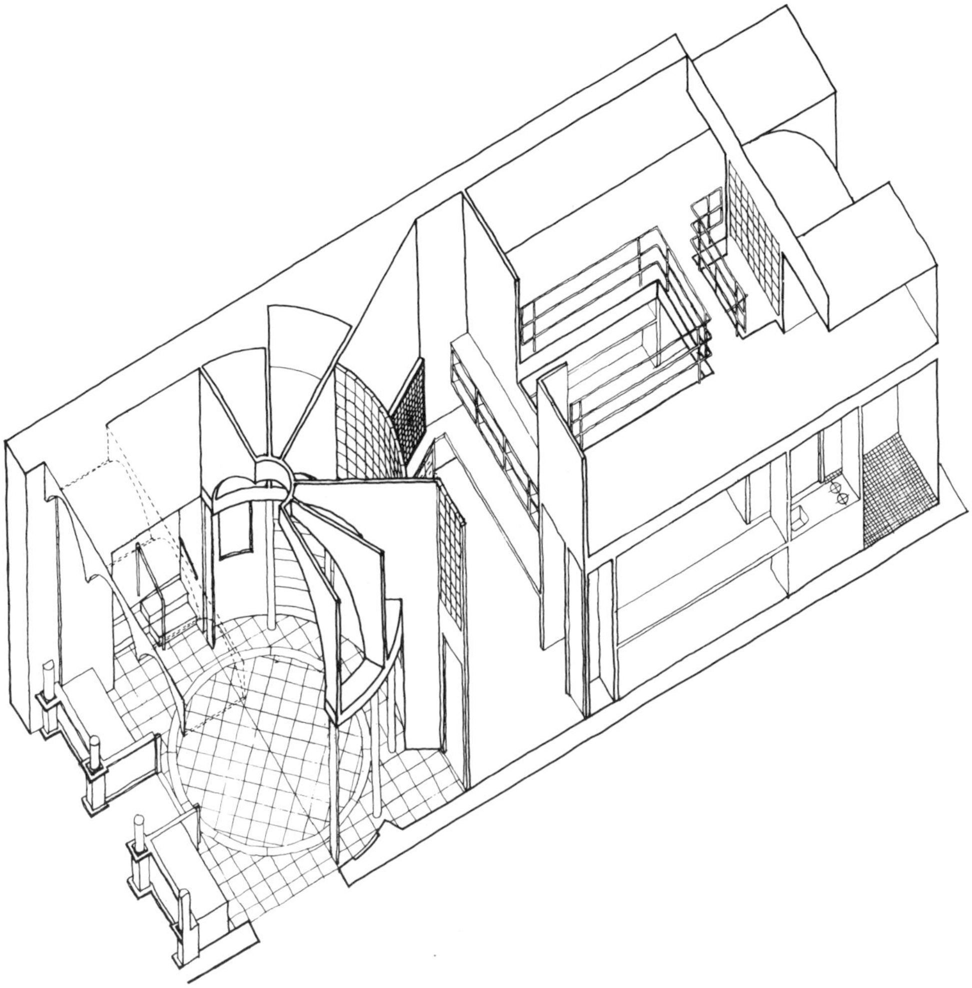

Designs for expanding the lobby and box office at the Grand Opera House in Wilmington, Delaware.

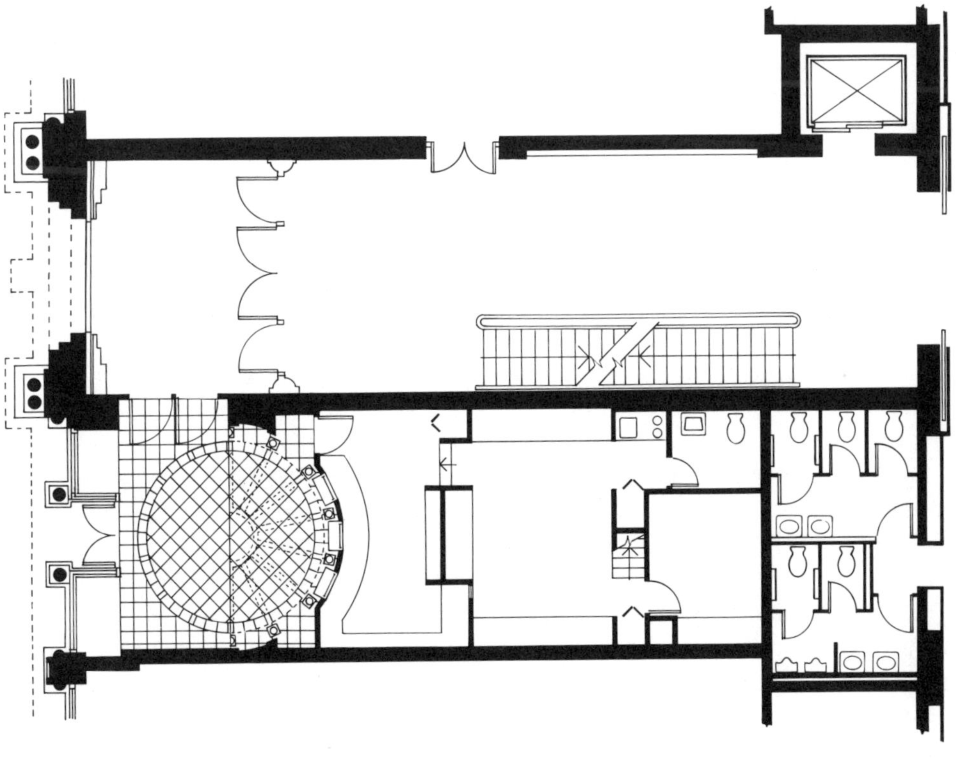

51

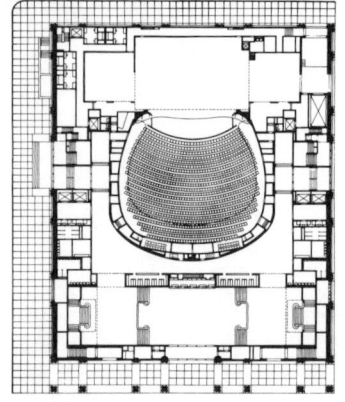

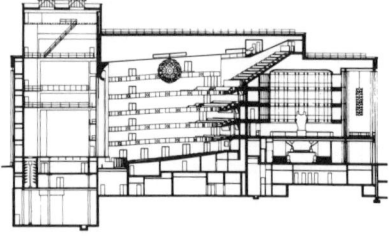

The 60-foot-high lobby at the New York State Theatre at Lincoln Center is large enough to accommodate two thousand people and to be used for a range of activities from formal receptions to spring carnivals. Yet the space is not overpowering. Elegant, yet inviting, the lobby permits ease of movement and is an ideal setting for the traditional intermission activity—watching and being watched. Bottom: Theatre plan and section.

baby-sitter or a traffic jam. A less punitive solution should be sought, such as a glass-walled room at the rear of the orchestra section or an unobstrusive standing rail behind the last row of seats.

Performers should not have to pass through lobbies in order to get backstage. Nevertheless, there should be an inconspicuous, lockable pass door that allows theatre employees to travel from the lobby to backstage without going outdoors.

Local building codes, under the heading "Places of Assembly," lay down minimum standards for the design and size of theatre lobbies. For example, the New York City Code states that the minimum unobstructed floor area shall accommodate the aggregate occupant load of all exits opening onto it, providing two square feet per person, not including space taken up by furniture or equipment. But this is a bare minimum for any lobby, and four to six square feet per person gives a more workable space. The New York Code also stipulates the minimum lobby ceiling height (eight feet); limits for stair risers and treads; number of risers per flight of steps; minimum exit-door widths; ramp slopes; and required fire ratings for floor, wall, and ceiling construction and their finish materials. It is essential for the architect to be familiar and comply with all governing building codes. In addition to setting standards for the safety of patrons, the codes provide important design guidelines.

COAT CHECKROOM

In cold or rainy climates, a coat checkroom is a public service, plus a source of revenue for the theatre. If a checkroom is included in the lobby, it should be easily accessible, and should hold at least half as many coats as there are seats in the house; the counter should be long enough to be manned by several employees. Coin-operated lockers, built into lobby walls or set in a separate, nearby room, let patrons check or retrieve their belongings without waiting in line, require no staff, and accommodate furs, which many coat rooms refuse to check. On the other hand, lockers are costly to buy, and are usually an inelegant addition to a theatre lobby.

PUBLIC TOILETS

Most building codes do not distinguish between the number of toilets that should be provided for men and women. Innocent architects tend to split the required minimum number equally between the sexes. Their first mistake is accepting the minimum; their second is to strive for equality.

At matinee performances in New York City, women patrons generally outnumber men seventeen to one, and matinees constitute twenty-five percent of the weekly performances in most performing arts facilities. As a rule, women require more toilets than men because it takes them longer to adjust their clothing. They need more wash basins, or at the least more counter space and mirrors, because women use restrooms to adjust their hair and makeup. To help shorten the lines outside lobby restrooms, plan on 1.5 women's toilets and 1.0 women's lavatory for every 100 seats in the house. For men, provide 1.0 toilet or urinal (within this ratio there may be 2 urinals for each toilet) and .5 lavatories per 100 theatre seats.

Architects overly fond of symmetry often place men's and women's restrooms at opposite ends of the lobby, an arrangement that separates couples for the better part of intermission. A more thoughtful approach is to distribute several pairs of small restrooms—the women's larger than the men's—throughout the lobby.

Toilets for handicapped persons can be combined with the general public's, but along with telephones and drinking fountains, they should be easily reached from handicapped seating areas in the house. Directions to these amenities should be as clear for blind or deaf patrons as they are for everyone else. Clear signage is important for all theatre-goers, not just handicapped persons; and a signage program should be part of the lobby design package. Criteria for restrooms, pay phones, and drinking fountains for handicapped patrons can be found in Appendix C.

CONCESSIONS AND SUPPORT SPACES

Stands for selling snacks, liquor, and soft drinks, as well as for souvenirs and subscriptions, can add to theatre revenue. Concessions are generally situated along lobby walls or in central islands. Plumbing is often required, so their location should be considered early in the design process.

Lobby support spaces should include a storage area for concession materials and theatre programs and a house manager's office opening onto the lobby. Each major lobby level needs a janitor's closet with a slop sink plus room to store cleaning supplies and equipment.

THE HOUSE

All good theatre designers strive to create a space that encourages intimacy between patrons and performers and provides each member of the audience an unobstructed view of the stage. Vertical and horizontal sightlines must be carefully planned, especially in spaces for dance.

The simplest way of ensuring clear vertical sightlines—elevating each row a step above the one before it—creates too steep a rake for dance performances, raising most of the audience well above the stage. Most choreographers want dancers' bodies seen in space or against a scenic backdrop, not against the floor. The rake in a dance theatre should be shallow, with vertical sightlines achieved by staggering seats, so occupants of each row look between the heads of persons in front of them.

Horizontal sightlines depend on the shape of the fan in which seats are distributed about the stage. If the seats fan out too widely, viewers at the sides of the theatre cannot see the nearest side of the stage. A sixty-degree fan usually works best for dance.

While most choreographers want their work seen from eye level, some dance enthusiasts seek proximity over perspective. They prefer sitting in a balcony near the stage even if it means watching choreography played out against the floor. But balconies need to be designed with care. Too often they loom so far forward that patrons in the rear of the orchestra cannot see the top of the stage. Building second and third balconies may solve that problem but substitutes another: occupants of too lofty a balcony may be unable to see the front of the stage.

Theatre seat widths range from 19 to 22 inches, with 21 inches a useful standard. Varying seat widths is a common way to achieve staggered seating while keeping the edges of rows flush at the aisles. In most theatres, the space from seat back to seat back is between 32 and 37 inches. Allowing 35 to 36 inches makes for more comfortable patrons. Combine that depth with a 21 inch width, and each seat in the house will occupy from 5 to 5½ square feet of space.

Most building codes cite 44 inches as a standard aisle width, or 36 inches for aisles serving only one side of the house. The Off-Off Broadway Association's useful book, *Will It Make a Theatre?*, written by Eldon Elder, suggests that aisle space should equal 23 percent of the total seating area. In larger theatres, push that figure to 25 percent.

Because conventional aisles and cross aisles tend to cut swaths through seating, creating discreet, disconnected groupings, many theatre planners advocate continental seating, in which there are no aisles from the front to the back of the house. Instead, widely spaced rows of seating run clear across the width of the orchestra.

"Probably the best-designed theatre, in terms of proportion and the relationship created between audience and stage is the Zellerbach in Berkeley. One needs only lift an eyelid or an arm and the gesture is in the lap of the audience. There is no need to belt a movement a quarter of a mile out, nor inch around the honeycomb of boxes lining the house. There is complete and direct connection with the audience."
Murray Louis, choreographer
<u>Inside Dance</u>
Copyright © 1980 by Murray Louis
St. Martins Press, Inc. New York

The "best seat in the house," located on the centerline of the auditorium, provides a clear view of the entire performing area and masks the wings.

If the angle of the seating fan is limited to 60 degrees, people seated at the extreme ends of rows will have an adequate view of the stage and will not see too far into the wings.

If the angle of the fan is widened in an effort to increase the seating capacity of the house, persons seated at the ends of rows cannot see a significant portion of the stage, and wing space cannot be masked. This illustration shows the angle at 80 degrees.

Keeping the 60-degree fan but increasing the width of the proscenium in order to increase the seating capacity is no solution because dance companies cannot increase the width of their performing area, as defined by their masking, because this would change the choreography.

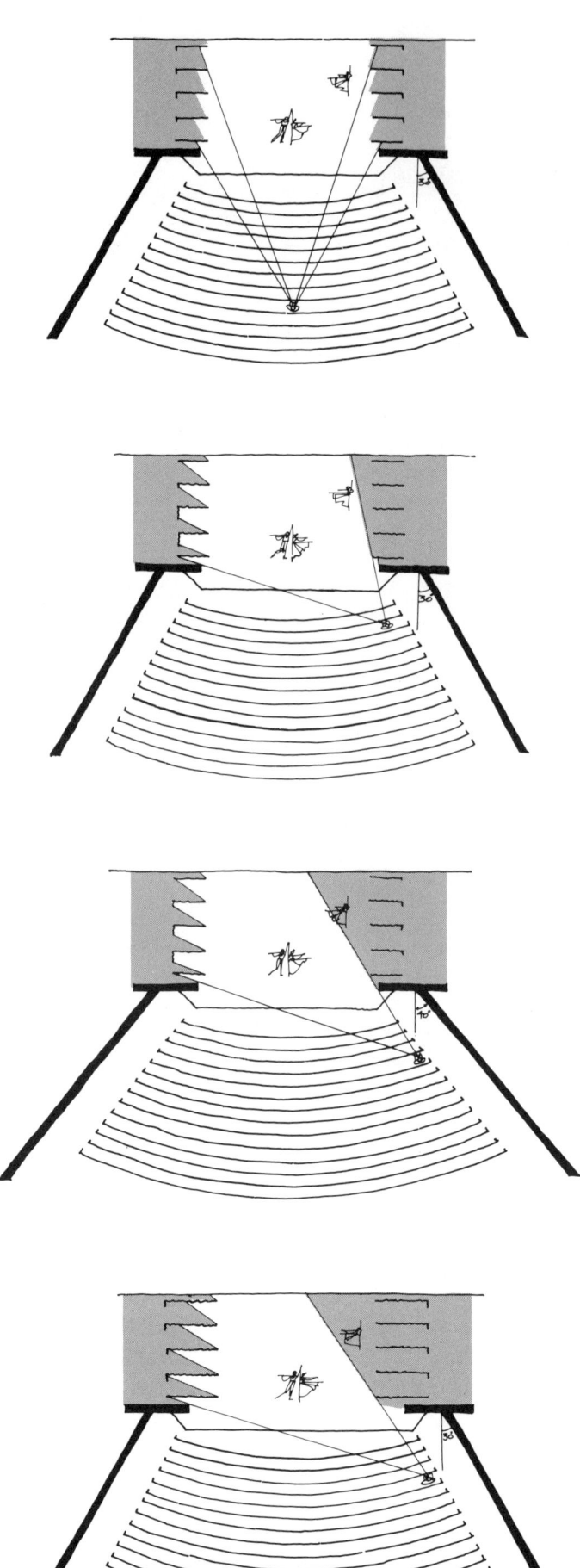

54

Most codes require that back-to-back spacing be increased to as much as 42 inches to permit easy egress from seating in the center of the rows. However, some patrons still feel reluctant to climb over twenty or thirty people to enjoy the amenities of the lobby during intermission. The lobbies of theatres with continental seating must be designed to accommodate the broad and usually stepped side corridors that give onto the multiple side doors to the house. This, in turn, may rob square footage from the main lobby. Also directing patrons to appropriate doors may require more ushers than are needed in a theatre with a conventional aisle plan. Because the number of seats per square foot of orchestra floor is virtually the same for continental seating as for traditional seating with aisles and cross aisles, the decision to use continental seating is a matter of preference.

ACOUSTICAL CONSIDERATIONS

Building a well-tuned theatre requires advice from an acoustical consultant with experience in designing for the performing arts. The acoustics of the house are a function of the size and shape of the auditorium; the angles of walls, floors, and ceiling; and the reflective or absorptive quality of architectural finishes and movable equipment, as well as other design features.

A slightly different species of expert, the sound-systems consultant, should be brought in to help plan where speakers, amplifiers, and sound control consoles will be located and to help decide what sorts of sound effects, backstage paging, and program-monitoring equipment will be needed in a particular theatre.

Since many dance companies depend on recorded music, any theatre designed for dance must have loudspeakers positioned to produce the best sound.

Many theatres otherwise right for dance have no built-in sound systems. If they do, the systems are often outdated, and dance companies using recorded music must cope with large and unsightly speakers stacked near the stage, and with exposed wires running to amplifiers, tape decks, and control consoles.

Sound systems are not cheap, and the state of the art changes constantly. However, recorded music is used throughout the performing arts today, not just in dance. In any new theatre, built-in speaker locations must be designated in the house and—at the least—empty conduits (for future wiring) must be run to pre-established locations for sound-control equipment and amplifiers.

TECHNICAL ELEMENTS IN THE HOUSE

Chapter 6 discusses in detail technical equipment that goes in the rear of the house. Space for projection, recording, and some lighting equipment should be allocated above and behind the back row of the orchestra section. Further, crew members working in these stations need access to backstage without passing through public areas.

In the house itself, near the center of the orchestra, a jack should be installed for headset connections with the control room and backstage, an essential convenience for the stage manager during rehearsals. Microphone jacks should be located in concurrence with the recommendations of a recording engineer or sound-systems consultant. Along the theatre walls and within the seating area, 115-volt outlets should be placed for electrical equipment needed during rehearsals and performances, as well as for the vacuums used by cleaning crews.

AUDIENCE ACCOMMODATIONS IN ALTERNATE SPACES

Seating arrangements in alternate spaces for dance range from semiformal to spartan, from folding chairs to foam rubber cushions. However one plans to accommodate the public, it pays to check local codes governing theatres and other places of assembly. Most building codes insist that when occupancy in a place of assembly

Patrons in the first row of seats should be able to see the entire surface of the stage floor, as in the top illustration.

A radial aisle seating plan

A continental seating plan

exceeds fifty persons, seating must be fixed. Some codes are more flexible. New York City's stipulates that when less than 8 square feet are allocated per patron, seats will be fixed to the floor. But when the audience space is 8 to 12 square feet per person, seats need only be ganged, that is, attached to each other side by side. And when the space goes beyond 12 square feet per person, seating may be loose, with chairs neither bolted to the floor nor ganged together.

COLORS AND FINISHES

Money often grows scarce as work on an alternate space draws to a close. The temptation arises to scrap the color scheme, so carefully conceived months before, and to spray paint walls and ceiling black or white. Yet most dancers find an all-black environment oppressive. And white rooms, while fine for rehearsals, are difficult to black out for performances, even after dark. Fortunately, there are inexpensive, less drastic alternatives.

The highly successful BeVard Community Room, at the Civic Center of Onondaga County, in Syracuse, New York, has been painted medium gray with a bright green overhead grid and catwalk system, draperies, and seats. Brown University's new dance studio was painted in two tones of beige, but its wall of casement windows and the trim around mirrors are painted bright red and green — to the delight of teachers, students, and audiences.

A pleasing color scheme, laid down with good paint, is more than a finishing touch in an alternate space for dance. It is an important design element, one that encourages performers and patrons to visit the theatre again and again.

Ashamu Dance Studio at Brown University in Providence, Rhode Island.

5 BACKSTAGE SPACES FOR PERFORMERS

Dancers may sleep at home or at the Holiday Inn, but—more than most performing artists—they live in rehearsal studios and theatres.

Large dance companies often set aside two six-week stretches each year to create new works and rehearse their repertoire. During these times when the company does not perform, its dancers spend their entire work week attending class and rehearsals. When the company's home season begins, daily performances go atop that existing work schedule. A nationally acclaimed company may perform eight times a week, thirty-eight weeks a year. When the company takes to the road, the class-rehearsal-performance routine continues, but now with the added rigors of touring. Throughout the long performance season, the cities and audiences change, but the dance company's hothouse athletes remain theatre-bound, twelve hours a day, six days a week.

Given the time they spend inside theatres, dancers develop a keen interest in well-designed houses. Every dancer interviewed for this book praised the theatres of Europe over those of America. The romance and history associated with those theatres partly explain their popularity. But the chief reason dancers appreciate them is that the European theatres were designed with evident respect for the artists who would use them.

A new theatre cannot recreate the mood of a nineteenth-century opera house, but it can respond sensitively to the needs of performing artists, and to the special needs of dancers. To understand those requirements, we will tour each room backstage. First, we should explain some general design problems that must be overcome to make the dance house a better home for dancers.

> What would I tell an architect who's designing a dressing room? Think of your bedroom.
> —Trisha Brown, dancer and choreographer

HEATING AND VENTILATION

Dancers need fresh air to replenish the oxygen they consume in class and rehearsals. However, they do not need air conditioning. In a room singers would find stifling, dancers will pull on layers of wool to retain body heat. "Dancers need to be warmed, not chilled," says Richard Le Blond, Jr., president and chief executive officer of the San Francisco Ballet.

In hot, humid climates, where backstage air conditioning is a must for other performing artists, cooled air should be pushed slowly through oversized ducts, to avoid drafts and noise. Relative humidity should be maintained at about fifty percent. Ideally, in a dance theatre the temperature on stage (which should match that in corridors, dressing rooms, and rehearsal areas) will be controlled independently of the air temperature in the auditorium and the rest of the building.

SOUND INSULATION

Of this country's new performing arts centers, the Civic Center of Onondaga County, in Syracuse, New York, earns some of the best marks from dancers. Joseph Golden, the center's executive director, attributes that popularity to the welcoming atmosphere backstage, to the clarity of the center's design, and to the fact that sound from one backstage area does not flow into others.

Increasing the thickness and mass of floors, walls, and ceilings is the simplest way to confine sound. But that can impose a heavy load on a building's structure. A less weighty, but more costly alternative is to build floors, walls, and hung ceilings in multiple layers, with each layer separated by air, insulation, resilient pads and/or

The most elegant dance in the world takes shape in simple rehearsal studios. They may be modestly finished and appointed, but they must have space, light, and warmth. Opposite: A rehearsal room for the Kirov Ballet, Leningrad.

A typical rehearsal schedule for the New York City Ballet calls for over 24 hours of rehearsal between mid-morning and early evening. Many ballets are in rehearsal simultaneously; and seven rehearsal spaces, including the stage of the New York Stage Theatre, are in constant use.

NEW YORK CITY BALLET

Date Tuesday, May 5

Time	Place	Ballet	Rehearsal Call Sheet
			TO KARINSKA: Gluck, Franceschi, Schetter, Trojaborg
10:30 — 11:30	Main	Class	Mr. Taras Barkagan
11:30 — 1:00	Main (Stage at 12:00)	Piano Pieces	Andersen, Franceschi, L. Roy Zimmerman/Robbins/Cook
11:45 — 12:30	Practice	Midsummer	BUTTERFLIES: All girls and available U's Barkagan/Dunleavy
12:00 —	Juil. #4	In G Major, Vienna Waltz, & Square Dance	Nichols, Lavery (Watts at 1:00) Boelzner (De Soto at 1:00)/Leland
12:00 — 2:00	Juil. #1	Histoire	Houston, D. Duell Poliakine
12:30 — 1:30	Main	Intro. & Fugue	Complete P's & U's Moredock/J. Duell/Dunleavy
1:30 — 2:30	Practice	Midsummer	TALL FAIRIES: All girls and available U's with hall Barkagan/Dunleavy
1:30 — 3:30	Stage	Concert	Complete, P's & U's in costume (girls in McBride Waltz leave at 3:00) Zimmerman/Robbins
1:30 — 2:00	Main	Apollo	Andersen Boelzner
2:00 — 4:00	Main	Mozartiana	Farrell, Andersen Boelzner/Balanchine/Dunleavy
2:30 — 6:00	Sofia	Stars, Apollo, Goldberg, Symphony in C	M. Roy (Calegari at 3:30; Lopez at 4:00; Lavery at 5:00) Moredock
4:00 — 4:30	Main	Vienna Waltz	McBRIDE WALTZ: All girls and U's De Soto/Dunleavy
4:00 — 6:00	Stage	5/4 Waltz	McBride, Tomasson, all girls and U's Zimmerman/Robbins/Cook
4:30 — 6:00	Main	New Ballet	WALTZ: All boys, girls and U's with Kistler, Lavery (without Scherzo couples) Poliakine/Martins/Hendl
4:30 — 6:00	Practice	Midsummer	DIVERTISSEMENT: All couples and available U's with Divet De Soto/Dunleavy
6:00 — 7:00	Stage	Apollo	Watts, Andersen Poliakine
6:00 — 7:15	Lower	Midsummer	Children Barkagan/Richardson
6:00 — 7:30	Main	Stars & Midsummer	Jennings (Alexopoulos, J. Duell at 6:30) De Soto

clips and hangers. The separate spaces absorb sound waves, rendering them too weak to travel from room to room.

Doors should be Sound Transmission Coefficient (STC) rated, according to the level of acoustical energy (decibels) that must be blocked. Backstage doors should also be fully gasketed. The heating-ventilating-cooling system should be designed so sound cannot travel from one space to another through continuous duct runs. Theatre planners on the quest for sound insulation will want to turn to an acoustical consultant for help in solving these and other problems.

LIGHTING

Warmth is essential to the physical well-being of dancers; good lighting soothes their souls. Proper backstage illumination consists of as much natural light as possible, supplemented by incandescent light.

Dancers use words like "snowblind" and "cooked" to describe the effect of twelve hours' exposure to backstage fluorescence. On the other hand, fluorescent lighting is efficient. A sixty-watt fluorescent lamp emits four times the light of a sixty-watt incandescent lamp. Fluorescent lamps not only offer more light per penny, but also generate less heat. Well-planned backstage lighting can provide the psychological benefits of daylight, the esthetic virtues of incandescent light, and the savings of fluorescence. However, help from an architectural lighting consultant may be needed to develop such a fine-tuned lighting scheme.

CORRIDORS

In most theatres, backstage corridors are pressed into service as parking lots. Instrument cases, wardrobe trunks, prop crates, and tables line the wall, encroaching on passage space. The American Guild of Musical Artists, the dancers' union, is aware of problems created by backstage traffic jams. The union's contracts stipulate that makeup cases and practice clothes will be at each performer's dressing station "no later than one (1) hour prior to performance time" and that "all dancers' costumes will be distributed in the dressing rooms no later than by half hour call, and theatre cases must be distributed one (1) hour prior to the first call of the day."

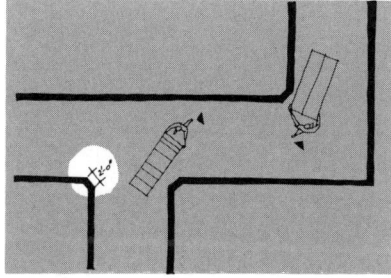

Chamfered corners permit easier movement of crates and equipment through backstage corridors.

If the stagehouse is part of a large-scale, multi-use facility, then the architect should size corridors in the vicinity of the stage no narrower than 8 feet. If the stagehouse is a part of a smaller facility, 5 feet is probably sufficient. The corridors should be designed with as few sharp turns as possible. Also, corridors leading to dressing rooms should be equally wide to allow for easy movement of costume racks and for dancers running to and from the stage.

Corners and right-angle turns in major corridors must be chamfered, that is, cut on a 45-degree bevel no less than 2 feet wide on the face. Chamfered corners make it easier to maneuver large pieces of theatre equipment and protect fast-moving dancers from injury. Vinyl wainscoting and steel or vinyl corner guards will protect corridor walls from damage by moving goods.

Touring dancers and their company's crew are often unfamiliar with a theatre's layout. Clear signage and color coding can help keep backstage strangers moving. Windows offering open vistas also help orient newcomers and can brighten a backstage maze.

WARM-UP ROOM

The speed and ease with which dancers are able to travel between backstage and stage can affect the smoothness of a performance and stands as a measure of good

Dancers in the studio rehearse on both permanent and portable barres.

theatre design. As we walk through the dancer's home away from home, each room will be visited in order of its need to be near the stage.

The warm-up room comes first. Giving dancers a private space for limbering up reduces offstage congestion. The room should be equipped with a barre and with full-length mirrors along at least one wall. The floor should have a resilient substructure and a nonslip finish. Even in multipurpose theatres, a warm-up room near the stage will rarely be empty. Musicians or actors can use the space for rehearsals, or it can serve as a spare dressing room.

DRESSING ROOMS

The heart of the dancer's second home is the dressing room. Unfortunately, many new American theatres have hearts of stone. Star dressing rooms tend to be concrete cubicles. Chorus dressing rooms are cell blocks minus bars. Ceilings are usually low, and floors are raw concrete or are covered with thin vinyl tile.

Dancers visit and revisit their dressing rooms throughout the day; between company classes, rehearsals, and meals and before, during, and after performances. "I live just a few minutes away from the [New York] State Theater, but I don't want to change clothes two, four, or six times a day so I can run home," says dancer Edward Villella. "So I move into my dressing room and live out of it. I need space for a refrigerator, a massage table, clothes, storage, theatre cases, shoes, makeup, and a place to lie down and rest."

Dressing rooms should be spacious enough for dancers to sit on the floor with their legs extended or to lie flat with their feet raised against a wall. Dancers reclining in corridors may be picturesque, but they disrupt backstage circulation. Whether the space is for a chorus of twenty or a single star, dressing rooms require the following fixtures:

- One dressing table per dancer, at least three feet wide and fitted with a mirror, incandescent makeup lights, and two lockable drawers
- One chair per dancer
- Separate, lockable storage space for each dancer's street clothes
- Hanging and shelf space near each dancer's station, for costumes and shoes
- One sink per three to five dancers
- Full-length mirror or mirrors
- Wastebaskets
- Cot or cots, depending on the needs of the performers
- Stage monitor with paging override
- Wall clock
- Telephone jack in star dressing room

Extra space should be allowed for each dancer's dance bag (a bulky carryall containing leotards, tights, leg warmers, practice shoes, salves, bandages, and other items), theatre cases (usually one per dancer), makeup cases, and several portable costume racks or carts. Most chorus dressing rooms end up being used by more performers than they were designed to accommodate. Increasing the number of dressing rooms can turn crowded spaces into cozy ones. Four rooms, each designed for twelve persons, are more congenial than two rooms for twenty-four.

DRESSING TABLES

Dressing tables are usually built as continuous counters with a laminated plastic surface. Separate mirrors, makeup lights, and drawers establish the breadth of each dancer's space. Standard dressing stations usually measure 2 feet 6 inches high (this is the vertical surface facing the dancer) by 3 feet wide by 2 feet deep; many dancers

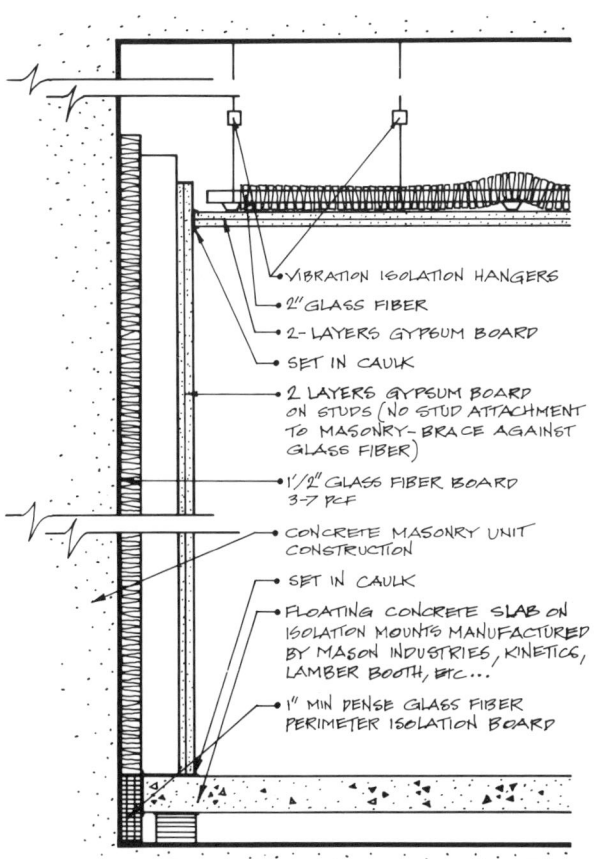
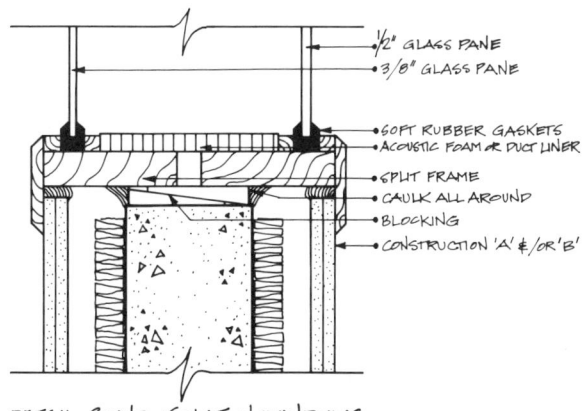

Top left, sound-isolating construction rated STC 65. Floors, walls, and ceilings must provide equal degrees of resistance to the transmission of sound.

Bottom left, balanced construction for dance spaces to provide noise reduction of approximately NC 57 between adjacent critical areas.

Above, vertical section through window sill separating two acoustically isolated spaces. (Drawings developed in collaboration with Klepper Marshall King Associates, acoustical consultants.)

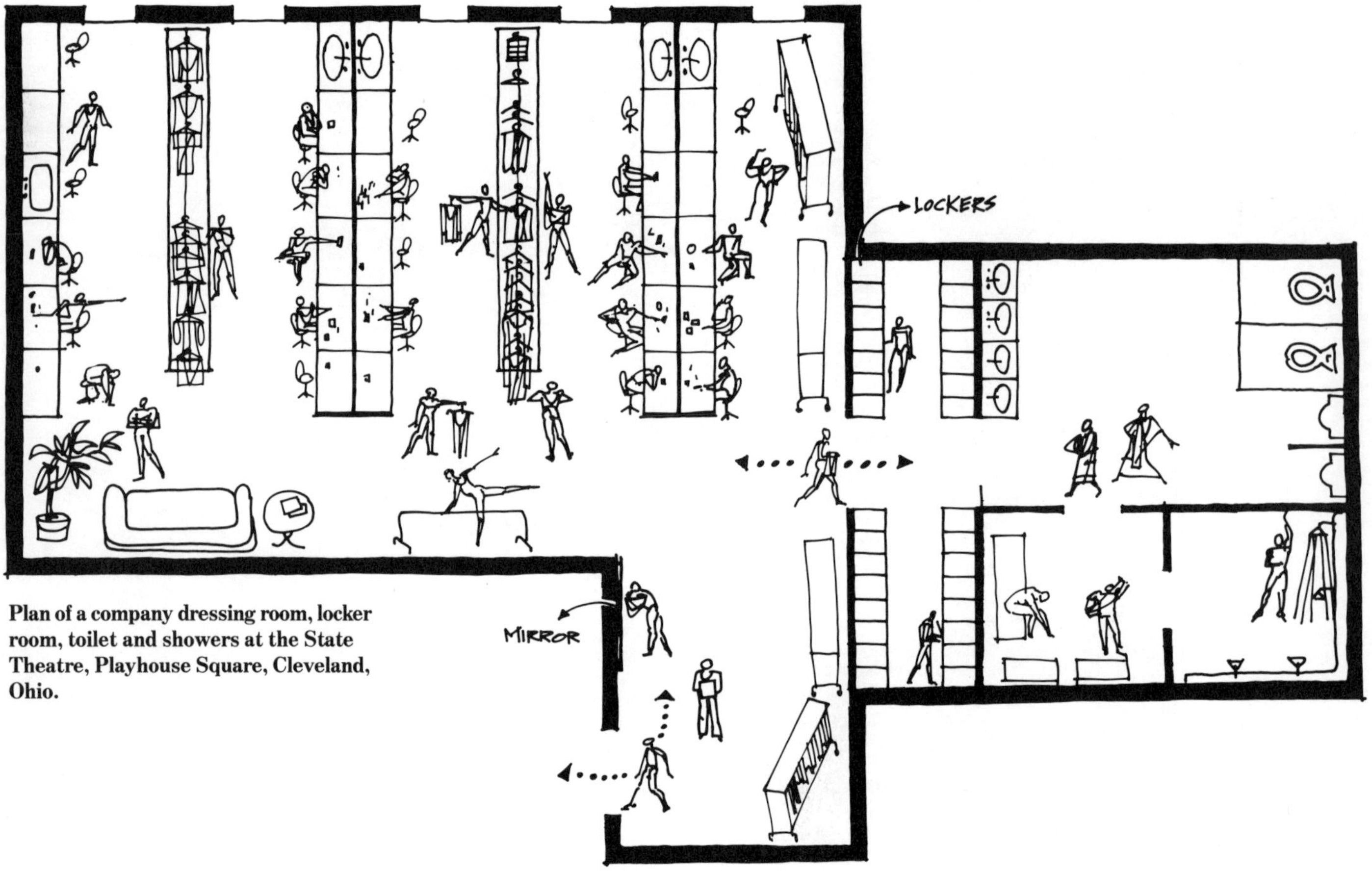

Plan of a company dressing room, locker room, toilet and showers at the State Theatre, Playhouse Square, Cleveland, Ohio.

Star dressing room spaces, left, can be rendered more flexible by dividing them with folding partitions so that they can be opened into a single large space.

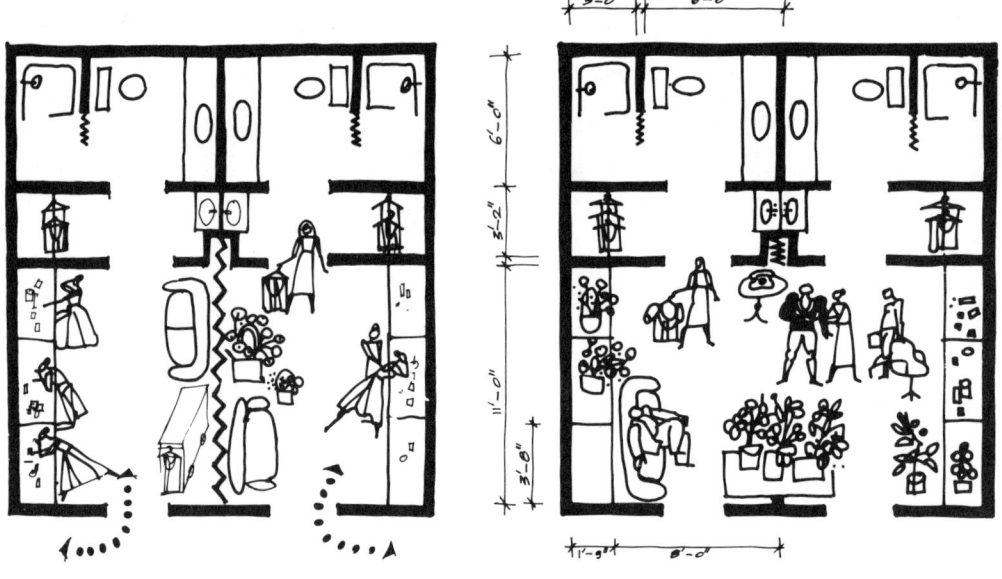

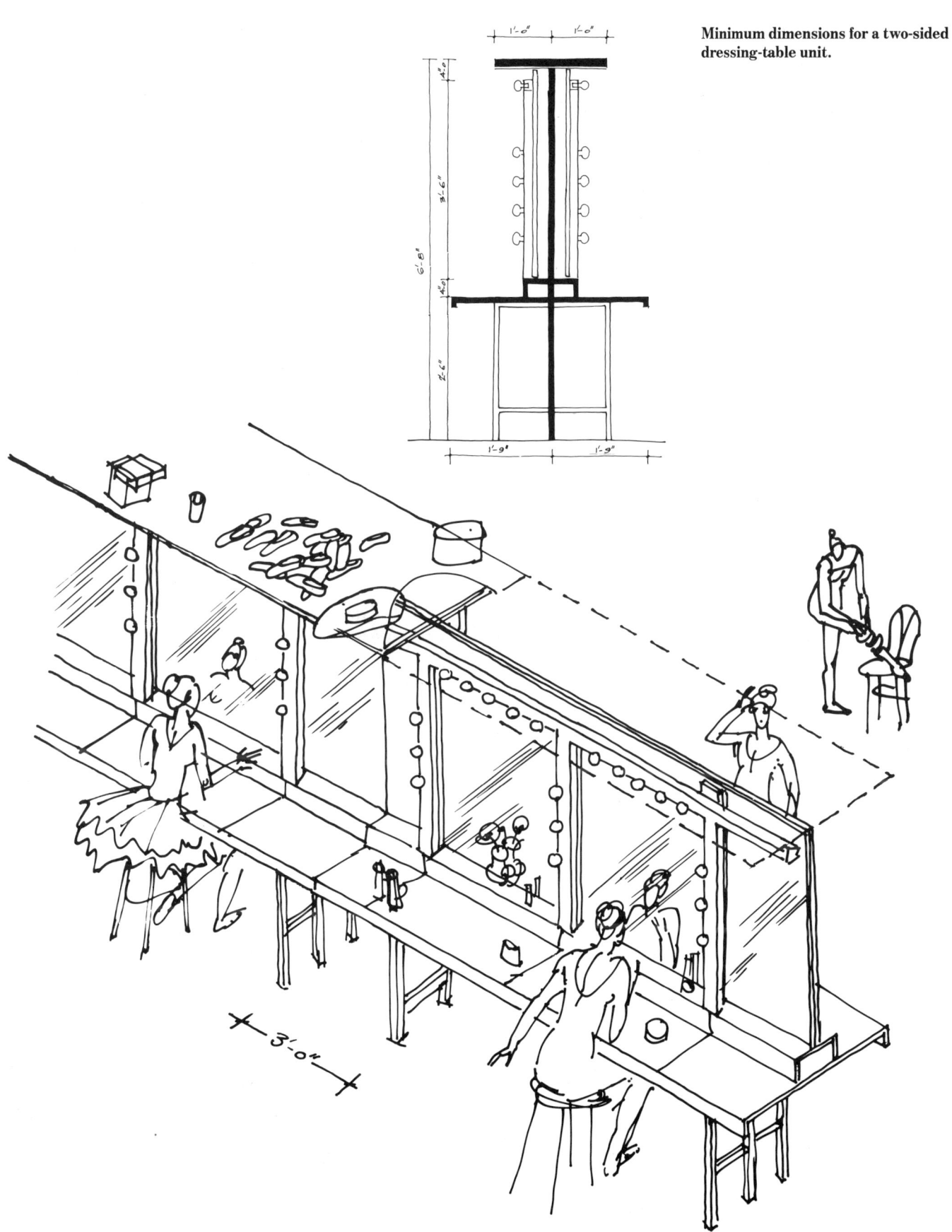

Minimum dimensions for a two-sided dressing-table unit.

Dancers at a two-sided dressing-table unit—an efficient way to provide table space in a large dressing room.

Dressing tables must be wide enough to accommodate a variety of make-up supplies, equipment, food, and personal gear.

find it easier to apply makeup at a shallower counter, but a depth of 1 foot 6 inches should be the minimum. Doing away with legs or columns at each station makes it easier to clean the floor beneath the counter. But the walls and brackets supporting the counter must be strong enough to bear the weight of cabinets, or of a dancer using a counter for a seat. Each dancer needs two lockable drawers beneath the counter; the drawers should be shallow enough to provide plenty of knee room.

LIGHTING

A continuous strip of incandescent—never fluorescent—makeup lights should run along the top and down both sides of each dressing station mirror. Standard catalog items, the lighting strips take either twenty-five or forty-watt bulbs. Each bulb should be covered with a wire guard to avoid burns or breakage. There should be a double electrical outlet at each station (for hair dryers and the like) or, better still, a continuous "plugmold" running below the mirrors the full length of the dressing table.

Dressing rooms require general illumination beyond that provided by makeup lights. If possible, there should also be natural light. Using makeup lights at full intensity for overall illumination is costly and generates too much heat. One option is to design the lighting so a third or half of the makeup lights, evenly distributed around the room, can be flicked on with one switch. Another is to use ceiling-mounted fluorescent fixtures to provide ambient light.

ACTIVE STORAGE

Along the walls or in the center of the dressing room, space must be set aside to hang costumes, and to park portable costume racks brought from the wardrobe room. Lengths of horizontal pipe hung from the ceiling, or standing racks anchored to the floor, can be used to hold costumes. Each dancer needs at least 2 linear feet of hanging space for costumes. Dancers also need room to sit and walk about in the aisles between dressing tables and costume racks. There should be 4 feet of space between the edge of each dressing table and the edge of a row of hanging costumes, and another 2 feet of depth for the costumes themselves.

While many modern dance companies perform barefoot, a single ballet dancer may tie on twenty-five pairs of shoes a week. Each dressing room should have permanent or portable shoe racks, individually labeled, designed to accommodate dancers' footwear, from slippers to sneakers, as dictated by companies' and dancers' needs.

Lockers for storing street clothes and theatre cases, one per dancer, can be spread throughout the dressing area or grouped in an anteroom. Dancers' bags are bulky, so the lockers should be 15 inches wide and at least 5 feet tall.

TOILETS AND SHOWERS

When planning performers' support spaces in a new theatre, be generous with plumbing, especially with showers. For dancers, says Edward Villella, "Showers are necessary as preventive medicine. When you perform eight times a week, which is the usual performance load for a corps dancer and is enormously tiring, your muscles become very tired and strained and your body swells up. The swelling is important. It is the body's signal to stop. When you swell, your circulation slows down. One of the best ways to get the blood circulating again, even before warming up, is to take a hot shower. It's not unusual for me to take six showers a day."

One shower for every five or six dancers is a good standard. As for other backstage plumbing ratios, Actors Equity has proposed one lavatory per three performers as a reasonable goal. Charles Rueger, project architect for the San Francisco Ballet's new studios, suggests one toilet per six women or five men, with urinals accounting for half the men's toilets.

Toilets and showers should connect directly to principal's dressing rooms, and should be convenient to chorus rooms. That way, dancers can bathe and then return to their dressing tables semi-clothed. The relative number of men and women in a visiting dance company may not correspond to the theatre's plumbing plan. Four medium-sized dressing rooms, each with their own toilet-and-shower stations, offer more flexibility than two twenty-person dressing rooms and two large bathrooms. There should also be toilets adjacent to the stage for use during performances or rehearsals.

Since one dancer may use as many as 25 pairs of ballet slippers in one week, dressing rooms designed for ballet dancers must have separate shelf space for storing slippers.

PHYSICAL THERAPY ROOM

Large dance companies often employ a full- or part-time physical therapist. Smaller companies on tour are apt to look up local practitioners who may make house calls. A dance theatre's physical therapy room need not be as near the stage as warm-up and dressing rooms. While a dance company building its own home may want to install a sauna, whirlpool bath, and one or more Pilates machines, standard fittings for a physical therapy room include:
- Massage table, measuring approximately 24 by 78 inches
- Floor mats, each approximately 24 by 87 inches
- Small barre, portable or fixed
- Full-length mirror
- Lockable cabinet for first-aid equipment and medicine
- Small refrigerator
- Desk and chair for therapist

LOUNGE AND CANTEEN

Throughout the day, dancers travel in flocks, going from company class to rehearsal to performance, and returning time and again to crowded dressing rooms. A quiet backstage lounge is the place for non-physical therapy, where dancers can savor solitude and recover a sense of individuality. Unfortunately, most such spaces offer only a few hard chairs and a bank of vending machines. A dancers' lounge, which can double as a greenroom for actors and musicians, should be provided with a comfortable couch and armchairs, a table, end tables, carpeting, windows or skylights, a clock, pay phone, wastebaskets, and — always — a stage monitor with paging override.

Because dancers often spend their whole day in the theatre, a canteen near the lounge is almost a necessity. The cost of building and running an in-house cafe is usually prohibitive. Vending machines will do, but they should be set apart from the lounge and stocked with fresh and healthful food, not potato chips and candy bars. A kitchenette should be included in the canteen plans; dancers and crew will use the cooking facilities, and so will caterers when the lounge accommodates cast parties or public receptions. Because it will occasionally be used by the public, the lounge should be accessible from the theatre lobby, as well as from backstage. If the lounge is built near the stage, it must be sound-isolated and provided with two sets of acoustically rated, gasketed doors.

REHEARSAL SPACE

"There never seems to be enough rehearsal space once the theatre is finished," says lighting designer and theatre consultant Gilbert Hemsley. "Most building committees plan for the rehearsal space for this week's performance, forgetting that next week's activities should also be rehearsing at the same time. There must be a space

The rehearsal studio must be larger than the performing area on stage in order to allow space for entrances and exits, for dancers waiting their turn to rehearse, for rehearsal instruments or sound equipment, and for the choreographer and rehearsal director to have an adequate view of the work in progress.

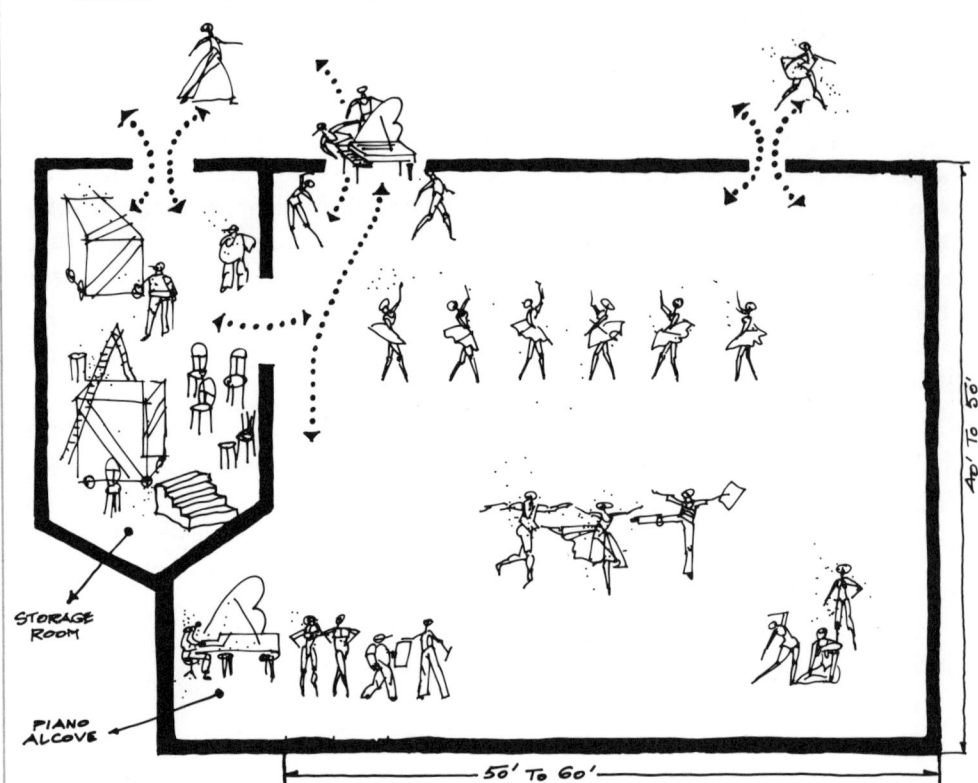

A well-equipped rehearsal studio needs barres, full-length mirrors (and curtains to cover them), a piano alcove, windows for fresh air and natural light, and ceiling fans for circulation.

large enough for full-scale rehearsals free of stage and stagehand requirements. Many architects forget that rehearsal rooms are occupied by artists for many long hours, and thus the need for windows and toilets is forgotten. Better chicken houses make better chickens, and better rehearsal rooms make better performances."

A rehearsal room smaller than the stage is almost useless for dance. Ideally, the room should be 1¼ to 1½ times as large as the performing area, to allow space for practicing entrances and exits and for dancers working alone while the company rehearses. Thirteen feet is the minimum clear height for the rehearsal room ceiling.

Still more space, beyond that dedicated to dancers, must be allowed for musicians—usually a pianist or small percussion or chamber group. Sometimes pianist and piano are squeezed into an alcove, although this only works well when the musician has a clear view of the choreographer or dance teacher. For times when live music is not possible or not desired, a small lockable room should be nearby, for storing tape decks, turntables, portable loudspeakers, and other sound equipment.

When planning new rehearsal studios for the Bella Lewitzky Dance Company in Los Angeles, architect Newell T. Reynolds designed a choreographer's niche, located front-and-center of the rehearsal area. A raised platform within the niche puts the choreographer or rehearsal director in full view of every dancer. Extra space is also desirable for observers in the rehearsal room—the company's artistic director, administrative personnel, or students. A gallery overlooking the room works well, provided the ceiling is high enough and the orientation is correct. It can be stacked atop the storeroom or musician's alcove, or above the corridor leading to the rehearsal studio.

The rehearsal room, or rooms, can be located beneath the stage, above or below the house, or almost anywhere in the theatre. As with lounges and canteens, rehearsal rooms must be sound-isolated. They should also be accessible to the public. Many companies use their rehearsal studios for public dance instruction; in such cases, students on their way to class should not be directed through backstage work areas.

FLOORING

The American Guild of Musical Artists, in its National Dance Basic Agreement, provides that "artists shall not be penalized for refusal to rehearse on a concrete floor even though it may have a linoleum covering." The AGMA agreement further holds that "when ten percent or more of the cast of any ballet are required to execute movements or kneel on the floor in any rehearsal room or on stage, the floor of such rehearsal room shall be maintained in proper condition for such work and cleaned prior to such rehearsal."

The rehearsal-room floor must offer the same resiliency that the stage does. (For guidelines on building resilient floors, see Chapter 3.) Studio floors that will accommodate both ballet and modern-dance rehearsals must be washable; rosin from ballet slippers is hard on bare feet. Because rosin is difficult to remove from wood, battleship linoleum or one of the newer sheet vinyl materials may work best for floors in multipurpose rehearsal rooms.

MIRRORS

A continuous panel of mirrors, 8 feet high, should be installed across the front of the rehearsal room. From 4 to 8 inches of space should be left between floor and mirrors to prevent damage from cleaning equipment. The mirrors should be double-silvered and mounted with mastic or adhesive on a rigid plywood backing no less than ½-inch thick. The silvering manufacturer will suggest the best adhesive. Exposed mirror edges should be polished and beveled; abutting edges should be polished but not beveled. Rehearsal room mirrors must be free of distortion. Each panel has to be perfectly aligned with the next to provide continuous and undistorted reflections.

Some time ago, Eliot Feld discovered that tilting rehearsal room mirrors slightly up reduced the shortening and flattening effect that occurs when dancers back away from their reflected image. In the Feld Ballet studios, the bottom of the mirror panels projects 2½ inches from the baseboard.

Draperies that can be pulled across the mirror panels should be installed. Dancers rely on mirrors during rehearsals, but need to be weaned of that dependency as the first performance date draws near. Also, if the studio will be used for theatre or opera rehearsals, or for readings and lectures, the expanse of mirror will prove distracting.

BARRES

Dance companies of almost every choreographic style use ballet barres during classes and warm-ups. To accommodate a full company, most rehearsal studios have barres along at least three walls. Permanent barres are preferred because they are more rigid and occupy less floor space, but several portable units should be kept in the storage room for use by especially large groups of dancers.

Permanent barres may be attached to walls with brackets or mounted on posts in the floor. When permanent barres are to be installed along mirrored walls, they should be floor-mounted if draperies are to close behind them. In either case, mountings must be strong enough to hold through years of steady use as well as occasional abuse, such as children swinging or hanging from barres.

Charles Rueger, project architect for the San Francisco Ballet's new studios, has studied rehearsal spaces at the American Ballet Theatre, the School of American Ballet, the Metropolitan Opera House, the National Ballet of Canada, and several other dance facilities. Each company Rueger spoke with agreed that ballet barres should be 1¼ or 1½ inch hardwood, with a slight give. Steel barres are unacceptable.

Typical dimensions for rehearsal studio barres, mirrors, and draperies.

LIGHTING

Rehearsal-room lighting should be incandescent, or at least a combination of incandescent and fluorescent. Whenever possible, daylight should complement the scheme. A minimal pipe grid with electrical wiring, for small-scale theatrical lighting, and a few portable dimmer packs, for live presentations or videotaping, can add to the studio's usefulness. Electrical outlets should be distributed generously throughout the rehearsal room, including the stretch of wall below the mirror panels.

CHANGING ROOMS

Changing rooms with toilets, showers, and lockers (but minus dressing tables, makeup mirrors, and costume racks) should be provided in the rehearsal area. The theatre's dressing rooms, assigned to whatever company is performing on stage, cannot absorb the overflow from rehearsal rooms, which may be used by dancers, actors, musicians, or dance students who do not belong to the visiting company.

MISCELLANEOUS AMENITIES

Like the dressing rooms and backstage lounge, the rehearsal studio should be equipped with a stage monitor and paging override. Also needed are a blackboard, bulletin board, a clock, wastebaskets, and movable seating. The studio requires two entrances: a single-leaf door for dancers, and a double-leaf, double-width door for pianos and other bulky equipment. Both sets of doors should be fully gasketed and acoustically rated. The door most often used by people should have a viewing window. Lockers, blackout curtains or shades, portable seating risers, and a foyer for dancers or the public are useful, if less critical, additions.

Two large rehearsal rooms and one small one are enough for most theatres. However, a large dance company or booking facility may need two or three full-size studios, plus additional spaces for small groups of dancers and other artists.

A NOTE ON ALTERNATE SPACES

The ideal alternate space for dance offers a comparable, if condensed, array of the same backstage facilities found in larger theatres. Dressing rooms, at least one per sex, as well as toilets and showers, are a must. However, once these backstage basics are squeezed in, there may be little or no space left for a lounge, canteen, or warm-up room. Each dance company, with help from its theatre-design consultant or architect, must decide which performers' facilities rank as necessities, and which as luxuries.

The studios at the New York School of Ballet offer dancers and dance students ample space, high ceilings, resilient wood floors, tall windows, and skylights.

SUPPORT SPACES FOR CREW AND STAFF

6

A well-designed backstage area is crucial if the work that takes place there is to be accomplished with ease and efficiency. The design will affect everyone from the truckers who take their turn at the loading dock to crew members attempting to erase the scuff marks from two hundred ballet slippers. Builders and their architects should talk with people who are thoroughly familiar with the workings of backstage—stagehands, scenery painters, wardrobe personnel, and other theatre employees—before the design is attempted. The time will be well-spent. A design that aids rather than hinders backstage operations will result in lower production costs, and every dollar saved backstage is a dollar earned for dance.

STAGE ENTRANCE

Leaving the stage door unguarded may be the quickest way to move a theatre's newly acquired technical equipment from the storeroom to the street. All theatre personnel should pass through a single entrance, where a doorman or security guard can discourage unwelcome visitors. The theatre's receiving and loading area should not serve as a separate stagehands' entrance unless it, too, is under the doorman's eye. The stage door should be located where it can be easily found by visiting artists, and must be accessible to handicapped artists and staff. Performers often work odd hours, leaving the theatre late and alone; putting the stage door at the end of a shadowy alley may make for a dangerous trek to the street or parking lot.

RECEIVING AND LOADING-IN

Urban performing arts facilities, especially renovated theatres in congested business districts, pose special problems during load-in and load-out. The forty-foot rigs that haul scenery and equipment should be able to enter and exit the receiving area with a minimum of maneuvering. When designing the loading area, the architect must consider the number of trucks that will have to be accommodated. A facility presenting the American Ballet Theatre must be ready to welcome ABT's half dozen tractor trailers. Ballet West often travels with three such rigs; smaller companies may tour with one truck or none. In areas where on-street parking is prohibited, a secure parking area must be available, around the clock, for company trucks.

When the loading dock is not level with the truck bed, as in these photos, road boxes must be pushed up from the front of the truck when loading-in, and controlled on the downward slope while loading out.

Information on truck lengths and heights, turning radii, and parking needs can be found in guidebooks such as *Architectural Graphic Standards* by Ramsey and Sleeper or *Time-Saver Standards*, edited by John Hancock Callender. (See Bibliography.)

The loading dock should be shielded from bad weather, for the crew's comfort and for the protection of scenery and equipment. It should be the same height as the bed of a standard highway trailer, generally 4 feet above street level. But at least one loading position should be equipped with a dock leveler, to match odd-sized trailers. Pushing and pulling equipment from trucks parked on an incline adds to the crew's already strenuous labor; in front of the loading dock, a level space stretching at least 45 feet will accommodate the longest trailers, and thus keep truck beds on an even keel during packing and unpacking.

Much of a touring dance company's equipment comes in heavy wheeled crates. Backdrops rolled on battens and long pieces of built scenery are bulky and not easily carried around corners. Thus, putting the theatre's loading entrance in a direct line with the stage, and as close to it as possible, saves time and effort backstage.

While many items from trucks are meant to go directly to the stage, others are destined for the wardrobe area, orchestra pit, rehearsal studios, or dressing rooms.

Cleveland's State Theatre, located in the heart of the busy downtown area, has a private driveway and an off-street truck parking area.

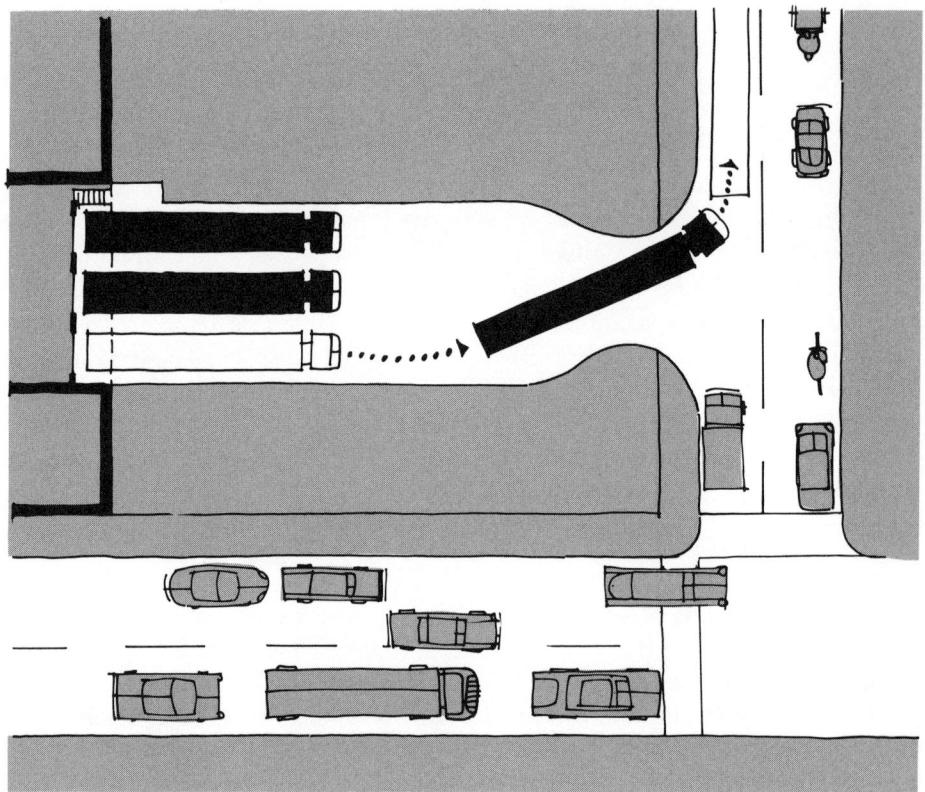

The receiving area must provide easy access to the stage, the wardrobe room, and all other areas to which equipment and scenery will be brought.

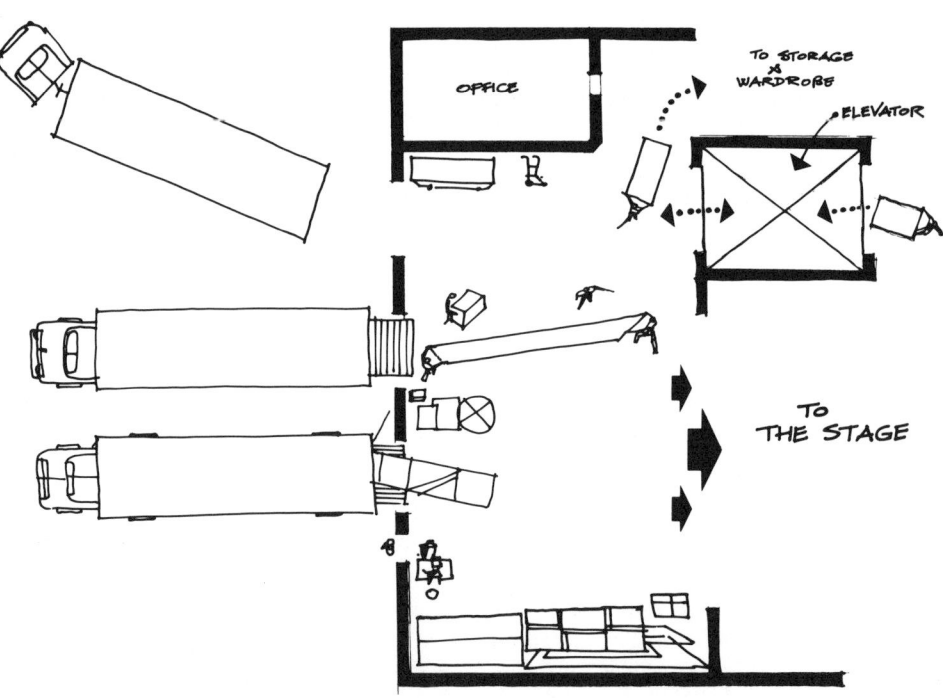

Sorting space adjacent to the receiving area can help in untangling the load; the space should be near any freight elevators and on a direct path to the stage. The receiving-area ceiling should be at least 12 feet high, and doors opening onto the loading dock at least as large as those on the trucks. Providing several truck bays allows different departments (scenery, lighting, props, and wardrobe) to unload trucks simultaneously. There should be a separate personnel door on the dock for stagehands.

A concrete floor with a topping of hard cement holds up best under scraping from heavy boxes and crates. There should be a drain to carry off rain or melting snow. Walls in the receiving area must be durable, and corners should be chamfered and protected with steel corner guards.

The areas connecting the loading dock to the stage should be built on one level. Ramps make it necessary to hire extra stagehands to maneuver heavy equipment over the slopes. Elevators cause time-wasting bottlenecks. If a ramp cannot be eliminated, its slope should be no steeper than one-to-twelve. If an elevator is required, its floor area should be as large as possible, so the maximum amount of equipment can be carried in one trip. The elevator should also move rapidly; twenty feet per minute is an acceptable speed.

Crates and boxes fill every available corner after a load-in.

CARPENTRY DEPARTMENT

Much like the masons, plumbers, and electricians on a construction project, a stage crew is divided into separate departments, all usually supervised by the house carpenter or production manager. The carpenter not only hires and schedules crew members, but is also responsible for general theatre maintenance. His office, large enough for a desk, file cabinets, and two or three chairs, should be near the stage. Close by, crew members need men's and women's showers, toilets, and lockers as well as a lounge.

A theatre presenting new productions requires well-equipped scenery, paint, and property shops, each with ample space. The shops should be clustered near the stage, so scenery can easily make the rounds. A theatre that does not construct its own scenery still needs a basic carpenter's shop for minor modifications and other work on visiting company's sets.

SCENERY SHOP

To gauge the best dimensions for the scenery shop, the architect should speak with scenic designers and technicians who will work at the theatre. Even an average shop requires 2,500 square feet of space, and a clear ceiling height of 30 feet to permit scenery to be assembled as it will appear on stage. So that scenery can be nailed down, the shop floor should be built of softwood tongue-and-groove strips (edge grain) of Douglas fir or yellow pine. Good ventilation and filters must be provided to remove sawdust from the air. A lockable tool room and a foreman's office (with space for a drafting table, plan files, and other furniture, and with a window looking out on the shop) should abut the working area.

High, wide doors are needed between shop and stage so assembled scenic units can be rolled through on wagons. Doors 20 feet wide and from 20 to 30 feet high are common here. If the shop will be used during performances, construction noises cannot be allowed to reach the stage. At some theatres, a bit of background noise is acceptable during rehearsals, but the shop is shut down during performances. Where complete acoustic isolation is required, architects should seek advice from an acoustician with experience in noise control.

SCENE PAINTING SHOP

Sawdust and fresh paint make poor company. Newly built scenic units and backdrops

Painting a drop for the New York City Ballet.

must be hauled to a separate shop for painting. The paint shop needs a large wooden floor where backdrops can be tacked down flat. There should be space enough to paint more than one drop (each of which may measure 30 by 60 feet) at a time.

Vertical paint frames are used infrequently these days. If a vertical frame is desired by a theatre owner, the frame must be built to accommodate the widest drops, and rigged to fly down into a slot in the floor along one wall. That way, the scene painter can stand on the floor and still reach any part of a full-height drop. Generally, such paint frames are furnished and installed as part of the stage-rigging equipment contract. Providing a vertical paint frame does not eliminate the need to accommodate flat painting.

PROPERTIES

Three backstage rooms may be needed for the work of the property department. If the theatre builds its own scenery, there should be a separate property construction shop. Putting it next to the scenery shop makes it easier for both departments to share tools.

Every theatre requires a running prop room, where stage furniture and hand props for current productions are kept. Its wide, double doors should open directly onto the stage, so crew members can readily shift props during a performance. In plays, and occasionally even in dance, food props are used. Thus, the running prop room should be outfitted with a double sink, refrigerator, and kitchen range. The room also needs shelves for storing small props and a workbench for repairs. There must be space at the center of the room for road boxes, trunks, and large props.

The running prop room serves only current attractions. Separate space should be set aside for storing reusable props. For a resident dance company, such space is especially useful. Without it, valuable props may have to be discarded to make way for new ones.

COSTUME DEPARTMENTS

Working from the designer's drawings, the costume-construction staff fabricates all costumes for each production and makes adjustments to costumes throughout technical and dress rehearsals. After the premiere, however, responsibility for those costumes usually shifts to the wardrobe department, which keeps performance apparel clean and in good repair. Each department requires separate facilities, but not every theatre needs both departments. A presenting organization bringing in attractions from elsewhere has little call for a complete costume construction shop, but does require wardrobe space. Even a producing organization developing its own works, and thus its own costumes, may prefer to subcontract the cutting and sewing to an independent costume shop.

COSTUME SHOP

In any costume construction shop, extra care should be taken with lighting. In areas where fabric colors are selected or compared (offices of the designer and costumier, fitting rooms, and painting and dyeing spaces), daylight and incandescent light are essential; other light sources distort fabric colors and cannot simulate the stage lighting under which costumes will be seen.

The sewing area must be bright and spacious. If fluorescent fixtures are needed —to save energy and achieve proper illumination levels—lamps with the warmest color temperature should be used. The shop's general work space should be fitted out with the following equipment:

- Cutting tables, at least 3 feet 6 inches high, 4 feet wide, and 8 feet long
- Sewing machines
- Ironing boards
- Steamers
- Dress forms
- Three-way, full-length mirrors
- Hanging areas and shelves for costumes and supplies
- Cabinets and drawers for small items
- Clock, tack board, and telephone

To bring dancers' costumes from the drawing board to the stage, the construction shop needs a few other work areas. The shop's fitting room should be large enough to accommodate a fitter, designer, and choreographer, as well as a dancer in full costume. A small changing room is needed nearby. A laundry area is also needed, with washers, dryers, and deep sinks, all sufficient to meet the shop's expected activity, plus counter or table space and room to park costume racks and clothes hampers.

The fabric dyeing area can pose special demands. Some costumiers will call for a stainless steel, commercial cooking vat, with integral heater and drain. Others prefer dyeing fabric in large pots heated over heavy-duty hot plates. (Dyeing can also be done in a standard washing machine used exclusively for that purpose.) The room may have to be specially ventilated to carry off noxious vapors. Vats should be placed so their tops sit at standard counter height; this makes it easier to gather up several yards of wet fabric. Space is needed for hanging wet costumes and cloth, and the entire area should have a watertight floor and non-staining walls. The dyeing room floor should also slope toward a drain, to let water run off. Level duckboards reduce the risk of slipping on the inclined floor.

As a dance company's repertoire expands, so grows its costume collection. The costume storage area, clean and well-lighted and ventilated, should be furnished with garment racks and cabinets, plus drawers and shelves for accessories.

On tour with American Ballet Theatre, wardrobe mistress May Shimoto mends a costume.

WARDROBE ROOM

Unlike the costume construction shop, a wardrobe room is required in every theatre. A visiting company's costume trunks are hauled here from the trucks. Members of the wardrobe crew immediately unpack costumes, air them out, and prepare them for the first performance. Plenty of space is needed for costume racks and boxes, as well as for sewing machines and other costume-care equipment. Nearby, there should be a fitting room, and an office for the wardrobe department supervisor. Because women dancers usually make more costume changes and wear more elaborate costumes than men do, the wardrobe room should be as near as possible to women's dressing rooms.

Costumes often have to be laundered after each performance. In theatres with a wardrobe room and a costume-construction shop, the same laundry facilities can serve both. However, because the costume-construction shop's dyes may remain in washing machines, each shop should have access to separate washers.

The wardrobe crew also tends to wigs and shoes. In a theatre that will be home to a large dance company, one room should be furnished with beautician's chairs, mirrors, sinks, a table, and shelves for wigs and wig stands. There should be space for two or three wardrobe crew members working at benches.

To touch up scuff marks or to match a new costume, dance shoes and ballet slippers are regularly spray painted. Too often, when a visiting company arrives at the theatre, a member of the wardrobe crew must rush for the nearest exterior door or fire escape, spray cans and slippers in tow. An isolated spraying room is a better idea. The room needs special ventilation to remove paint fumes, incandescent and natural lighting for color fidelity, and racks for drying shoes. Some companies have dancers spray their own shoes. In this event, there should be a bench or counter space for six dancers working at one time.

ELECTRICAL DEPARTMENT

The theatre's electrical department keeps all stage-lighting, sound, and projection

Lacking a proper booth for spray-painting shoes and slippers, dancers must find a remote corner for the job and endure the noxious fumes.

gear in good working order, and operates the equipment during performances. The crew does most of its work in the following quarters.

CONTROL ROOM

The control room is best situated at the rear of the orchestra or balcony seating, where it affords a clear view of the stage. During performance, sound and lighting system operators in the control room may work elbow-to-elbow with the stage manager. The room must accommodate a stage-lighting console, the stage manager's control station, and the sound-system console with its associated tape decks, amplifier racks, and patch bays. Other electronic gadgetry may require wall or counter space, plus one or two storage cabinets.

The control room needs large windows that overlook the stage. The glass should not be tinted: technicians must see stage lighting just as the audience does. Walls should be finished in a dark color. The room requires dimmable incandescent lighting during performances, but bright fluorescent lighting for equipment maintenance sessions. The floor should be carpeted and the walls and ceiling covered with sound-absorbing material.

At theatres without elaborate sound requirements, sound and lighting control facilities can go in the same booth. But where there is a great deal of audio equipment, or where precise, live mixing is handled by an independent sound engineer, separate booths may be needed. Combining sound- and lighting-control systems in one space allows one technician to operate both systems—a strong argument for building a single booth. If the theatre owner prefers having two booths, they should interconnect. The sound booth needs a window that can be opened (so the technician can hear, and better adjust, the same amplified sound the audience hears), and it should be acoustically isolated from the lighting booth.

VIEWING ROOM

Choreographers, designers, and their guests need their own space for viewing performances. The best location for the viewing room is at the rear of the orchestra floor, where the choreographer sees the performance as the public does. The viewing room needs a window that opens and closes quietly, comfortable chairs, lights that can be dimmed, speakers that monitor the performance, and adequate ventilation.

FILM PROJECTION BOOTH

While spaces designed solely for dance do not need a film projection booth, operators of multipurpose theatres may wish to show movies. Presenting commercial films calls for a projection booth dead center at the rear of the auditorium. The height of the booth must be such that the down angle of the projection beam is no more than nine degrees from a perpendicular line extended to the center of the screen. A sixteen millimeter projector can share space with the theatre's followspots. But thirty-five or seventy millimeter film projectors, harder to move and readjust, require their own permanent space and ventilation system.

FOLLOWSPOT BOOTH

Followspots also go at the center-rear of the auditorium. Up to four followspots may be needed in demanding theatre-lighting situations. The window in the followspot booth must be large, untinted, and with any required mullions placed to allow free rein to moving spotlights. Technicians in the booth must be given a clear shot over the heads of patrons to a dancer standing at the edge of the stage apron. Balcony railings, parapets, and catwalks should not interfere with spotlight angles.

Locating the control room: The control booth must offer a view of the entire performing area. In the drawing on the left, a control booth located anywhere between the two dots would afford a full view of the stage. Right, locating the booth in extreme corners results in a partially obstructed view.

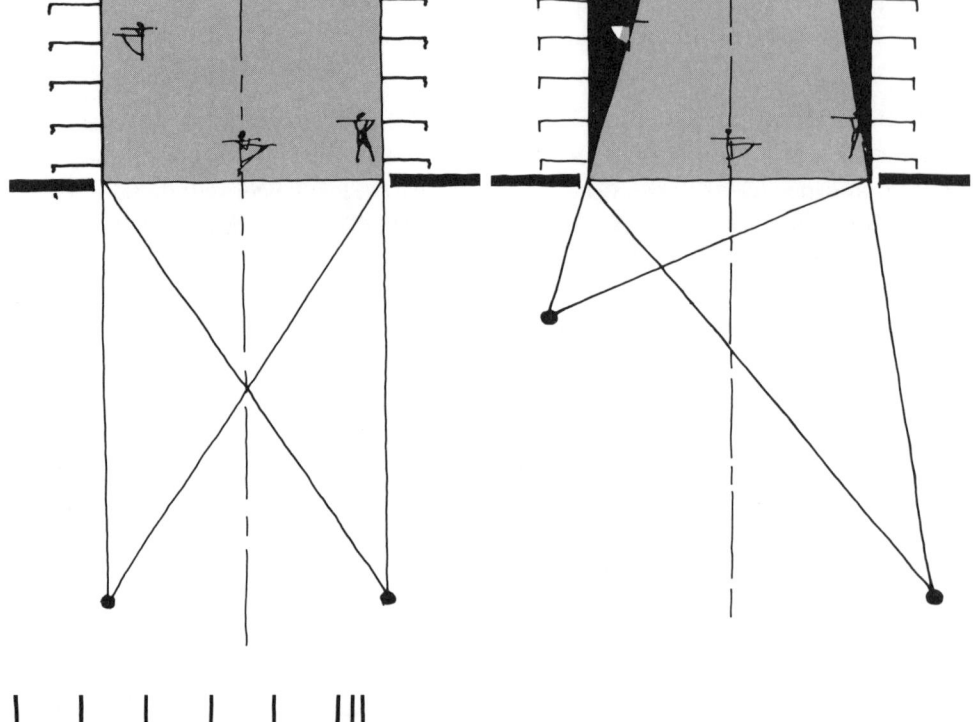

The control room may be located either at the rear of the orchestra or the rear of the balcony. It must be high enough to offer a clear view over the heads of people seated in the back row but not so high as to have the view of the performing area obstructed by the balcony overhang or the front line of stage masking.

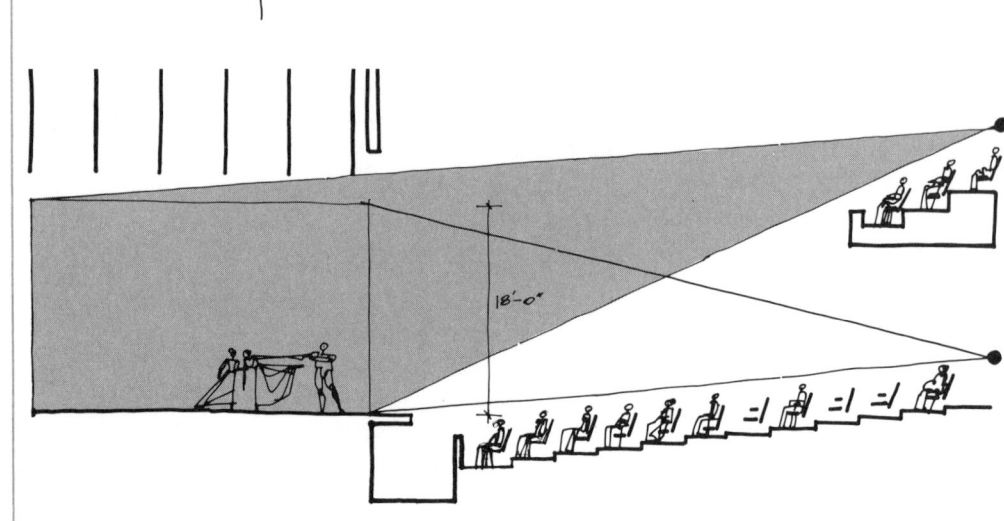

Plan of a typical control room in which the sound technician is acoustically isolated. Storage and work space are combined into the same space, and sound-equipment racks are easily accessible from the back for maintenance.

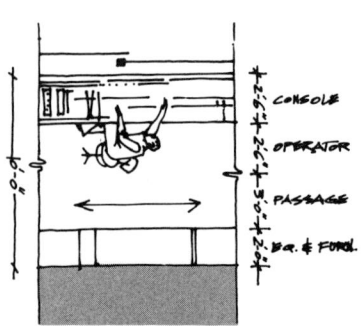

Minimum depth requirements for a full-scale control room.

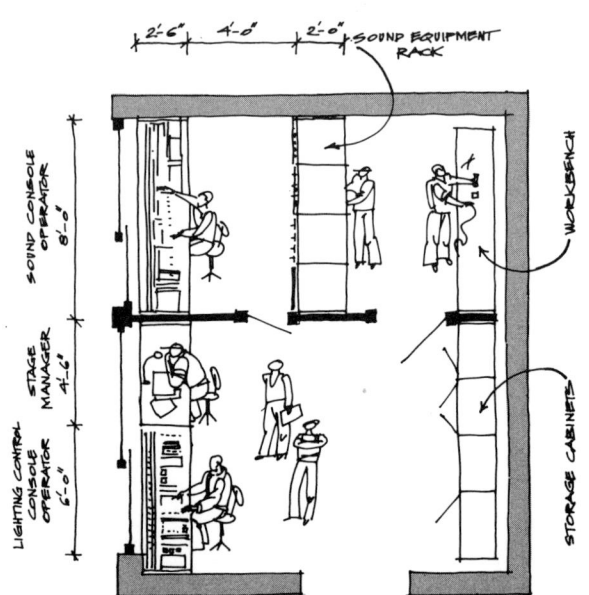

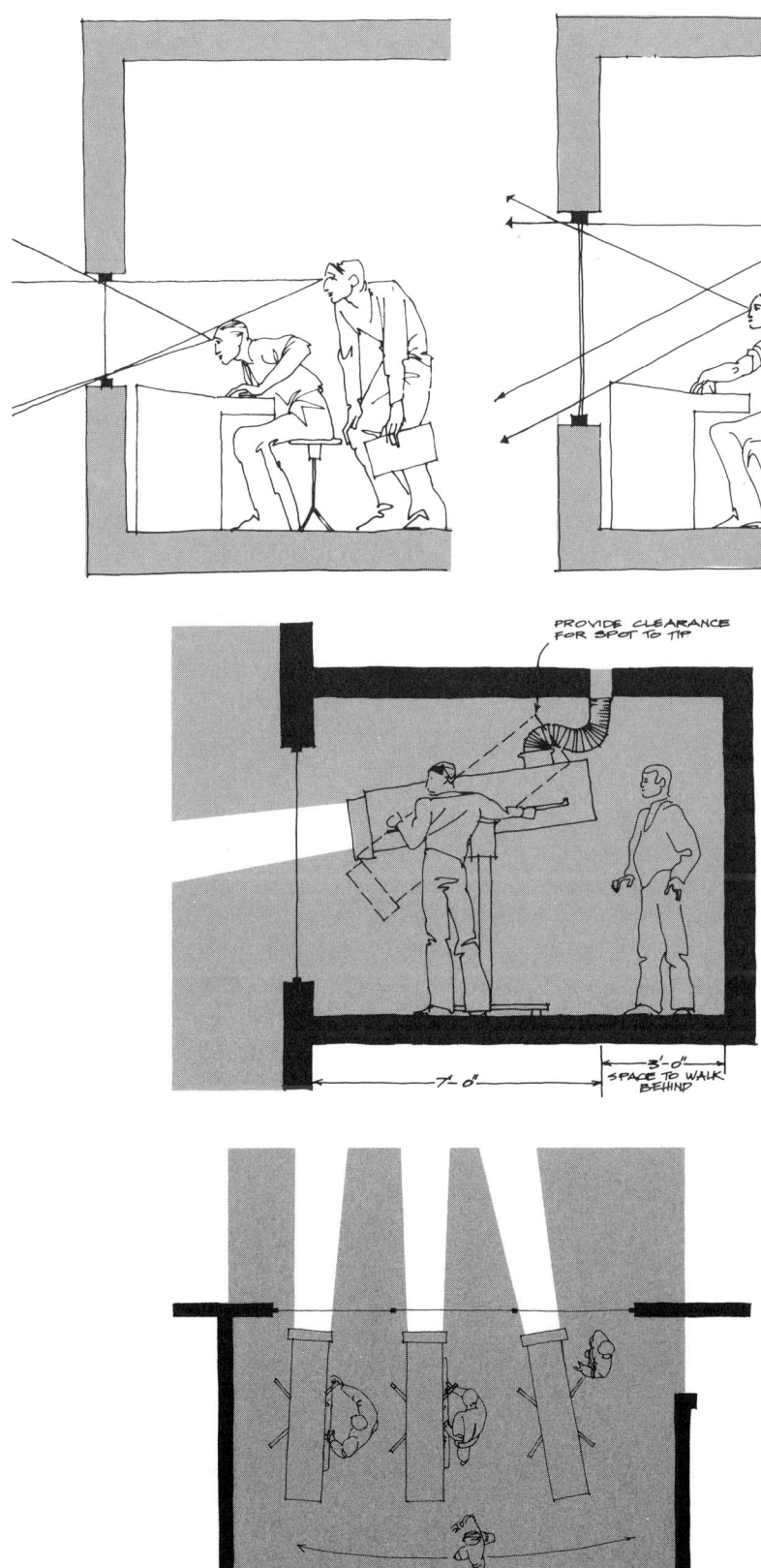

Windows in the control room must not be so small that they restrict the view of control-booth operators (left). Although architects sometimes object to the appearance of large windows, it is essential for control-booth operators and standing observers to have a clear view of the performing area (right).

Followspots need enough floor space so that they can swing horizontally without colliding, and enough room height and window height to allow them to be aimed as low as the first few rows of the orchestra and as high as 18 feet above the upstage limit of the performing area.

The booth itself should be acoustically sealed so that spotlight operators can converse without disturbing members of the audience nearby. All followspots produce heat, and carbon-arc lamps emit harmful gases. An appropriate ventilating system is essential; if carbon-arc spotlights are used, fumes must be expelled outside the theatre.

Architects trying to accommodate followspots, a film projector, a control booth, and a viewing room encounter an obvious problem. There is only so much space at the rear of the auditorium, less still along the center line. Advice on priorities should be sought from a theatre-design consultant. By studying the particular needs of the house, the consultant can establish the best site for each booth.

DIMMING EQUIPMENT ROOM

The theatre-design consultant, with help from an electrical engineer, can also suggest the proper size and location for the theatre's dimming equipment room. The heart of the dimming system is the dimmer rack, which regulates power to stage-lighting fixtures. The scale of productions planned for the theatre determines the number of dimmers needed, and thus the size of the room that will house them. The room itself should be dry and well-ventilated and readily accessible to stage electricians making emergency repairs.

LIGHTING WORKSHOP AND STORAGE

At large theatres or facilities where one or more theatres are grouped together, the lighting storeroom is apt to be combined with the electricians' workshop. Because lighting equipment is heavy and unwieldy, the space, or spaces, should be near the stage. Electricians need a bench where they can repair light fixtures, plus storage space for spare lamps, color media, tools, and electrical hardware.

SOUND REQUIREMENTS

A room next to the control booth or near the stage, where speakers, tape recorders, and other equipment can be kept, and where minor repairs can be made, should satisfy the needs of the sound department. However, if sound effects or music will be recorded and dubbed at the theatre, separate recording space should be set aside. The sound control booth is usually neither large enough nor acoustically designed for such work.

ACCOMMODATING FILM AND TELEVISION

More and more theatres are using closed-circuit television to monitor performances from backstage. Dance companies are videotaping their repertoire, to help teach choreography to new members of the company, or to present works to the public. Almost any live or taped television production will rely on a control truck parked outside the theatre. A convenient power source (in the form of a two-hundred ampere, three-phase, four-wire switch) is needed to operate the truck's electronic gear and heating-ventilating-air conditioning system. Temporary cables carry audio and video signals from auditorium to truck. Providing small cable openings in an outside wall eliminates the need to leave a door ajar. Because the audio and video signals are low voltage, the cables need not be run to the auditorium through conduit.

The local television crew taping two minutes of dance for the evening news, or the video company recording a performance on stage, will each rely on what theatre technicians call a "clean feed." Sound collected by microphones, or from recorded music, is fed into the house amplifying system. A clean feed, in the form of a separate jack in the control booth or on stage, lets the television team pick up a preamplified sound signal to accompany its visual recording. Without the connection provided by a clean feed, extra microphones may have to be positioned on stage or next to the theatre's loudspeakers, and more wires must be run to the control truck in the parking lot. To ensure a clean feed in the house sound system—a major need for electronic media—theatre planners should seek help from a sound-systems consultant or from a theatre technician with extensive experience in sound.

Television technicians usually make frequent trips between cameras and truck. They need a convenient parking place for the control truck. The parking place should also offer protection from bad weather and from thieves. The stage-loading dock may serve the purpose, provided the television truck does not block trailers hauling equipment for other theatre productions.

OTHER BACKSTAGE SPACES

Backstage, there should be two or three small offices for visiting stage managers, technicians, and designers, plus a reasonable amount of unassigned storage space. As the seasons pass and the theatre's stock of scenery, props, and costumes piles higher, resident dance companies are sometimes driven to rent outside storage space. Moving company property to a warehouse costs less than eating into prime theatre space. However, estimating the company's projected annual gain in costumes and other production accessories can ensure a decade or two of growing room. Unassigned storage spaces should be basically rectangular and convenient to the stage.

ADMINISTRATIVE OFFICES

The administrative offices of the San Francisco Ballet are located above the entrance to their new building.

Relegating administrative offices to some netherworld far from backstage reinforces the tendency of performers and stagehands to look down upon non-production theatre employees. It is better to strike a balance, one that draws office workers into backstage life but leaves ample space for dancers to dance and clerks to clerk. Office plans should allow for growth: as success overtakes the theatre, more administrative space will be needed. One solution is to build a minimum number of enclosed offices for management and an open "office landscape" for support staff. Offices should be airy, with as much sunlight as possible.

The theatre's executive, artistic, and managing directors should have lockable, private offices, each large enough for a desk, file cabinets, and four to six visitors. The managing director may also need a safe for storing box office receipts overnight. Support staff, whether in separate offices or a common area, each need about 120 square feet of office space.

Most performing-arts facilities also require a meeting room. It should be large enough to seat twenty people—at least three hundred square feet. In addition to being used for staff, board, or executive committee gatherings, the space can serve as a reference library or be used as a workroom for collating theatre mailings.

MAILING AND DUPLICATING ROOMS

Theatre mailrooms are busy places, usually crowded with employees and volunteers handling everyday correspondence, promotional literature, and box office orders. Because address printers and postage machines are noisy, the room should not open onto office space without an intervening sound baffle. Duplicating rooms tend to be equally noisy and busy; it may be a good idea to combine both functions. As duplicating and photocopying equipment grows increasingly sophisticated, theatres are finding it practical and inexpensive to copy, collate, and bind printed matter on the premises. Here, as in other backstage space, planners should leave room for expanding operations and runaway success.

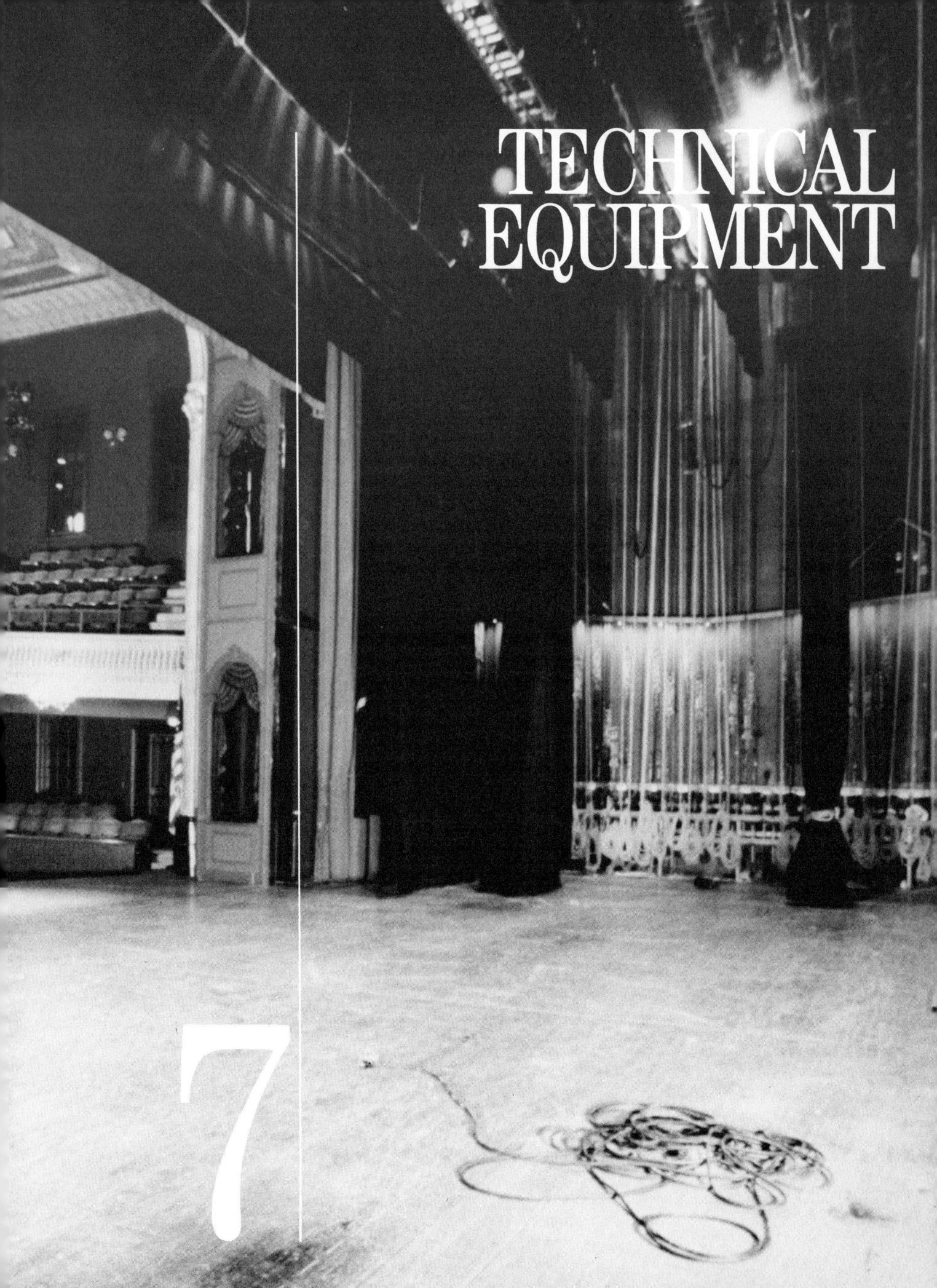

TECHNICAL EQUIPMENT

7

Technical requirements for dance vary from company to company and from piece to piece. For the theatre designer, choosing the best rigging, lighting, and sound system becomes a thorny problem; learning which dance companies are apt to use the theatre, and which of those relies on the most stage apparatus, points the way to proper choices. But for the newcomer to dance, understanding the difference between borders and battens, or counterweights and catwalks, stands as a more immediate hurdle. This chapter, a field guide to the parts and principles of modern theatre magic, should smooth the path of the builder or architect creating a well-equipped space for dance.

DANCE COMPANIES AND THEIR TOURING EQUIPMENT

Company	Company Size	Music	Staff Size	Touring Equipment
American Ballet Theatre	90	Full-time orchestra	50-60	MINIMUM of six semi-trailers (50 tons of sets and costumes
Ballet West	40	Uses Utah Symphony Orch. on a part-time basis	25-30	Three semi-trailers
Twyla Tharp Dance Foundation	16	Usually uses live musicians in NYC, taped music on tour	Twyla Tharp plus 10	16 trunks (no trucks on tour: trunks fly as excess baggage)
Laura Dean/ Dancers and Musicians	6	Two full-time musicians	Laura Dean plus 1	16 trunks (one small truck)

SCENERY AND MASKING

Because choreography requires a large open performing area to accommodate the movement of dancers, dance sets its own standards for scenery and masking. Where theatre and opera often fill the stage with bulky, floor-supported, three-dimensional settings, dance tends to rely on thin, painted backdrops and other two-dimensional elements that preserve clear and uninterrupted floor and overhead space. In plays, doors that open and shut and other scenic devices provide precise entrances and exits for performers. Dancers, entering or leaving the stage on the run or in flight, have similar needs for precision, but must satisfy them more simply.

To meet these requirements, dance depends upon a standard system of masking for treating the edges of the performing area. Masking consists of a series of fabric borders and legs, gathered or stretched flat and usually black. Borders hang across the top of the stage picture, concealing lighting equipment and flown scenery. Legs are vertical fabric panels that hang down to the floor of the wings and hide the backstage area from the audience. In combination, borders and legs create a receding series of mats (on the same principle as the mat that frames a painting), beginning downstage and ending at the cyclorama, or large, flat backdrop that forms the background for the performing area. To provide ample room for dancers' exits and entrances, legs are usually hung at intervals of 6 to 10 feet.

Opposite: Looking into the stage-right wing of the Grand Opera House in Wilmington, Delaware. The lines of the rigging system and the pin rail can be seen in the background.

STAGE RIGGING

Scenery and masking for dance are rarely freestanding. The traditional dance stage requires an overhead rigging system from which borders, legs, and drops can hang. In turn, every dance company develops a hanging plan indicating positions for the masking, lighting, and scenic elements used in each of its works. Any theatre the company plays must be able to accommodate its hanging plan.

Some elements in the company's hanging plan remain stationary; others are used for one scene but raised out of sight—flown—for the next. Flying scenery quietly during a performance is possible only in a high proscenium stagehouse equipped with motorized or counterweighted rigging. In theatres with a low-grid stagehouse, scenery, masking, and lighting equipment cannot be flown out of sight, but it can be raised and lowered for easy installation and adjustment. In many modern theatres of modest size, small scenic elements and all lighting fixtures are hung from an overhead catwalk system or from a fixed network of pipes reached by ladders.

RIGGING SYSTEMS FOR A HIGH-GRID STAGEHOUSE

Old-style rigging systems use a network of ropes, with each line running up a side wall, across the ceiling, and then down through a grid floor to a rigging batten—the length of pipe from which scenery is hung. The load on each batten is counterweighted by attaching sandbags to the ropes. Rope systems are still found in many older theatres and in some new ones, but a system referred to as T-bar counterweight rigging is widely preferred today.

The newer rigging arrangement gets its name from the T-shaped steel tracks arrayed along a side wall of the stagehouse. The tracks guide the system's counterweight arbors or carriages (filled with steel bricks) and prevent the carriages from colliding with each other as they slide up and down. The system's battens hang from braided steel cables connected to the arbors.

T-bar systems are operated by hand. Motorized winch systems, although used in some theatres, are more expensive than hand-operated systems and are considered by many technicians to be less safe. When a batten fouls in the rigging, the T-bar

Stagehands hang lighting fixtures on a rigging batten at the Carrier Theatre in the Onondaga County Civic Center in Syracuse, N.Y.

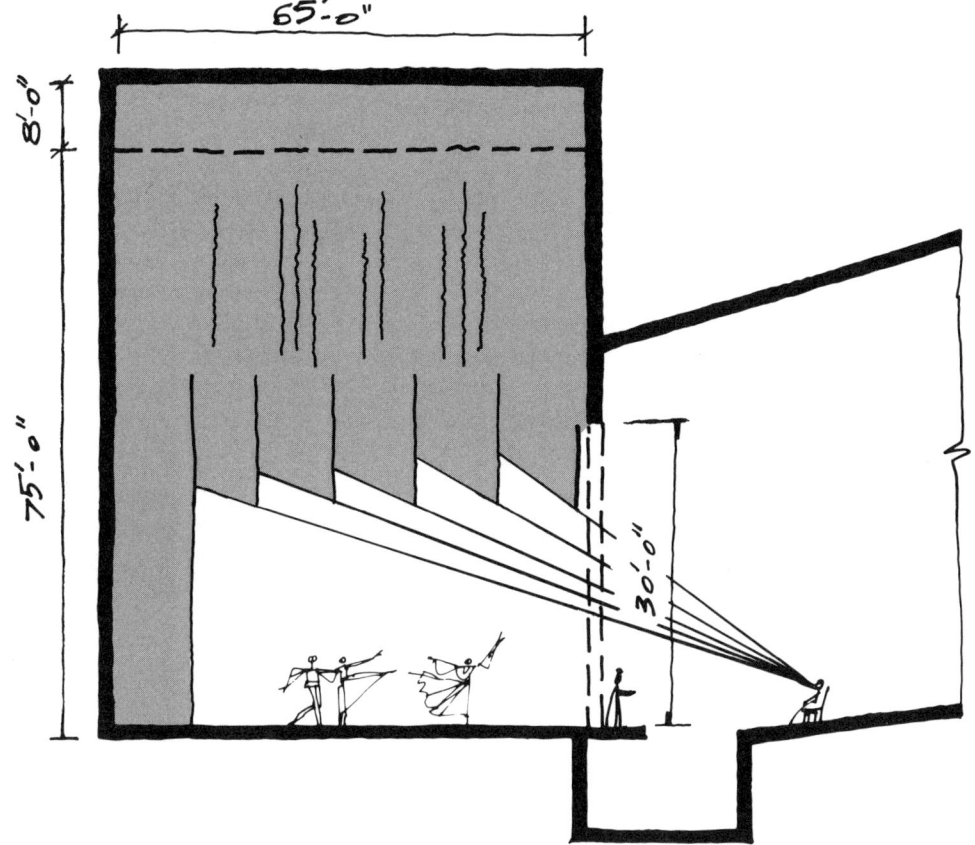

A high-grid stagehouse has a grid of at least 2½ times the height of the stage picture.

Stagehands at the Metropolitan Center in Boston rig a backdrop for American Ballet Theatre.

A full-height proscenium stagehouse showing the components of a T-bar counterweight rigging system.

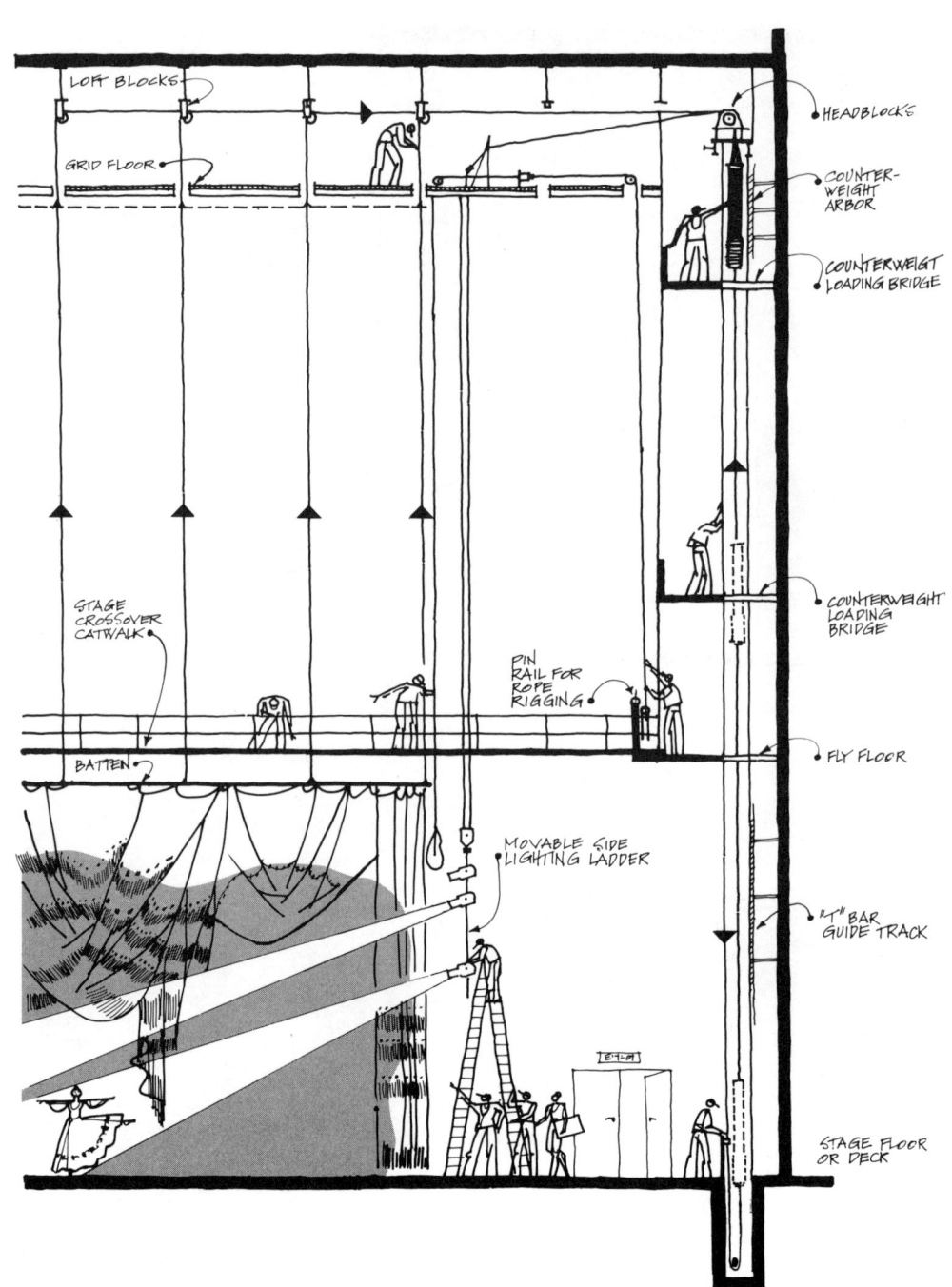

operator feels resistance in his hand line and can stop to investigate. An electric motor simply pours on more power when it senses an overload.

The stagehouse needs enough rigging sets—battens and the lines that support them—to handle the greatest anticipated load of scenery and lights. One ballet can require four or five groups of painted legs and borders, as well as a special backdrop. Five or six such settings, in place for a weekend's booking, can claim twenty-five to thirty rigging sets. Stage lighting may require another dozen battens. The sets themselves are usually spaced 6 to 8 inches apart. If rigging sets are installed too close together, flying scenery may sideswipe lighting. When that happens, it can take hours to readjust lights bumped askew.

The following architectural elements and equipment must be included in the stagehouse to accommodate the rigging system:

Fly Floors—When spotting lines, stagehands stand on narrow platforms called fly floors, on the sides of the stage. One or more rope lines are spotted (rigged to a single, movable pulley) when a full-length batten is not used—for example, to hang a banner or chandelier. A single line may also be used to gather up bundles of lighting cables as they pass from the ends of battens into the wings. The rope is then tied off at a pin rail, a long, hollow pipe fitted with belaying pins. Fly floors should be built as low as possible but still high enough to permit scenery to pass beneath—thus about 30 feet above the stage floor.

Loading Bridges—Upper and lower loading bridges are used by stagehands stacking counterweights into arbors. The loading bridges must be carefully located. The upper one sits approximately 9 feet below the headblock beam, which is at grid level; the lower bridge should stand next to the arbor when the batten is at normal playing trim (30 to 35 feet above the stage floor).

Grid Floor—The grid floor is located 7 to 10 feet below the structure supporting the stagehouse roof. It consists of steel girders supporting a steel floor grid to which rigging sheaves are attached; rigging lines run over the sheaves and down through the grid to battens. Each time a new arrangement of scenery is installed, crew members climb out on the grid floor to adjust the equipment. Thus crew members need standing room between the grid floor and the underside of the roof steel. In addition to supporting the roof, the roof steel bears the weight of the rigging system, counterweights, and scenery and lighting equipment. Roof-steel beams must be spaced to mesh with the rigging system, since rigging loftblocks (pulleys) are usually attached to the beams' bottom flanges.

Headblocks and Loftblocks—Rigging-system cables run up the stage wall to headblocks, over the headblock wheels, then across the grid floor to loftblocks. Each headblock (a pulley unit consisting of several parallel sheaves or a grooved drum) transfers a loftblock's horizontal load down to a counterweight arbor. One headblock is linked to each rigging set in the system; the headblocks are usually spaced evenly along the headblock beam. Since the scenery and lighting equipment that hangs from rigging battens change with each new production, the distribution of weight along the headblock beam varies—a fact engineers must take into account when designing the structural system. The headblock beam sits directly above the array of counterweight arbors. The beam's elevation must be carefully calculated, so that cables from loftblocks enter each headblock at the proper angle. The top of each headblock cannot be higher than the top of loftblocks. Headblocks can be somewhat lower, assuming loftblocks are hung from the bottom of the roof-steel structure.

A straight lift, or single purchase, counterweight-rigging system balances each pound of batten weight, plus its hanging load, against an equal amount of counterweight. A stagehand pulling in one foot of operating line moves the attached batten one foot, and both line and batten travel at the same speed.

Installing a single-purchase rigging system requires that an entire side wall of the stage be given over to counterweight arbors and their guide tracks. The wall must be plumb, and its height must equal the distance each batten travels *plus* the additional height of counterweight arbors. Furthermore, the wall cannot contain any floor-level opening larger than a single small door. Otherwise, counterweight arbors must be installed above the opening and a double-purchase system has to be used, or the counterweight approach may have to be abandoned and a motorized winch system installed.

The double-purchase system requires that the arbors travel only half the vertical distance that the battens travel. But twice as much weight is needed to counterbalance loads, and the battens move twice as fast as the arbor. Because its cables run through more sheaves, the double-purchase system introduces more friction. Sets thus "run" stiffer than with single-purchase rigging. Also, headblock beams and loading bridges must be sized to accommodate a double burden of counterweights. For all these reasons, a double-purchase system should be installed only as a last resort.

Since motorized winches may be placed at grid level, they may not require the use of a side wall or loading bridges. However, a pin rail should still be provided for spotting lines. Some winch systems also eliminate the need for a headblock beam and remove horizontal loading. Thus, a motorized winch can result in savings in the way of less structural steel and other equipment. But purchasing and installing the system can cost two to three times as much as a comparable counterweight array.

A LOW-GRID STAGEHOUSE

Not every space for dance has room for a high stagehouse. In restoration and renovation projects, the theatre roof may have to stay at an existing, low level to comply with historic preservation standards or local zoning codes. Or a dance company may decide that the stagehouse, and thus scenery, can fly no higher than its budget. Sometimes the decision to build a low-grid stagehouse is founded on esthetics—the less scenery the better.

While scenery cannot be flown in and out of a low-grid stagehouse (it can only hang), rigging battens can be lowered to the stage floor, allowing the crew to attach or remove scenery and lighting fixtures quickly. A low grid should still stand between 30 and 45 feet above the stage floor. As in high stagehouses, 7 to 10 feet of space must be left between the grid floor and the theatre roof, so stagehands can stand on the grid to adjust rigging battens and lines.

CATWALK RIGGING SYSTEM

An overhead catwalk system can be installed where the stagehouse is too shallow for even a low-grid rigging system. In this instance, floor-supported flats, rather than hanging fabric panels, are usually used to create the wings. Overhead masking is omitted (part of a catwalk's cachet is that the theatre's rigging system stands boldly in view of the audience).

Catwalks must cover the entire performance space and project over a portion of the seating area. The system should allow crew members to reach every part of the space above the stage, and should be designed so scenic or lighting elements can be attached to guard rails, to walkways, and to fixed battens suspended from the ceiling alongside catwalks.

STAGE LIGHTING

Just as a dance company's hanging plan tells stagehands where and how to

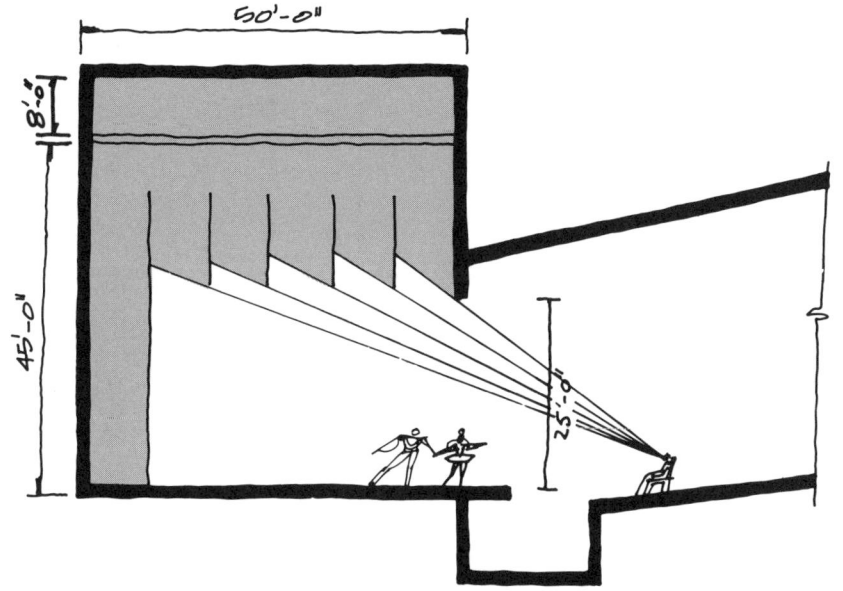

While it has no flying capabilities, the low-grid stagehouse offers many of the advantages of a high-grid stagehouse.

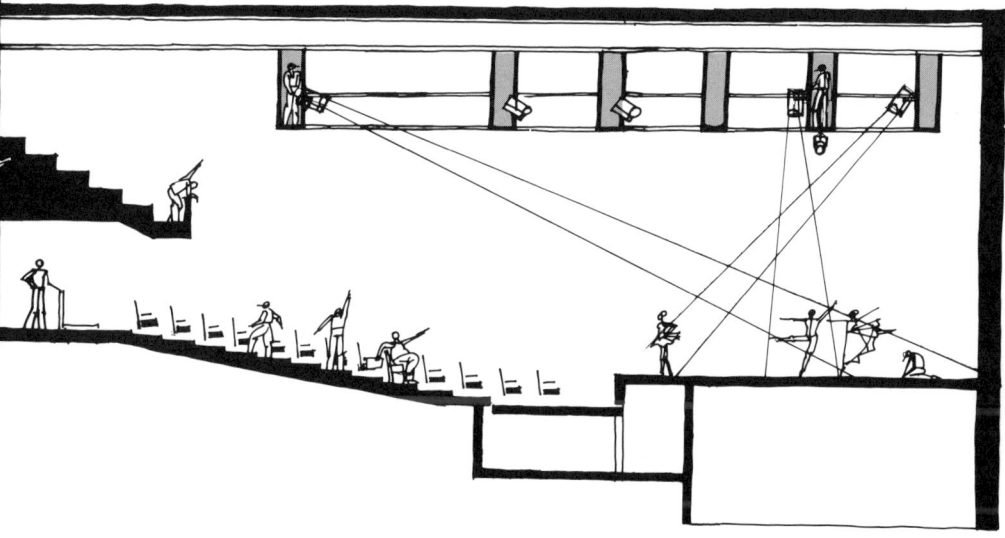

A catwalk rigging system affords efficient, convenient access to almost any point in the theatre ceiling for hanging stage lighting, scenery, or masking.

The performing area must be illuminated from the front of the house as well as from the stage. The most common front-of-house lighting positions are in the ceiling, the balcony rail, and the box boom positions on the side walls.

The light plot above was laid out by lighting designer Jennifer Tipton for a small modern dance company on tour. The light plot below, also by Tipton, is for the same size performing area but for the American Ballet Theatre.

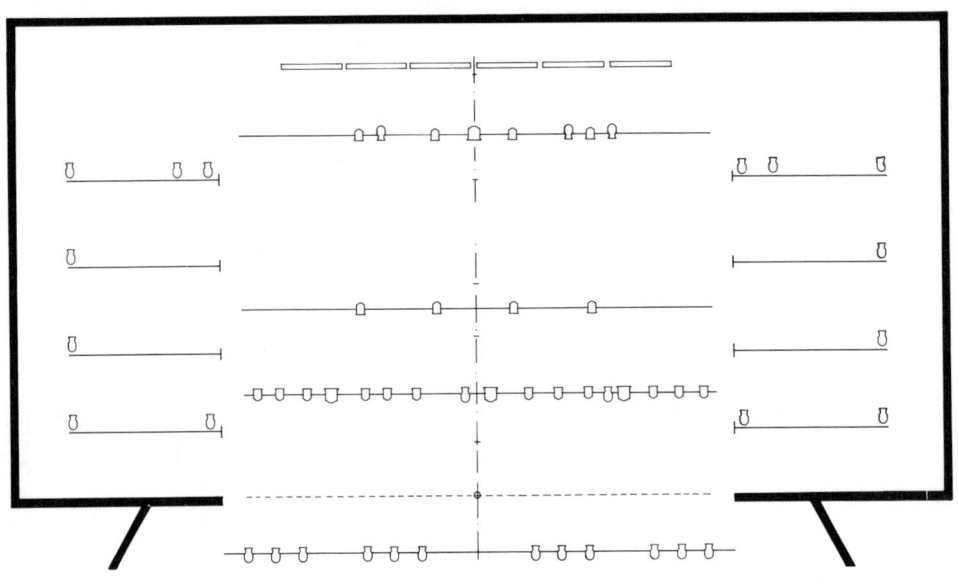

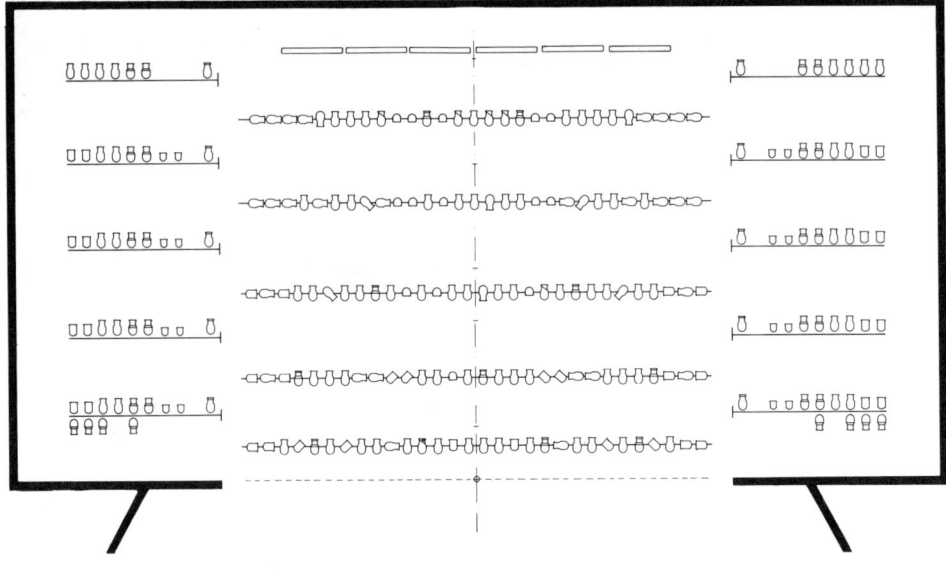

arrange scenery, its "light plot" guides them in distributing luminaires (lighting instruments). Almost every dance theatre must be well-stocked with stage-lighting fixtures—catalog items that are easily installed. Luminaires may be furnished as part of the construction package, or purchased separately by the theatre owner. How much and what kind of equipment is needed depends on the size of the theatre and its stage and the requirements of companies that will dance there. A theatre-design consultant can compile an appropriate shopping list. Theatres presenting only major touring companies may choose not to purchase any stage-lighting fixtures since these dance organizations arrive at the door with a full complement of company lighting gear.

EQUIPMENT MOUNTING TECHNIQUES

On stage, most lighting instruments are clamped to pipe battens and hung overhead among scenery and masking. There should be enough rigging battens to accommodate complex lighting designs, with plenty of hanging and flying space remaining for other equipment. In dance, many lighting instruments are attached to "tormentor booms" or "lighting ladders" that hang or stand in the wings: side lighting is needed to model dancers' bodies; without it, they appear two-dimensional.

The crew must be able to rearrange fixtures to comply with company lighting plots. Thus, lighting instruments on stage, unlike those in the front-of-house, are never permanently installed.

FRONT-OF-HOUSE LIGHTING

Front-of-house lighting fixtures are installed in the auditorium, rather than on stage. When a new theatre is built or an old one renovated, precise front-of-house lighting positions should be established during the design process. Studying sample light plots from companies that will use the theatre will help in determining front-of-house needs.

The Illuminating Engineering Society of North America, in its *Guide in the Planning of Theatres and Public Building Auditoriums*, provides a lighting primer for the front of the house:

> The most common high front position is located in the auditorium ceiling, usually referred to as the ceiling cove or beam position. Ideally, this is plotted on a 45-degree angle from head height (five feet) of a performer standing at the proscenium line to the auditorium ceiling. Lights located in this position provide the basic illumination for the downstage area. This is the most important front position. In larger facilities, several auditorium ceiling slots may be necessary to provide adequate lighting on the forestage or apron and the area just behind the front curtain.
>
> Lighting ports or mounting slots must provide sufficient openings to allow unobstructed maneuverability for flexible focusing of lighting instruments. Horizontal slots should allow a *minimum* of thirty inches of clear space for up to ten-inch ellipsoidal spotlights. Three feet is preferable.
>
> Vertical slots should be at least 24 inches wide, but this may vary depending on the type of units used. It is desirable that ceiling units or wall units in the house be hung with the front of the units behind the slot to prevent wall or ceiling spill light on architectural surfaces.
>
> Secondary positions at the sides of the auditorium (side slot or box boom positions located vertically below the beam positions) supplement the primary ceiling positions. Low-angle lighting from these side positions adds three-dimensional qualities to the performer and setting.
>
> Low-angle lighting from the front, usually from a balcony (balcony rail), provides flat fill and wash lighting. This position is also required for certain types of projected effects.
>
> Performer highlighting may be done by follow spots generally located at the rear of the auditorium.

FOLLOWSPOTS

Followspots are used extensively in dance lighting, and three to four may be required in a large proscenium theatre. The spotlight booth must be located on the center line of the theatre, and each spotlight must be able to illuminate any portion of the performance area. If the followspots' angle of throw is too shallow, light will reflect onto the backdrop; if it is too steep, a beam aimed upstage can be obstructed by a portal edge or border at the proscenium opening. Downward followspot angles of thirty to forty-five degrees are preferable. Chapter 6 sets out design standards for the theatre's followspot booth. In theatres with catwalk rigging systems, incandescent or enclosed-arc followspots can go on the catwalks rather than in a special booth.

WIRING DEVICES

The theatre-design consultant, together with the electrical engineer, provides the plan which the electrical contractor follows to install the wiring system that feeds power to theatrical lighting. Electrical outlets in the auditorium are usually installed in fixed positions. Backstage, flexible cables are often run to the rigging battens that support lighting fixtures.

While only experts should install wiring, understanding some basics of theatrical circuitry can help the architect and theatre owner coordinate the work of the design consultant and electrical engineer. The standard theatrical circuit is 20 amps at 120 volts. This means a maximum of 2,400 watts of lamp load may be placed on a given circuit. Thus, for example, two 1,000-watt lamps, three 750-watt lamps, or four 500-watt lamps can be fed from one circuit.

Circuits must be installed at potential stage-lighting fixture locations throughout the theatre even when stage lighting and dimming equipment will not be purchased by the owner. Local building codes usually require that circuits in the auditorium be permanently wired, with a circuit breaker provided for each one. In houses with no fire curtain, all stage-lighting circuits must be permanent. But in houses with a fire curtain, flexible cables, rather than fixed conduit, are usually permitted backstage. These provide a temporary means of distributing power from the dimmers to stage-lighting fixtures. But this method is appropriate only in theatres used primarily by touring companies that carry their own lighting equipment. Since few theatres present only major touring companies, it is generally wise to install permanent wiring backstage. A visiting company may choose to disregard the system in favor of its own wiring. For such cases, the theatre must be furnished with a front-of-house disconnect panel, where the company's portable dimming system can be linked to permanent circuits in the auditorium.

DIMMING SYSTEMS

Dimmers, which may be portable or permanent, regulate the power flowing through stage-lighting circuitry. Because it will be remotely controlled, a permanent dimming system can be installed at whatever place the electrical engineer deems best. Portable systems must go offstage and at the stage level, near a source of power. The front-of-house disconnect panel must be placed adjacent to the portable dimming system.

Until recently, all branch circuits of a permanent stage-lighting system were run to a "patch panel" similar to an old-fashioned telephone switchboard. Each cluster of branch circuits was controlled by a single, large-capacity dimmer in a dimmer rack. New dimmer-per-circuit systems provide an electronic dimming device for every branch circuit in the theatre; patching is done electronically at the lighting console.

LIGHTING-CONTROL CONSOLE

These days, even a simple lighting console can control forty-eight dimmers and will permit reasonable flexibility in operating stage lighting for small-scale theatrical productions. Where more than sixty dimming units are required, it makes sense to install a custom-made dimming equipment rack, plus a control console with an electronic memory. A single technician seated at a memory-equipped console can create sophisticated lighting effects unheard of a few years ago. On the other hand, a component failure in the electronic console can shut down the entire stage-lighting system. Each theatre needs a back-up unit that can stand in for a crippled console; the system should also have a comprehensive manufacturer's guarantee. While the wiring for the lighting-control system is usually installed by the theatre's electrical contractor, an engineer representing the manufacturer should make final connections at the console and test the system.

Auxiliary equipment is available from major manufacturers to extend control of the stage-lighting system to theatre locations other than the lighting booth. A portable remote-control module permits a designer to adjust lighting levels and cues while sitting in the auditorium. Control panels for house, rehearsal, and work lighting may be furnished on stage at the stage manager's position; subsidiary control devices may also be provided for crew members, house management, and maintenance personnel.

SOUND SYSTEMS AND EQUIPMENT

Because many dance companies perform solely to recorded music, a first-class sound system is a must in every space for dance. The overall sound system consists of separate subsystems (sound effects, sound reinforcement, stage fold-back, performance monitoring-and-paging, and intercom), all generally installed under a single contract. Theatres designed for four-walls bookings (rental houses without any movable production equipment) usually possess only performance monitoring-and-paging and intercom systems. Amplifiers, control consoles, loudspeakers, and other equipment required for performance are brought in by the visiting dance company.

SOUND EFFECTS

The theatre's loudspeakers broadcast the sound of recorded music and special effects. The speakers are connected to an amplification system operated from the sound-control booth. Around the stage and in the auditorium, there should be additional outlets for portable loudspeakers and microphones, to allow for unusual production needs.

SOUND REINFORCEMENT

In theatres presenting musical comedy and similar productions, and seating a thousand or more patrons, a sound-reinforcement system may be needed. The system amplifies sound from the stage and carries it to the auditorium, so singers and actors can be heard over music from the pit orchestra. Sound reinforcement is also needed in theatres so vast that an actor's voice cannot fill the house.

FOLD-BACK

What sound reinforcement does for the audience, a fold-back system does for performers; loudspeakers carry the sound of the orchestra or recorded music to the stage. Without fold-back, dancers in most theatres cannot hear music as well as the audience does, because neither the pit nor the loudspeakers direct sound toward them.

Lighting ladders suspended from the rigging provide necessary side lighting without taking up valuable floor space in the wings.

PERFORMANCE MONITORING AND PAGING

The monitoring system broadcasts the sound of a performance backstage to dressing rooms, toilets, corridors, and other areas. By hearing what is happening on stage, dancers and stagehands know when to be on hand for an entrance or a scene shift.

The paging system lets the stage manager override the performance monitor in order to make announcements backstage. Some paging systems can also be used to broadcast into the auditorium, to address the audience or make announcements during rehearsals.

INTERCOM

To coordinate the work of stagehands during performances and rehearsals, the stage manager speaks over an intercom connected to headsets worn by key backstage personnel. The intercom, which is distinct from the paging system, may be augmented by a cue-lighting system, for the benefit of stagehands not wearing headsets. Jacks for headsets are usually installed in the rigging area, at other points along the perimeter of the stage, and in the followspot and lighting-and-sound booths. Two or more jacks should also go in the center of the auditorium, where the lighting designer sets up a production table during rehearsals.

MINIMUM REQUIREMENTS FOR ALTERNATE SPACES

Satisfying technical requirements for presenting dance can seem well-nigh impossible on a modest budget. Even secondhand lighting and sound equipment is expensive. Each dance group, on considering its resources, will set its own goals for equipping an alternate space.

DRAPERIES AND MASKING

Drapery and masking requirements for alternate spaces are essentially the same as in large theatres, except that the basic elements are scaled down to fit a dance company's space and budget. Draperies should be uniform in height, so they can be used anywhere in the room. If framed, velour-covered flats will serve as masking, provide a few extra ones to allow for a variety of configurations. "Two-fold" flats are the easiest to use since they stand by themselves. So they can be shifted easily, flats should be short enough to stay clear of lights hanging from overhead mounting positions.

RIGGING SYSTEMS

Where ceiling height allows, a catwalk rigging system of the kind described earlier in this chapter should be provided. If the alternate space is being newly built, the extra room height will not add greatly to construction costs. However, in found spaces ceilings are often too low to provide headroom above the catwalks, or the roof may be unable to support their additional weight.

The next best rigging alternative is a system of suspended pipes. The pipes hang at a fixed height over the stage and much of the seating area. While intended mainly for stage lighting, the pipes can be used to support loudspeakers, minimal scenery, and masking. Because the pipes do not move, they can be reached only by using ladders or scaffolding, a time-consuming process, since each luminaire must be hauled up, attached, connected to an electrical circuit, and then focused. But suspended pipe grids work well with limited budgets and in places where the ceiling height is less than 28 feet, rapid changeovers are not required, and labor is inexpensive.

The grid should be built of continuous lengths of 1½ inch (inside diameter)

A dead-hung pipe-grid system provides an easy, inexpensive solution to rigging problems for alternate spaces or other theatres with limited ceiling height.

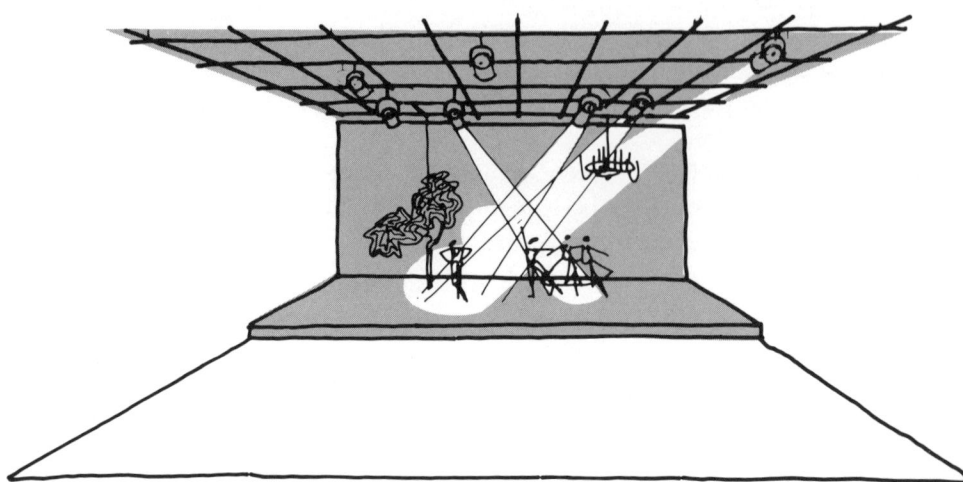

"Schedule 40" pipe, suspended at least 12 to 18 inches from the ceiling. If seats for the audience will remain fixed to the floor, and thus in a constant position relative to the stage, the pipes can be hung parallel to seating rows about 4 feet on center. If the position of the audience will vary, more flexibility is needed; two layers of pipe, each 4 feet on center, should be hung perpendicular to one another to create a pipe grid. Distribute electrical outlets across the grid, using rigid conduit or bundles of cable. Before the grid is installed, the ceiling may have to be reinforced to support the weight of the pipes, plus lighting and scenery.

PERFORMANCE LIGHTING

A new dance organization may be wise to rent lighting equipment for its first season or two. With time, the company can form a better idea of what fixtures best suit its needs. Whether rented or purchased, only standard theatrical equipment made by a recognized manufacturer should be selected. Fixtures should come with standard C-clamps and related hardware, so they will be interchangeable with any equipment rented to supplement house luminaires.

DIMMING SYSTEM

For dancers and their audience, few events can be more disconcerting than to have the stage plunged into darkness due to a sudden loss of power to the dimming system. Using an undersized electrical panel to power dimming equipment can cause blown fuses or tripped circuit breakers at mid-performance. Any electrical equipment should be installed by a licensed electrician, working from guidelines furnished by the theatre's lighting designer.

Many small performance spaces are well-served by modular theatrical dimming systems. These frequently come in groups of six dimmers (called six-packs) that can be easily expanded to systems of forty-eight dimmers or more. Each about the size of a small suitcase, the six-packs are usually parked next to a power source; branch circuits are brought to this location.

Because modular dimmer packs are portable, they lend themselves to touring. But if dimming equipment will be taken on the road, it should be chosen with care. Inexpensive dimmer packs may not stand up to the punishment that comes with being loaded in and out of theatres and trucks. Finally, if dimmer packs will be regularly moved from a company's theatre, as for touring, a three-phase electrical outlet should be installed for each pack. Otherwise, the theatre's main electrical panel will have to be opened every time dimming equipment is disconnected and reconnected.

HOUSE LIGHTING

A dance company trying to hold down the house electric bill may want to install a mix of fluorescent and incandescent lighting for rehearsals. During performances, dimmable incandescent fixtures—a modest number placed in a regular pattern at or above the level of overhead stage lighting pipes—are a must. If the alternate space is large and the seating pattern will change, house lighting should be adaptable. Circuitry should be arranged so any combination of circuit breakers can be turned on or off to meet a particular evening's lighting needs. House-light dimmers should be located where they can be easily reached by the operator of the stage-lighting console; an inexpensive house-light control system consists of a cluster of standard household wall dimmers.

SOUND SYSTEM

Most small dance companies rehearse and perform to recorded music. Their sound system may consist of no more than a portable tape recorder with built-in speakers. When special effects are called for, two tape recorders may be necessary, so sounds can overlap. If loudspeakers will be distributed throughout the space, it should be possible to relocate them to meet future performance requirements. The size of the alternate space determines the proper size of the loudspeakers.

CONTROL BOOTH

Although often overlooked during the planning of alternate spaces for dance, the control booth merits nearly as much attention as the stage. Whether the booth is tucked above the seating area, or stacked above a low storage room, it must provide a clear view of the stage. Inside the booth, there should be space for the stage manager, for lighting and sound control operators and their equipment, and for additional technicians as needed. Because the booth contains the theatre's most valuable equipment, sturdy locks should be installed on doors and windows. See Chapter 6 for guidelines on designing control booths.

RENT OR BUY?

Sound and lighting equipment for the theatre can be leased or purchased. Each approach has benefits and drawbacks.

For a new dance company, or one with very little money, buying equipment may be out of the question. But rental fees add up, and purchasing often proves cheaper in the long run.

However, what you own, you fix. The company that purchases technical equipment may discover it cannot afford a staff electrician to maintain its gear. In most rental agreements, the supplier assumes responsibility for periodic maintenance or for replacing defective equipment.

Also, rental equipment can be easily replaced to meet the dance company's changing needs. A company that buys equipment can accumulate a cumbersome supply of outmoded items, purchased at the insistence of last year's lighting designer.

Each dance company crafts its own compromise—whether to rent with an option to buy, or to purchase dimming racks and control consoles but lease stage-lighting fixtures. A group just starting out should seek advice from another company a bit farther along the path to prosperity.

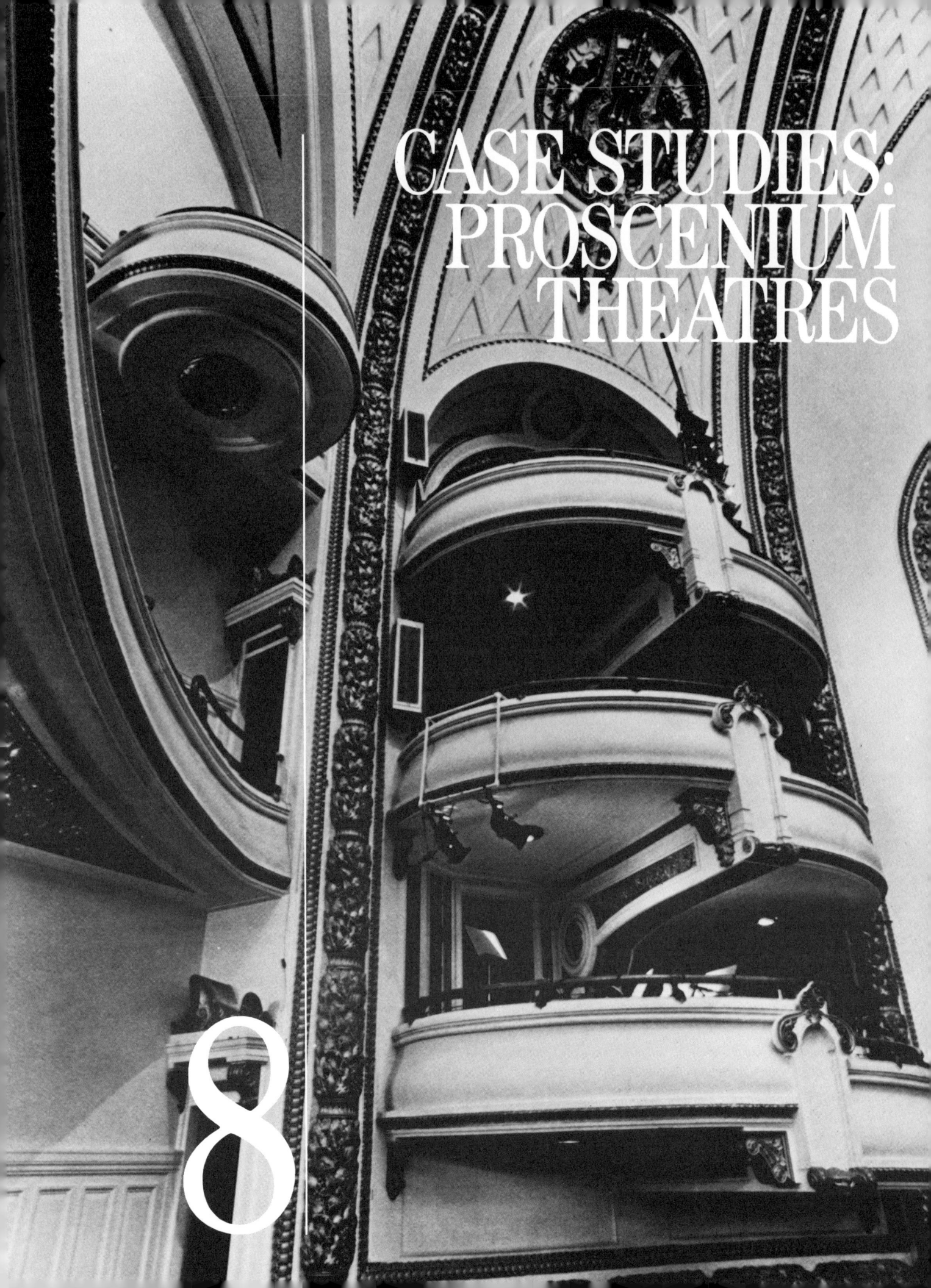

8
CASE STUDIES: PROSCENIUM THEATRES

Most big American cities have at least one large proscenium theatre. In those theatres, for better or worse, usually on stages too shallow and floors too stiff, the nation's dance companies perform. Touring dance companies play poor theatres because architectural hand-me-down's are often the only stages around. And they tour secure in the knowledge that for every space even partly remodeled to suit the needs of dance—a stage floor made more springy, a proscenium widened, the wings expanded—there remain scores of unrepentant, unforgiving houses.

The rule is bleak. There are also noteworthy exceptions. Of the seven case-study theatres that follow, a sampling of the nation's best performing arts facilities, two were designed specifically for dance; the rest are multipurpose theatres, large or small, newly built or renovated. Each theatre heeds the needs of performer and patron. Each can serve as a working definition of space for dance.

THE JOYCE THEATER
Home of the Feld Ballet

Until the Joyce Theater opened in 1982, the Feld Ballet had searched for years for an affordable place to perform in New York City. High rental costs at uptown theatres can break the budget of a relatively small company like the Feld. "Each time you venture into such a space, it's a life or death situation," says Cora Cahan, the company's executive director. "A bad uptown season in any given year can put you out of business."

A particularly generous donor came to the company's rescue. Lu Esther T. Mertz, who had funded construction of the company's studios, paid for the purchase of the Elgin Theatre, an old two-story movie house at Eighth Avenue and Nineteenth Street, in a neighborhood far removed from Broadway or Lincoln Center.

Next, the Feld negotiated a contract with the stagehands' union that allowed the company a long season (to better present its repertoire) and a small seating capacity (to avoid audience saturation) at an operating cost the ballet could afford. "The day after we bought the theatre," says Cahan, "we went to Local One [of the stagehands' union]. We had in mind one Local One stagehand as reasonable representation for a theatre of under five-hundred seats. They suggested one union stagehand and one apprentice from their apprentice rolls." With the latter arrangement settled on, the balance of Joyce stagehands are nonunion. Further, says Cahan, "They work cross-departmentally, which means electricians can handle props, and so on," an unusually flexible arrangement that she calls "extremely helpful."

The architectural firm of Hardy Holzman Pfeiffer and theatre consultant Robert Davis, of Jules Fisher Associates, were engaged to do the renovation (funds for the project came from several sources, including loans from a bank and from New York City, and grants from the Dance and Design Arts Programs of the National Endowment for the Arts and from private foundations). The theatre was gutted and rebuilt, and the building was extended the full length of the original movie house lot. A new stage, 67 feet wide by 36 feet deep and with a flexible (43 to 52 foot wide) proscenium opening, was constructed across the full width of the building. A 4-foot crossover was created where a back alley had been; stairs leading from the crossover go beneath the stage and on to dressing rooms, a wardrobe, and a laundry.

No fly tower was built above the stage, says Eliot Feld, because "there is no need for the technical capabilities of Broadway in an off-Broadway house." There are occa-

New York's City Center, originally a Masonic temple, was for many years the only theatre suitable for dance in the heart of the city.

Detail of the Opera House in the Brooklyn Academy of Music, a performing-arts center that has consistently had a strong commitment to dance.

sional regrets over the lack of a fly tower, but Cora Cahan says, "We know if we had tried to raise the added half-to-three-quarters of a million dollars [to build the fly tower] we might not have been able to do it. It might have been too much. Also, we might have had to use more union stagehands."

The Joyce has a fixed grid and small battery of electric winches. In the house, there are two overhead catwalks and multiple side-lighting and followspot positions. Built specifically for dance, with a basket-weave floor, the fully equipped theatre is used not only by the Feld Ballet, but is rented to other companies throughout the year.

Renamed the Joyce after Lu Esther T. Mertz's late daughter, the theatre is simple in design, rich in detail. The rake is gentle at the front of the house, then rises sharply to leave space below the seating for the lobby. Light, sound, and stage manager's booths are tucked away between the back of the house and the building's front face. The auditorium's 474 seats are upholstered in dark, geometrically patterned fabric, and the walls are exposed brick. Overhead trusses, catwalks, pipe railings, and exposed steel columns supporting descending side galleries are painted in a scheme of dark green, grey, and salmon.

The Joyce Theater, an off-Broadway space for dance, was once a decrepit movie house known as Elgin Theatre. Completely renovated in 1982, the Joyce is one of the few theatres designed specifically for dance.

Inside the Joyce: Above, the stage is set for rehearsal; left, looking toward the stage.

The rear of the house and the control room.

Orchestra and street level, Joyce Theatre
1. Lobby
2. Box office
3. Stage
4. Crossover
5. Loading-in platform

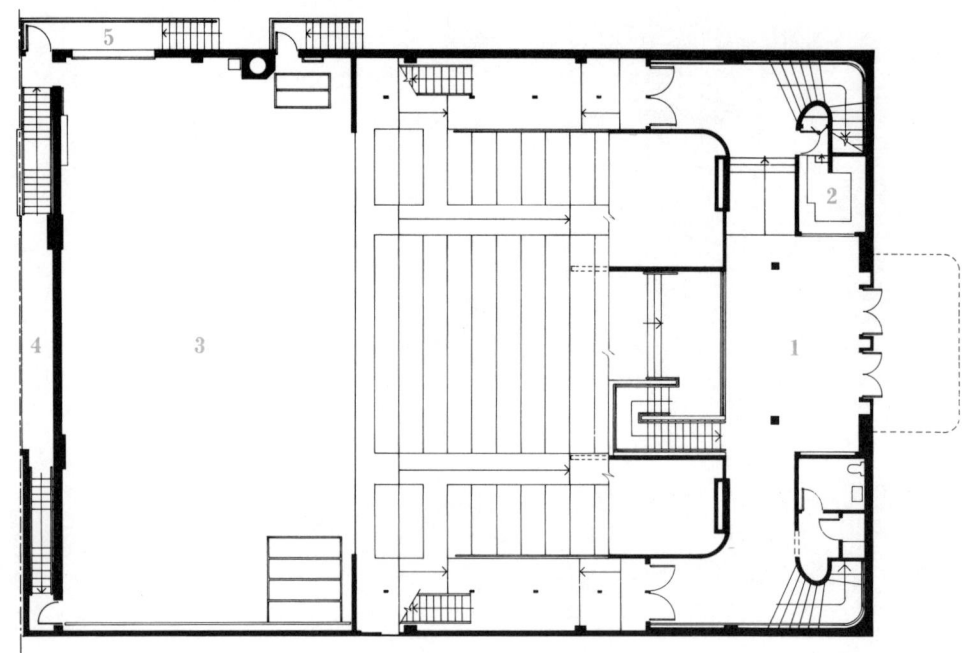

Upper level, Joyce Theatre
1. Upper lobby

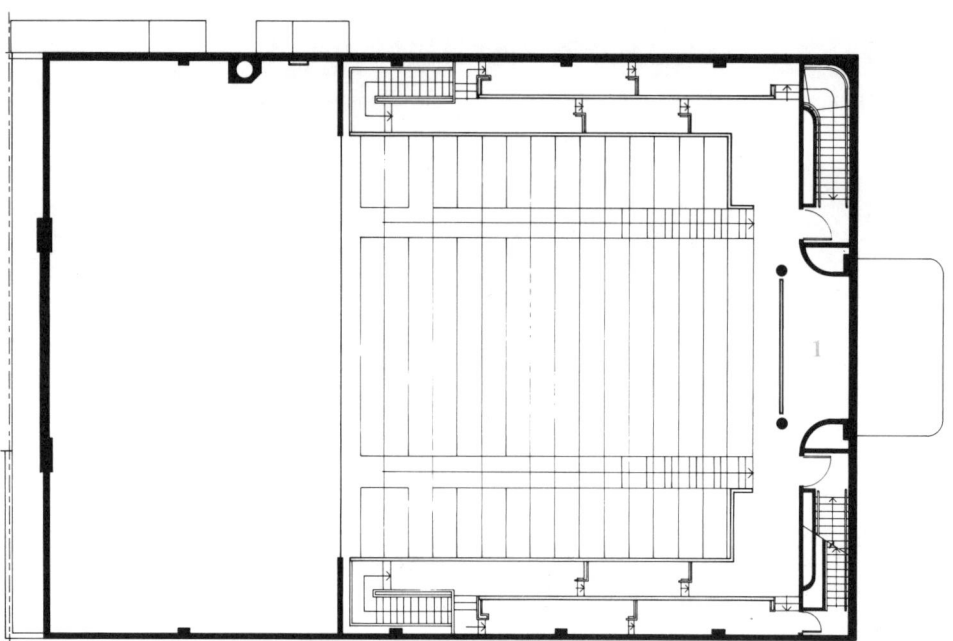

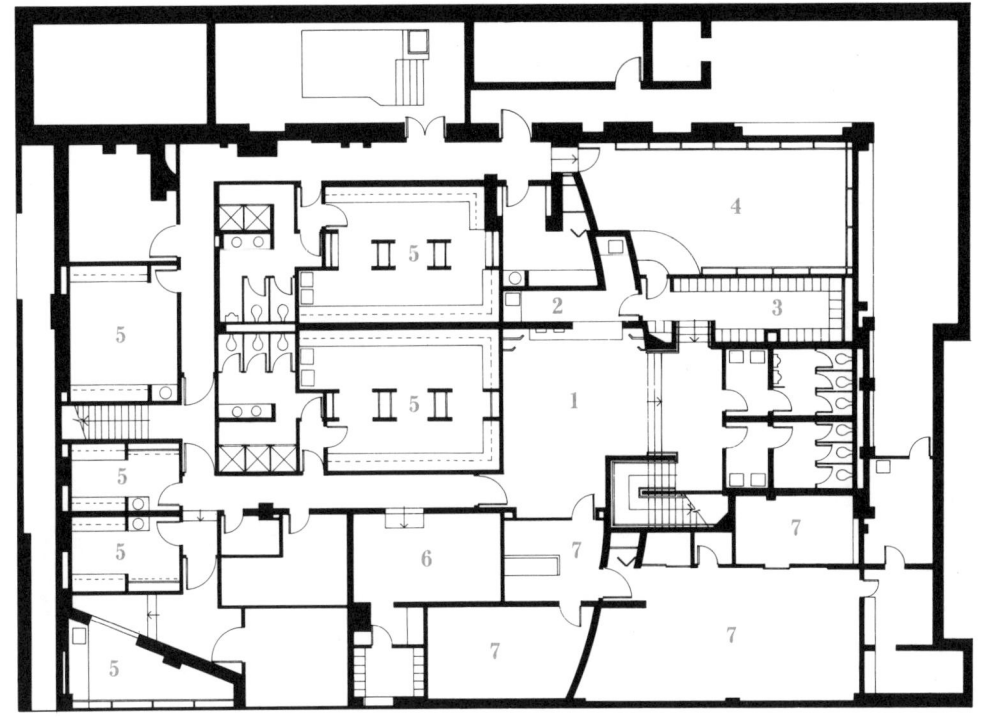

Basement level, Joyce Theatre
1. Lower lobby
2. Concession
3. Coat locker room
4. Warm-up room
5. Dressing rooms
6. Wardrobe and property rooms
7. Administrative offices

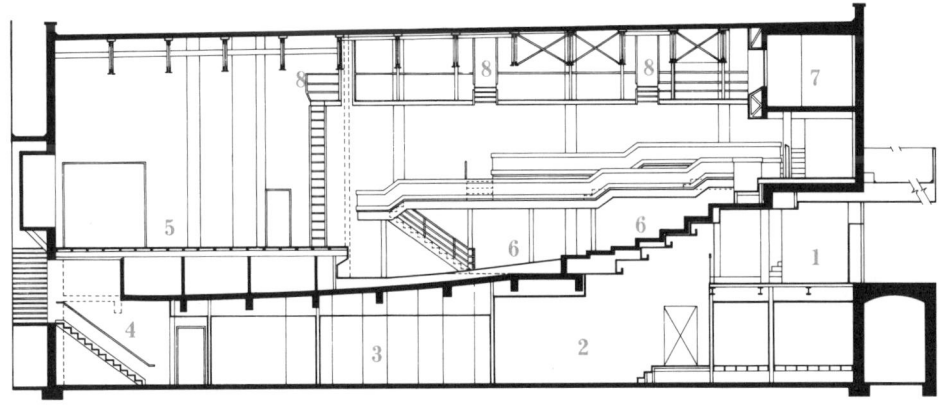

Longitudinal section, Joyce Theatre
1. Lobby
2. Lower lobby
3. Dressing rooms
4. Passage to stage
5. Stage
6. Orchestra seating
7. Control room
8. Catwalks

The Capitol Theatre in Salt Lake City, Utah, was once a vaudeville theatre. The Venetian-Italian facade and the equally ornate lobby and house were restored in 1978.

THE CAPITOL THEATRE
Home of Ballet West

Before the opening of the Capitol Theatre in 1978, Ballet West, Utah's foremost dance company, performed on the tiny (45 by 28 foot) stage of the University of Utah Theatre. Ballet West's wardrobe and offices were in a church.

When Salt Lake County's plan for a $20 million performing arts complex foundered for lack of voter support, a less expensive alternative—restoring a 1913 vaudeville house—was chosen to accommodate local dance and theatre groups.

The Capitol Theatre was redesigned by architect Steven T. Baird and theatre-design consultant Roger Morgan to meet the needs of Ballet West (now its chief user), the Utah Opera Company, the Ririe-Woodbury Dance Company, and the Repertory Dance Theatre. The theatre's stagehouse, newly constructed from precast concrete panels and now extending to the property lines, grew from its original 86 by 38 feet to a more spacious 100 by 50 feet. The original proscenium opening, 29 feet high by 35 feet wide, now measures 45 feet wide.

The stagehouse has been furnished with a new grid floor and single-purchase counterweight rigging system. On each side of the stage, electric motors raise and lower lighting booms in the wings; this allows Ballet West to fly out lighting booms during intermissions, which, in turn, leaves more space for quick scenery changes.

In addition, a resilient, basket-weave stage floor was constructed, an electronic-memory dimming system was installed, and a service elevator and theatre storage space were added to the building. To save space in the theatre, scenery and costume construction shops are located in other buildings. But all other support facilities are at the Capitol, including administrative offices for Ballet West and other resident companies. New support spaces for dancers include one large rehearsal studio (which, at 60 feet wide by 50 feet deep, exceeds the size of the performance space), one smaller studio, warm-up rooms, and showers.

Dance patrons have also benefited from the renovation work. Audience capacity was increased from 1,800 to 1,943 seats, and the theatre's narrow lobby was enlarged by claiming adjoining spaces previously leased to commercial tenants.

The original proscenium arch at the Capitol Theatre, above, was so low that it flattened the stage picture. The new proscenium arch, left, provides a higher and wider rectangular opening, closer in proportion to the ideal square, and suitable for the presentation of dance.

Orchestra and street level, Capitol Theatre
 1. Lobby
 2. Box office
 3. Coat room
 4. Concession
 5. Control room
 6. Viewing room
 7. Orchestra pit
 8. Stage
 9. Loading-in
10. Lighting trough

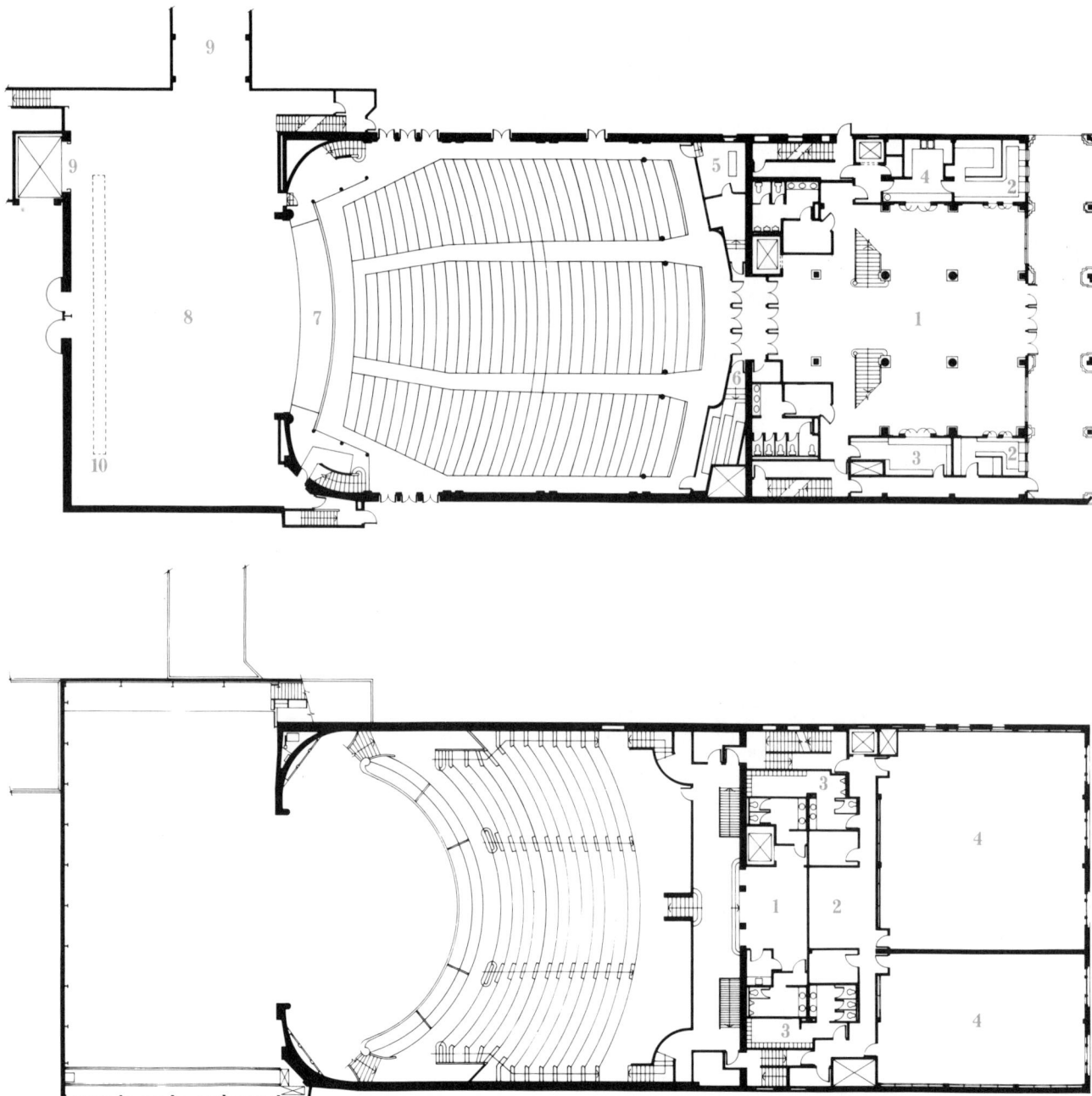

Balcony, Capitol Theatre
 1. Lobby
 2. Concession
 3. Dressing room
 4. Rehearsal rooms

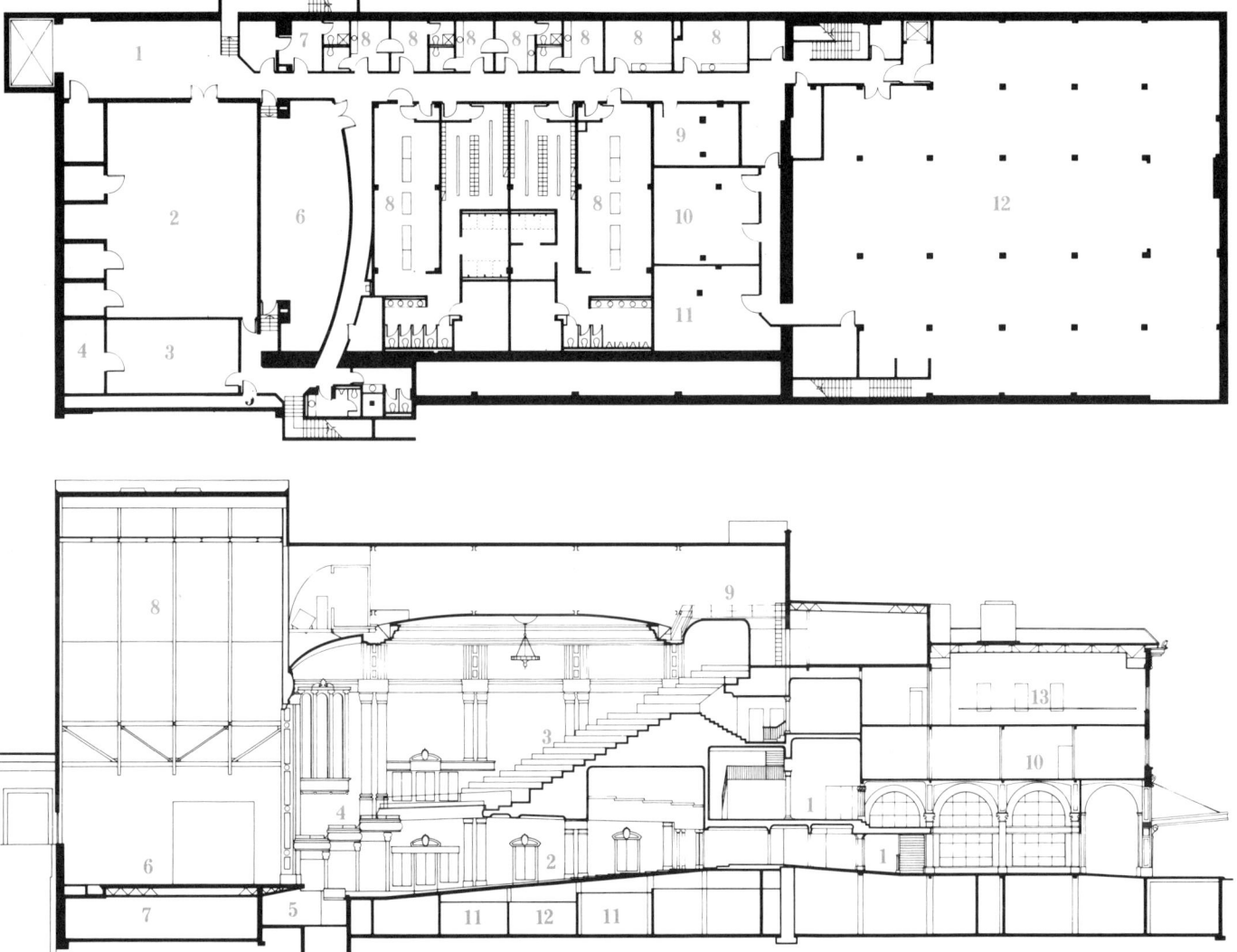

Basement, Capitol Theatre
1. Receiving area
2. Rehearsal room with piano alcove
3. Musicians' room
4. Music and instrument storage
5. Rigging arbor trough
6. Orchestra pit
7. Conductor's suite
8. Dressing rooms
9. Career room
10. Costume and wardrobe
11. Therapy
12. Unfinished

Longitudinal section, Capitol Theatre
1. Lobby
2. Orchestra seating
3. Balcony seating
4. Box seats
5. Orchestra pit
6. Stage
7. Rehearsal room with piano alcove
8. Fly tower
9. Catwalks
10. Board room
11. Dressing rooms
12. Costume and wardrobe
13. Studio

The marquee for the Civic Center of Onondaga County, Syracuse, N. Y.

CIVIC CENTER OF ONONDAGA COUNTY
Syracuse, New York

The Civic Center of Onondaga County in upstate New York sponsors a wide range of cultural events, including performances of music, theatre, and dance. Its construction budget was ample but not lavish; its architecture is clean and unadorned. Other multipurpose facilities of comparable complexity and scale include the National Arts Center in Ottawa, Canada; the Kennedy Center in Washington, D.C.; Meany Hall in Seattle; Hanscher Auditorium in Iowa City; and Zellerbach Hall at the University of California at Berkeley.

With 2,117 seats, the Crouse-Hinds Concert Theatre is the largest of the civic center's three spaces. A proscenium theatre, it has a removable orchestra shell. The large orchestra pit is adjustable and sits on hydraulic lifts.

Next down in size is the Carrier Theatre, seating 463 on a steeply raked floor. The Carrier presents a full range of drama, dance, and music, but on a smaller scale than in the Crouse-Hinds.

The civic center's most compact space is the BeVard Community Room. A "black box" with 200 movable seats, the BeVard measures 40 by 60 feet, with a 34-foot ceiling. Designed primarily for dance and orchestra rehearsal, the space has been used for all the performing arts, as well as for lectures, meetings, films, and bar mitzvahs. Stage lighting is hung above the room's chain-link grid system; dance amenities include mirrors along one long wall and portable barres.

Together, the three theatres present some sixteen hundred events each year. Entirely a roadhouse, the civic center mounts no productions of its own. Joseph Golden, executive director of the facility and the man chiefly responsible for its construction and success, attributes the civic center's popularity with artists to its logic and clarity of layout and its spacious backstage. There are three floors of dressing rooms, variously sized to hold four, eight, sixteen, or thirty-two persons, and accommodating one hundred twenty performers in all. Each dressing room has its own shower and toilet facilities. There are also three backstage musicians' locker rooms.

Performers have not been the only ones to benefit from the civic center's intelligent design. The facility's enclosed truck dock is "great for stagehands," says Carol Jeschke, director of programming and public relations. Able to accommodate "two semi's and a van" the dock is arranged so equipment from company trucks can be moved directly to stages and other backstage spaces.

Dancers perform at the Carrier Theatre, one of the Civic Center's three performance spaces.

The Crouse-Hinds Concert Theatre, largest of the Civic Center's auditoriums, seats 2,117.

Street and stage levels, Crouse-Hinds Concert Theatre, Carrier Theatre, and BeVard Community Room
1. Lobby
2. Box office
3. Coat check
4. Administration
5. Crouse-Hinds orchestra pit
6. Crouse-Hinds stage
7. Conductor's suite
8. BeVard community room
9. Storage and workshop
10. Dressing rooms
11. Offices
12. Carrier Theatre stage
13. New county office building
14. Loading dock
15. Existing office building
16. Existing court house

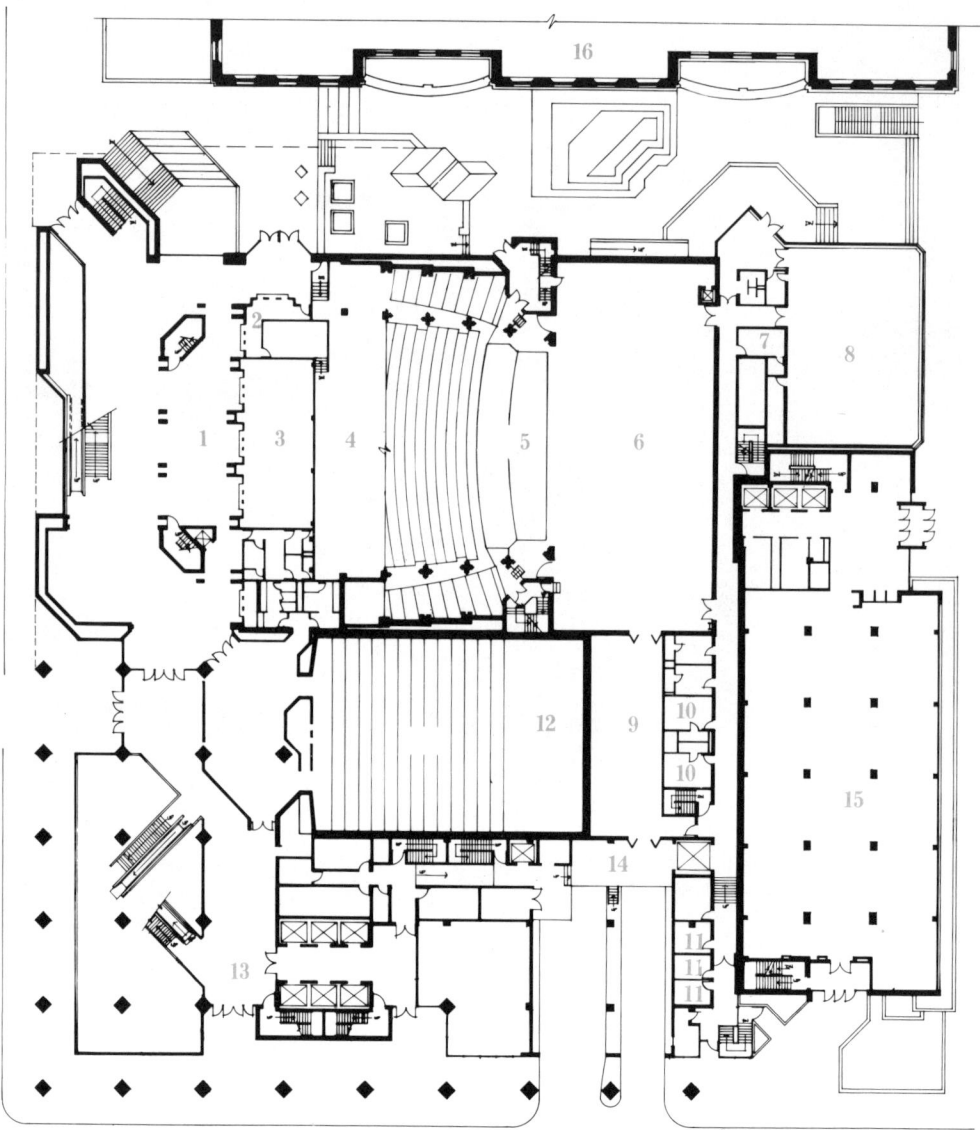

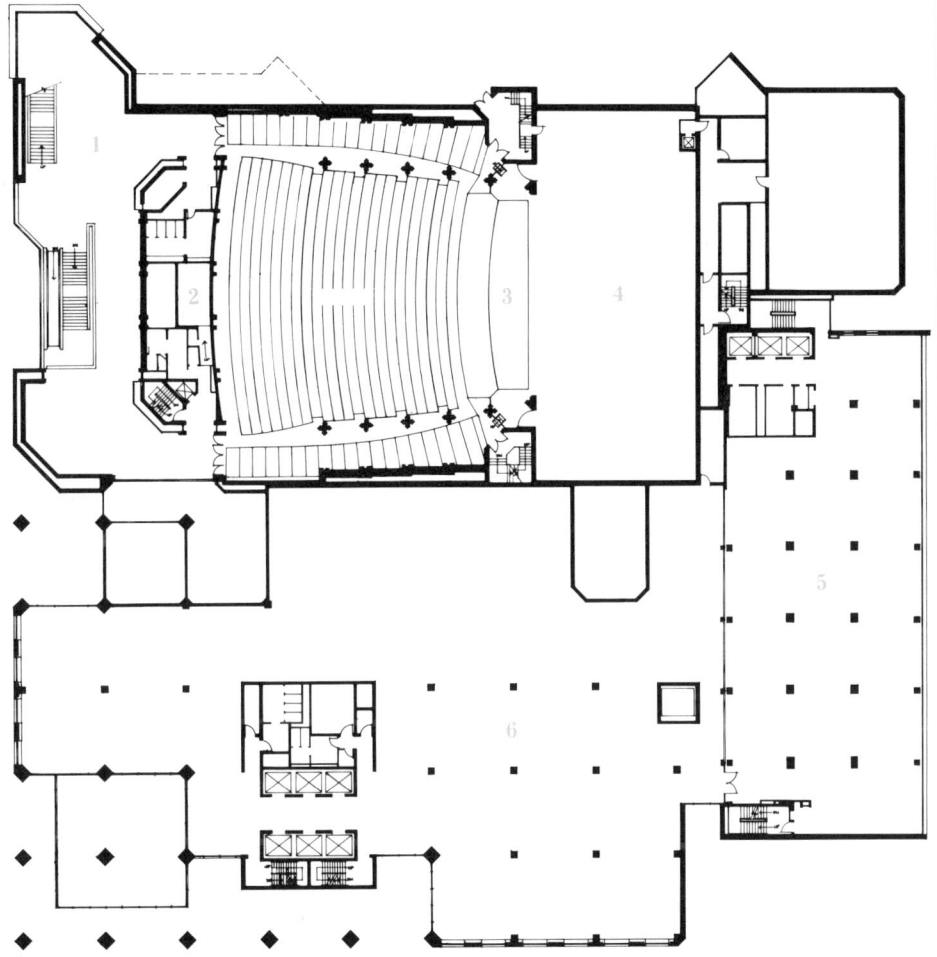

Entry level, Crouse-Hinds Concert Theatre, BeVard Community Room, and first floor of the county office building
1. Lobby
2. Projection
3. Crouse-Hinds orchestra pit
4. Crouse-Hinds stage
5. Existing office building
6. New county office building

Balcony level of the Crouse-Hinds Concert Theatre and terrace of the county office building.
1. Lobby
2. Sound booth
3. Light booth
4. Existing office building
5. New county office building

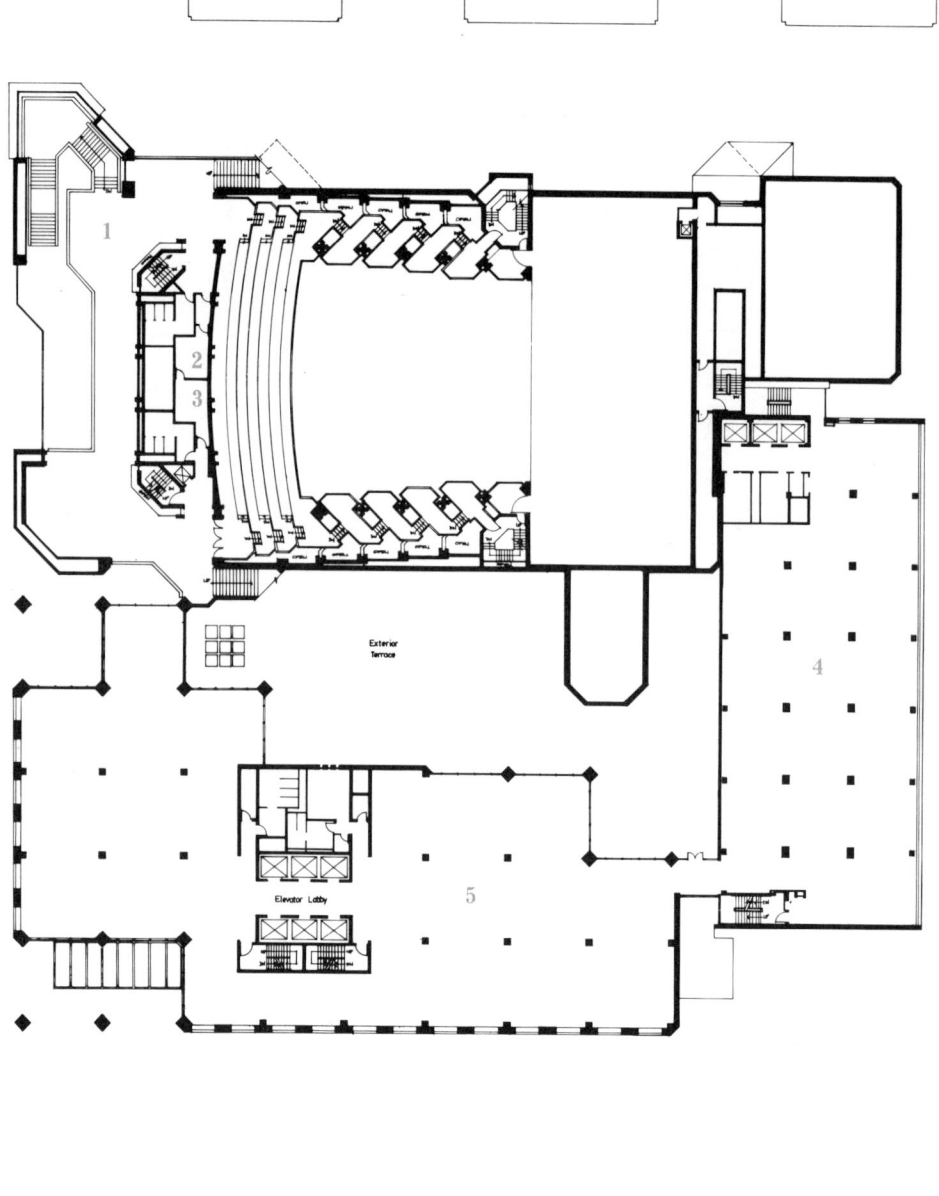

Longitudinal section through the Crouse-Hinds Concert Theatre and the BeVard Community Room.
1. Lobbies
2. Coat room
3. Orchestra seating
4. First balcony seating
5. Second balcony seating
6. Orchestra pit
7. Stage
8. Fly tower
9. BeVard Community Room
10. Dressing rooms
11. Orchestra pit elevator
12. Offices
13. Projection
14. Sound room
15. Spot room

A view from the wings at the Crouse-Hinds Concert Theatre.

THEATRE C, CENTER FOR THE ARTS
State University of New York at Purchase

Theatres seating more than four hundred but fewer than twelve hundred patrons are ideally suited to dance companies that do not need big box office receipts to break even. Yet, while many such theatres are scattered across America, few offer the performance area or the resilient stage floor needed for dance. An exception is Theatre C at SUNY-Purchase's Center for the Arts.

Dance companies perform on other stages at the Purchase Center, but Theatre C is the only facility with a sprung floor of double-layered pine. Its stage is approximately 45 feet wide by 43 feet deep; its proscenium is 30 feet high. The theatre has an orchestra pit on a hydraulic lift (converting to 84 audience seats when the pit is not in use) and a counterweight rigging system.

On each side of the 476-seat auditorium, there are four triangular boxes, equipped with lecterns and desk lamps for students and scholars following scripts or scores of performances. Depending on the type of performance, sound-absorbing draperies behind the boxes can be drawn to reduce reverberation time in the house. The house is paneled in white oak, and the seating is continental, with thirty seats per row.

Theatre C has its own rehearsal space, and principal and chorus dressing rooms. Technical equipment is shared by all of the Purchase Center's performance spaces, as is a basement-level scenery shop and storage space. Backstage lower levels are color-coded to match the theatres they serve, so visiting performers can easily find their way along the concrete block corridors.

Top left, fly towers of the Center for the Arts at the State University of New York (SUNY) in Purchase, N.Y. Below, the main lobby of the performing-arts complex. Right, the site plan, which shows the three principal performing spaces grouped symmetrically around a central lobby.

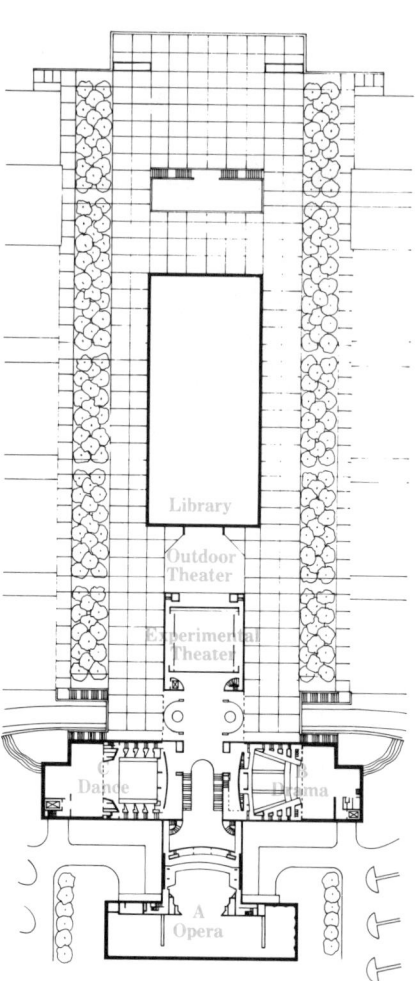

Looking toward the stage of Theatre C, a performing arts facility designed especially for dance and music. Below, the rear of the house, side boxes, and control room.

Main and stage level, Theatre C
1. Main lobby
2. Passage to theatres A and B
3. Administration lobby
4. Offices
5. Orchestra pit
6. Stage
7. Loading dock
8. Dressing rooms

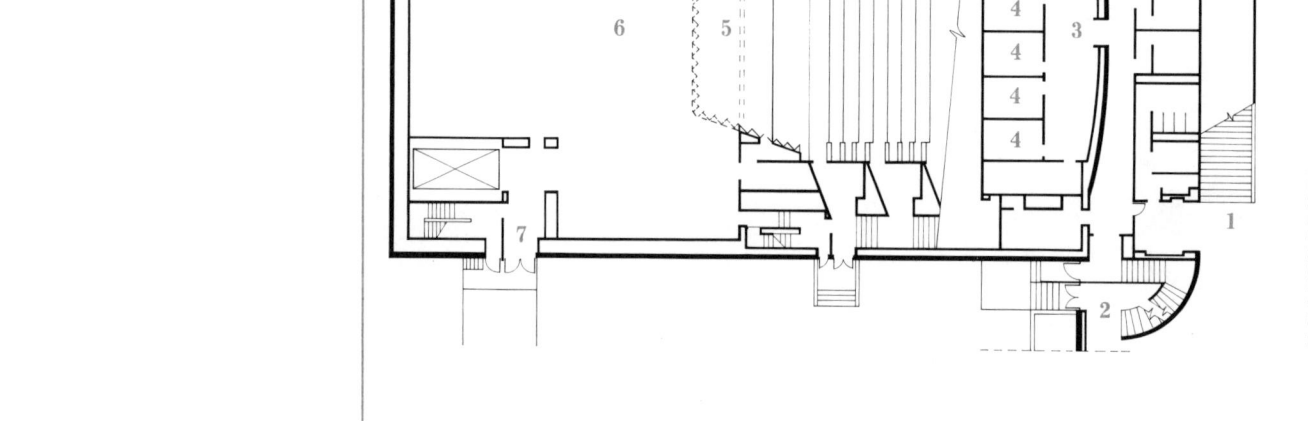

Entry and control-room level, Theatre C
1. Main lobby
2. Theatre C lobby
3. Orchestra pit
4. Stage
5. Stage elevator—loading-in
6. Production shop and office
7. Costume and wardrobe

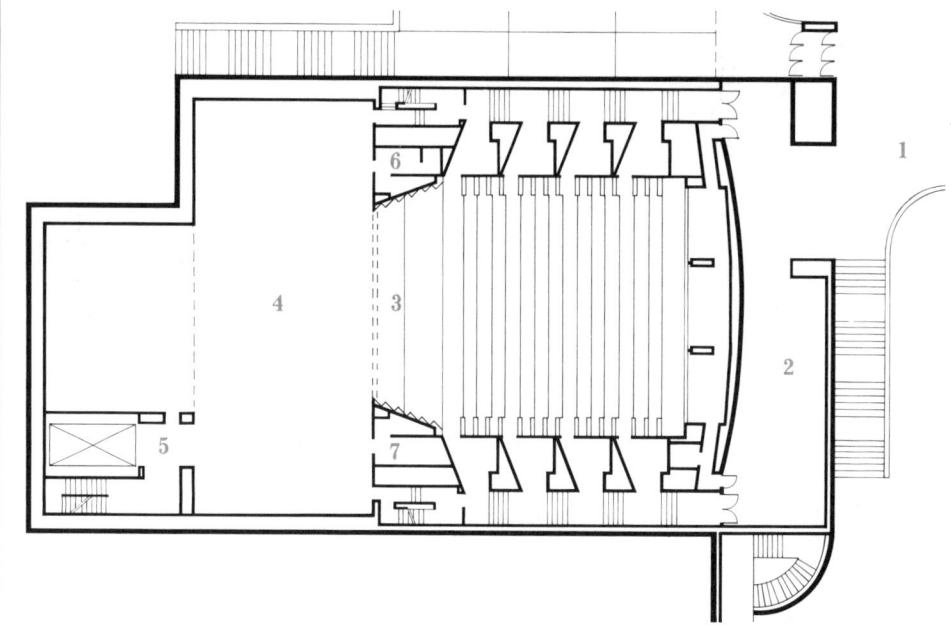

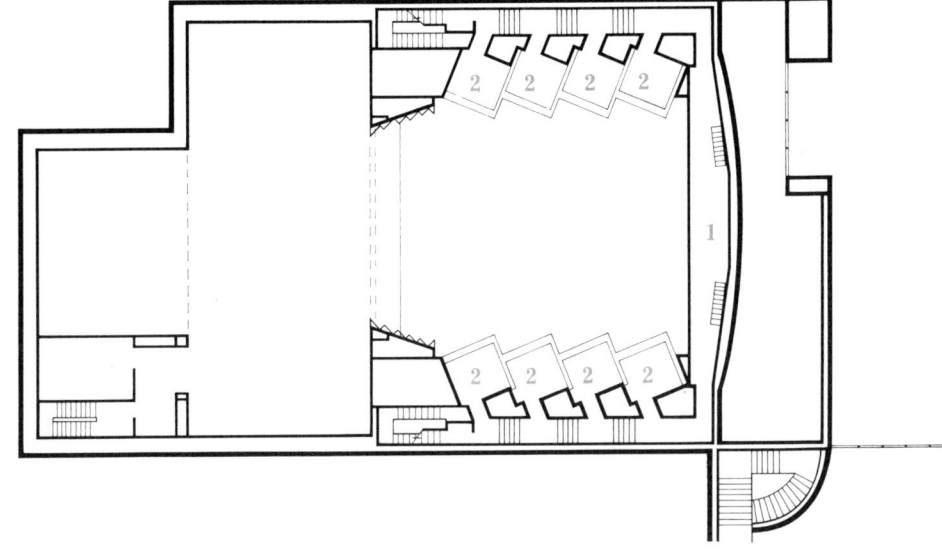

Box level, Theatre C
1. Upper lobby
2. Box seating with lecterns

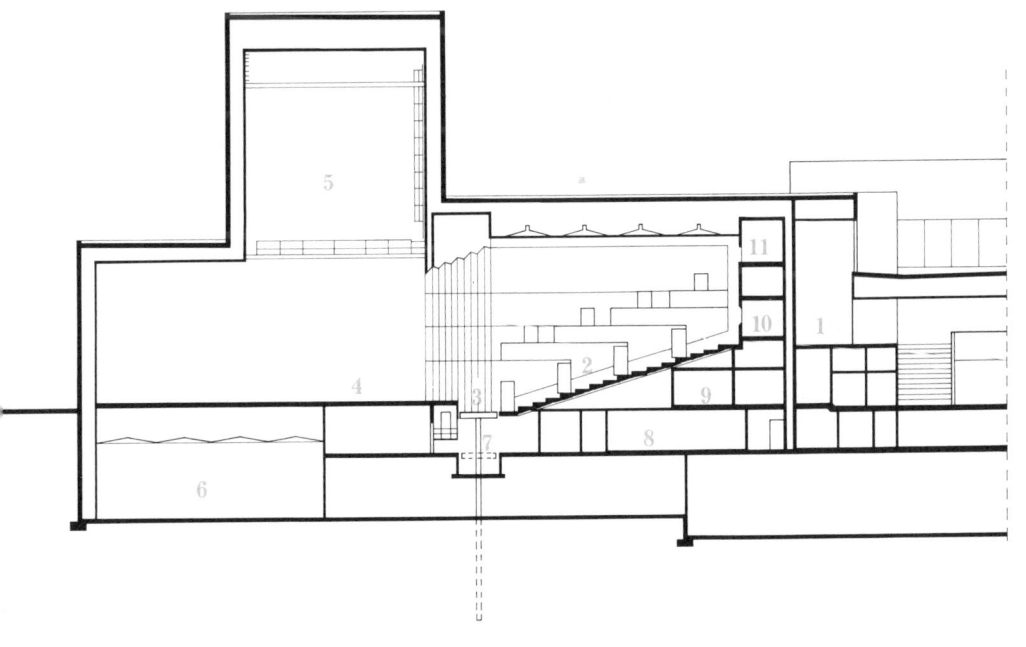

Longitudinal section through Theatre C
1. Lobby
2. Orchestra seating
3. Orchestra pit
4. Stage
5. Fly tower
6. Rehearsal room
7. Orchestra pit elevator
8. Dressing rooms
9. Offices
10. Control room
11. Follow spot booth

Grand lobby staircase at the State Theatre, Playhouse Square, Cleveland, Ohio.

THE STATE THEATRE, PLAYHOUSE SQUARE
Cleveland, Ohio

New life for old theatres can be sparked by a dance company's search for a home, or by community interest in architectural and urban preservation. In 1972 in Ohio, four magnificent 1920s theatres that make up Cleveland's Playhouse Square were threatened with demolition to make way for a parking lot. A grass-roots push to spare the theatres and revitalize sixty blighted acres downtown yielded plans for a $12-million performing-arts complex expected to draw a million patrons annually. The four theatres are being restored, with painstaking attention to their original detail, by architects Dalton, van Dijk, Johnson and Partners and by theatre-design consultant Roger Morgan.

The most extensive element of the project has been the renovation of the 3,300-seat State Theatre. The lavish movie palace was designed by Thomas Lamb, dean of American theatre architects. In 1921 its opening was attended by two trainloads of film celebrities.

The first challenge in restoring the theatre was to determine appropriate uses for a space so vast. The building program developed for the State envisioned the theatre being used by major touring dance companies and as the Cleveland Ballet's home. The State would also accommodate performances by the Cleveland Opera and touring opera companies, and of musical theatre. The theatre's public spaces were ideal for such purposes. The ornate lobby, one of the longest in the world and decorated with huge James Dougherty murals, was largely intact. The auditorium, while it needed new seating, air conditioning, and a coat of paint, was structurally sound and afforded good sightlines and acoustics.

The stagehouse, however, presented problems. Designed for cinema and vaudeville, it had a tiny stage, sufficient neither for dance nor opera. The theatre's technical equipment was also inadequate for the new program. Worse, there was no space inside for expansion.

The solution was drastic. The entire stagehouse was demolished and a new one built in its place. The new design pushed the side walls of the stagehouse to the property line and more than doubled its depth by building on a vacant lot behind the theatre. At stage level, the design includes a new receiving area with a loading dock for three trucks, plus scenery storage, "star" dressing rooms, and an upstage extension for scenery assembly and film projections.

A second level above the stage provides space for two full-size rehearsal studios with resilient flooring, plus changing rooms and administrative offices for the rehearsing company. When not needed by the State's current attraction, the rehearsal complex can be rented to other companies without disrupting theatre activities.

In the basement, dressing rooms for one hundred performers, space for musicians and musical instruments, and storerooms for house equipment have been provided. A freight elevator carries equipment between basement and stage.

Finally, the theatre's new, enlarged orchestra pit can comfortably accommodate ballet and opera orchestras; and its modern counterweight rigging, stage lighting, and sound systems fulfill the technical demands of contemporary productions. The depth of its stage, the capacity of its dressing rooms, and the attention devoted to its rehearsal space render the State one of the few American theatres designed not only to accommodate dance but to honor it.

Most renovation projects are less successful. Old theatres may present problems that cannot be corrected without radically altering the building. Restorations, especially of sites that are designated historic landmarks, are a challenge of another order. A study of the restoration of the 1,100-seat Grand Opera House in Wilmington,

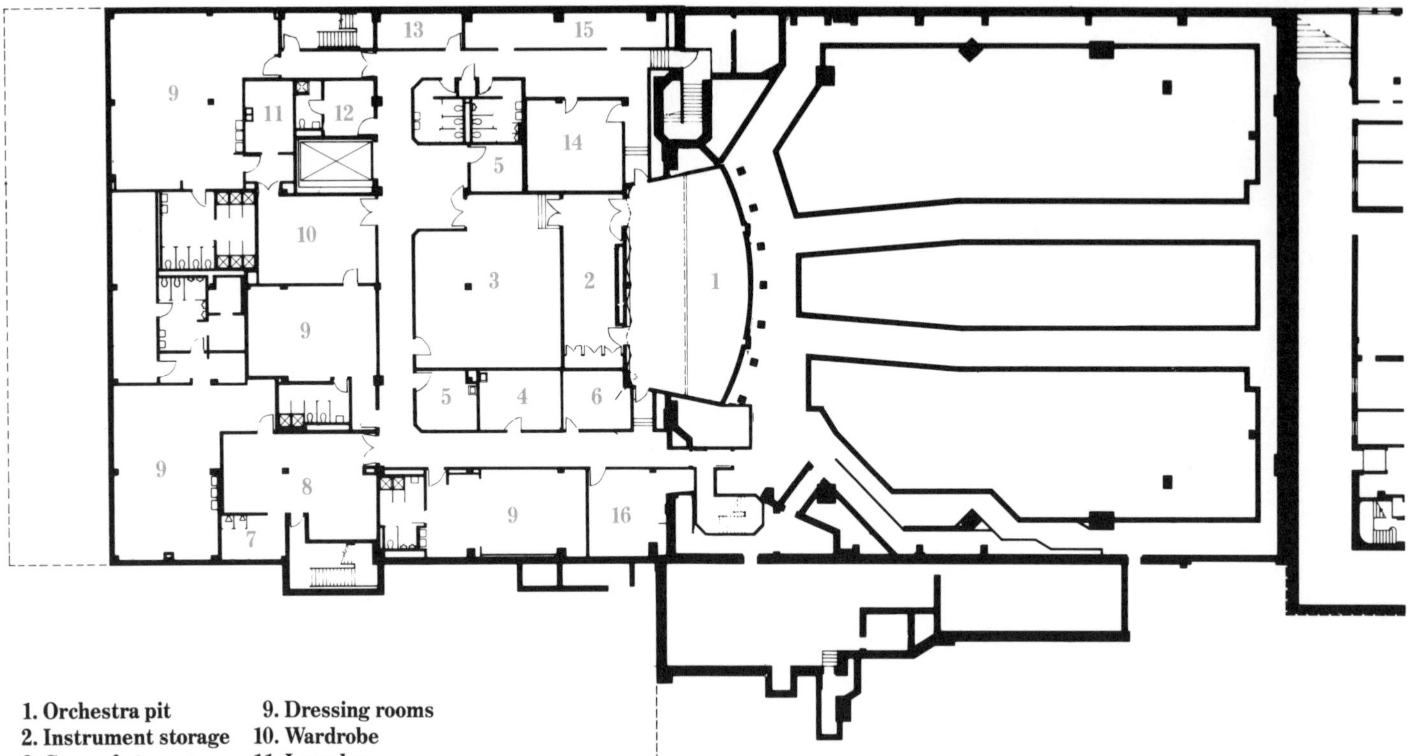

1. Orchestra pit
2. Instrument storage
3. General storage
4. Hairdressing room
5. Shoes
6. Office
7. Canteen
8. Lounge
9. Dressing rooms
10. Wardrobe
11. Laundry
12. Conductor's suite
13. Library
14. Musicians' room
15. Musicians' lockers
16. Dimmer room

The grand lobby of the State Theatre at Playhouse Square in Cleveland is one hundred yards long—one of the longest in the world. It is decorated with huge murals and can be used as a performance space in its own right.

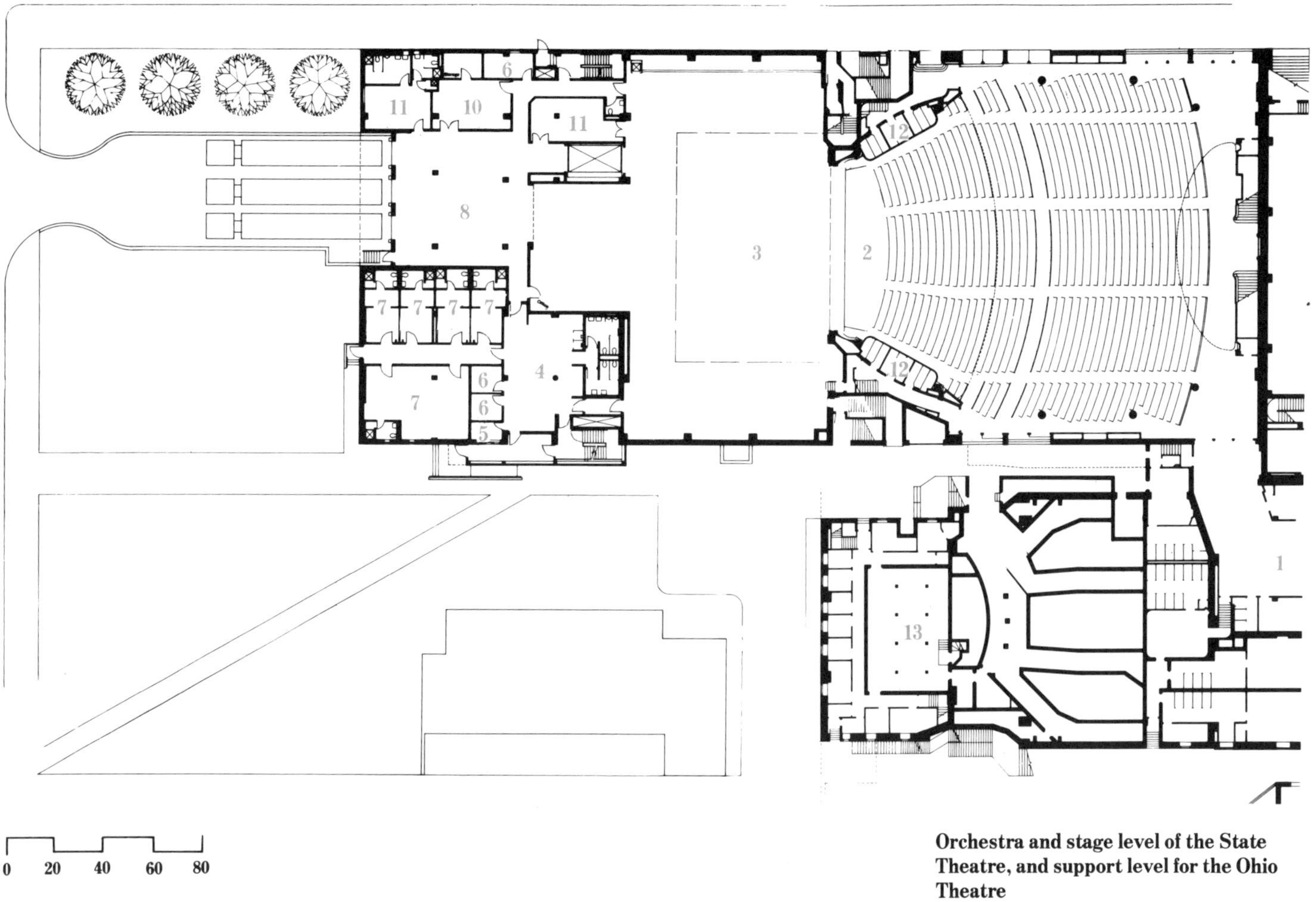

Orchestra and stage level of the State Theatre, and support level for the Ohio Theatre
1. Lobby
2. Orchestra pit
3. Stage
4. Stage lobby
5. Doorman
6. Offices
7. Dressing rooms
8. Receiving area
9. Crew room
10. Carpentry shop
11. Property shop
12. Box seating
13. Ohio Theatre—basement

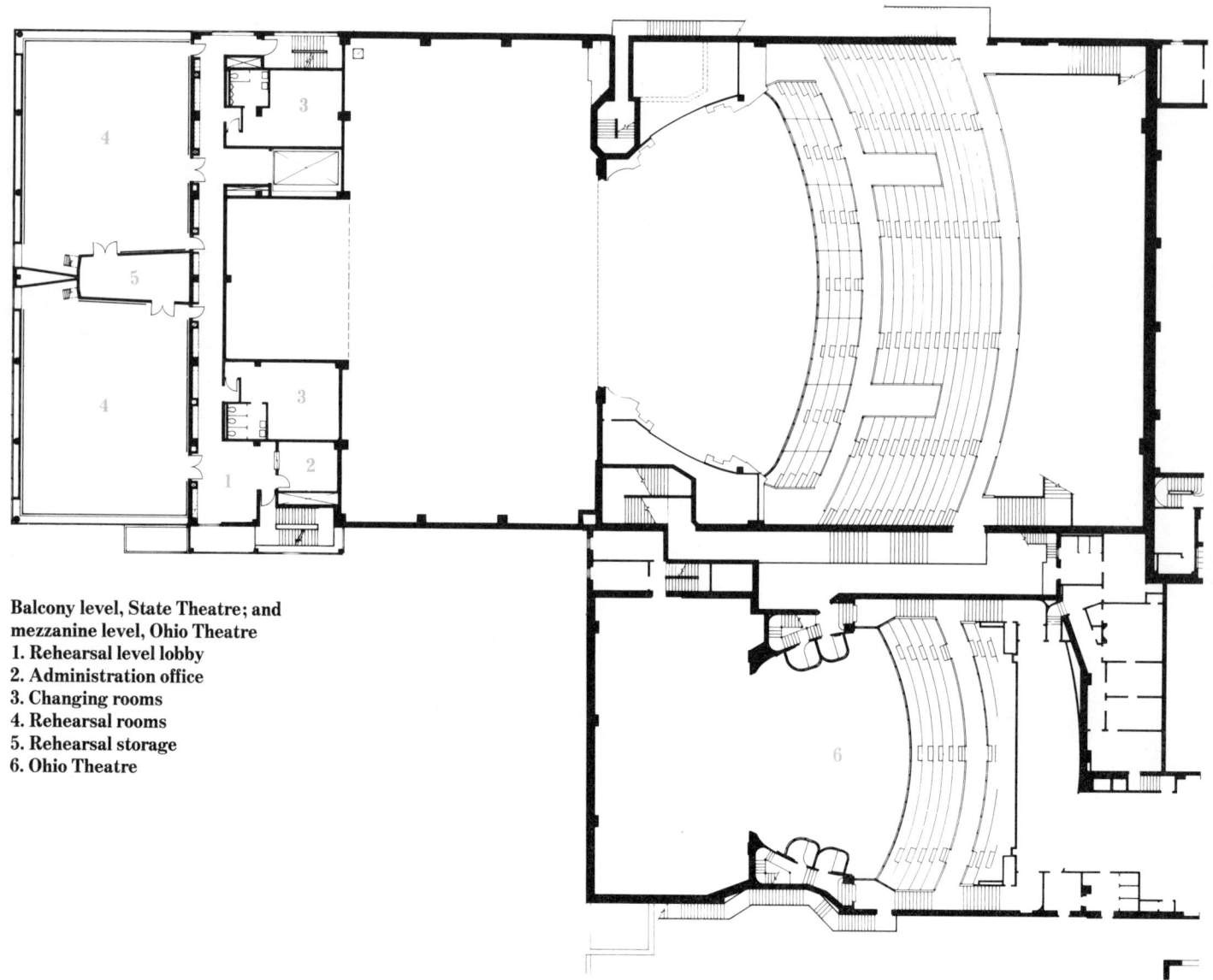

Balcony level, State Theatre; and mezzanine level, Ohio Theatre
1. Rehearsal level lobby
2. Administration office
3. Changing rooms
4. Rehearsal rooms
5. Rehearsal storage
6. Ohio Theatre

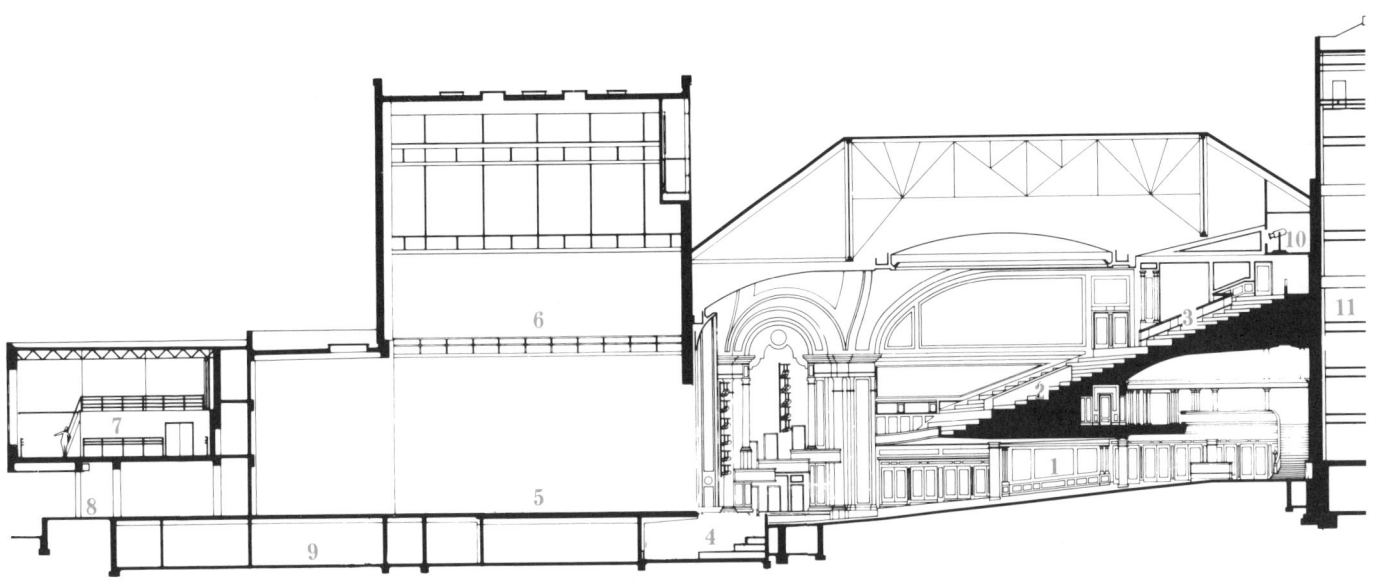

Longitudinal section, State Theatre
1. Orchestra seating
2. Balcony seating
3. Mezzanine seating
4. Orchestra pit
5. Stage
6. Fly tower
7. Rehearsal room
8. Receiving area
9. Dressing room level
10. Follow booth
11. Palace Theatre dressing rooms

The historic Grand Opera House in Wilmington, Delaware, built by the Freemasons in 1871, was recently restored as a center for the performing arts.

Delaware, reveals some of the problems posed by historic buildings and suggests how they may be dealt with.

THE GRAND OPERA HOUSE
Wilmington, Delaware

In 1871 the Freemasons of Wilmington, Delaware, built the Grand Opera House to enhance their city's image as a center for culture, as well as to house their fraternal society's lodge and offices. The lavish, gaslit Victorian theatre was constructed of masonry, plaster, and cast iron. Frescoes on the walls and ceiling depicted the Muses and Masonic symbols, and five bays of cast-iron arches and columns, comprising the theatre's elegant facade, dominated Wilmington's Market Street.

For the next forty years, the Grand Opera House was the performing-arts center for all of Delaware. However, Wilmington's anticipated meteoric growth did not occur. As the city was outpaced by Philadelphia and New York, the evening fare at the Opera House slipped from drama to vaudeville, and ultimately, to exploitation films.

In 1974 the city government decided to rehabilitate the theatre. The Masons consented to a complete restoration on condition that they would still occupy the front of the third floor and the entire top floor, which extends over the stage of the Opera House. Architects James R. Grieves, Leslie Armstrong, and Russell and Kirsten Childs were hired to guide the restoration. Roger Morgan was brought on as theatre-design consultant. The goal of the project was to restore the historic Opera House as accurately as possible while meeting contemporary standards of safety and comfort and the technical and economic requirements of modern theatre production.

Under the direction of cast-iron expert Steven T. Baird, who later served as architect on the Capitol Theatre in Salt Lake City, a movie marquee and assorted other commerical artifacts were stripped from the Opera House's ornate facade and mansard roof. Missing cast-iron elements were copied and bolted on, and the completed front painted its original off-white.

Inside, the small lobby was restored, and transverse lobby spaces added to improve circulation and to conform to local building codes. Onstage proscenium boxes, popular in nineteenth-century theatres here and abroad, had to be reduced in size to bridge the gap between the last downstage entrance and the downstage edge of the apron. After careful study of sightlines and viewing distances, the orchestra's original horseshoe seating configuration was reconstructed, but with a new rake and wider aisles. Reproducing the Victorian theatre's cast-iron seats proved too costly. However, cast-iron panels were fashioned to go on the outside of aisle seats, and new cast-iron combings were fitted to the top of modern theatre seating.

Before the renovation, seven-foot-deep trusses and a hung ceiling had been installed below the ceiling frescoes to reinforce the floor structure of the Masonic spaces above the theatre.

A catwalk mounted above a movable section of the frescoed ceiling provides access to the front-of-house lighting beam.

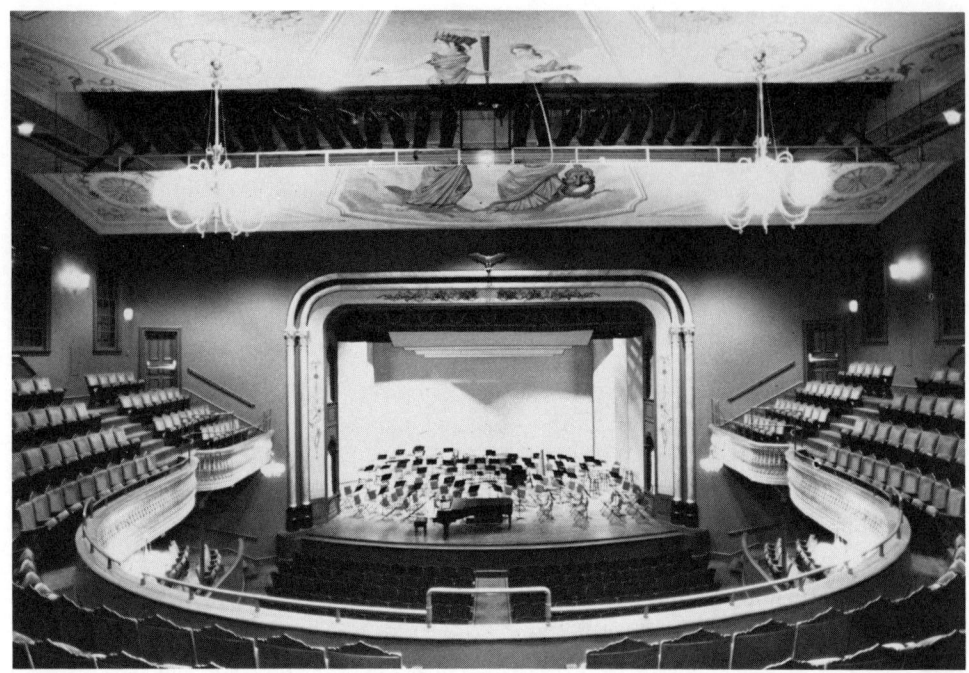

The original Opera House plans, discovered in the Masons' vault, as well as initial demolition work, revealed useful information about the vintage look of the theatre. Furthermore, the design committee and the architects consulted old newspaper accounts of opening festivities at the Opera House, and tracked down successors to firms that made many of the theatre's original fittings and furnishings. While nothing remained of the original wall and ceiling frescoes, written descriptions were reinterpreted by scenic designer Dale Amlund. The fresco designs were then painted on canvas and applied like wallpaper.

Since the Masons would still occupy the space above the theatre, building a full-height stagehouse was impossible. Instead, a low-grid rigging system, with room for stagehands to work above it, was installed for hanging scenery and lighting equipment.

Another Opera House limitation became apparent when front-of-house stage lighting was being planned. The auditorium's ceiling predated the introduction of electric lighting, and a faithful historic restoration ruled out modern ceiling ports or exposed catwalks or pipes. Yet stage-lighting positions in the auditorium are essential for presenting dance. The solution was to mount a long-beam lighting position between the underside of the floor above and the new ceiling. A catwalk giving access to the light pipe was installed above a movable section of the frescoed ceiling. This section was sloped slightly toward the stage, to create a slot through which the light could pass during performance. For changing or focusing instruments, a motorized winch lowers the sloped section and the catwalk above it to where it can be reached by crew members from either side of the house. When the sloped section and catwalk are pulled flush to the ceiling, the frescoed surface looks almost as it did to audiences of 1871.

The Opera House's minimal wing space and low grid preclude its use by large ballet companies. But the theatre's resilient new stage floor, state-of-the-art lighting control system, convenient dressing rooms, and other facilities make it an ideal space for smaller dance groups, and reestablish the Victorian landmark to its rightful role as a center for the performing arts.

Above: A view from the opera-house stage, an ideal space for small dance groups. Below: The original cast-iron balcony rail was stripped of layers of ornamental plaster and restored. The original horseshoe seating plan was retained, but with improved sightlines and more generous spacing.

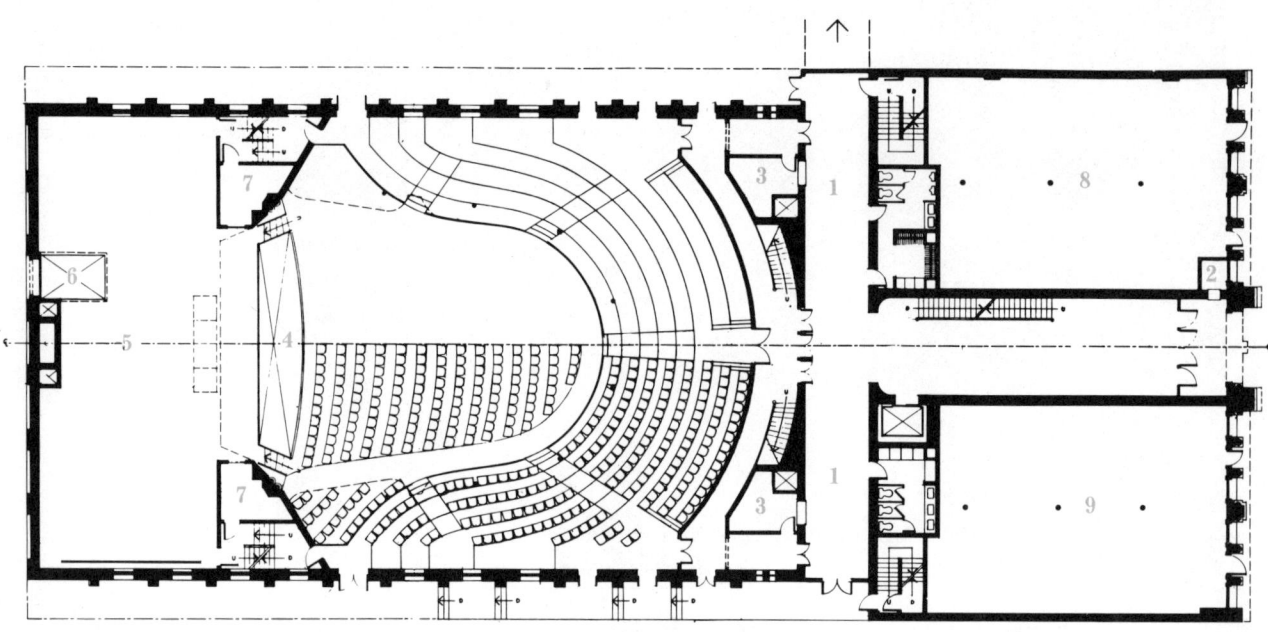

Orchestra and street level, Grand Opera House
1. Lobby
2. Box office
3. Concession
4. Orchestra pit lift
5. Stage
6. Freight
7. Proscenium boxes
8. Retail space
9. Restaurant

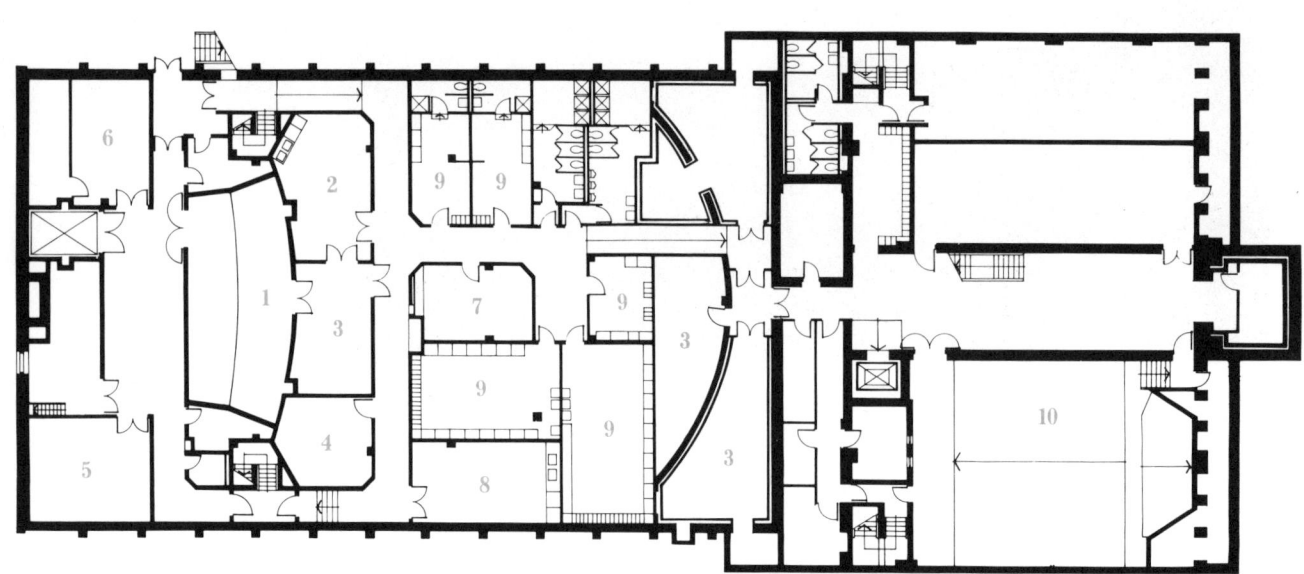

Basement level, Grand Opera House
1. Orchestra pit
2. Carpenters' room
3. Storage
4. Lighting storage
5. Musical instrument storage
6. Dimmer room
7. Career room
8. Wardrobe
9. Dressing rooms
10. Film theatre

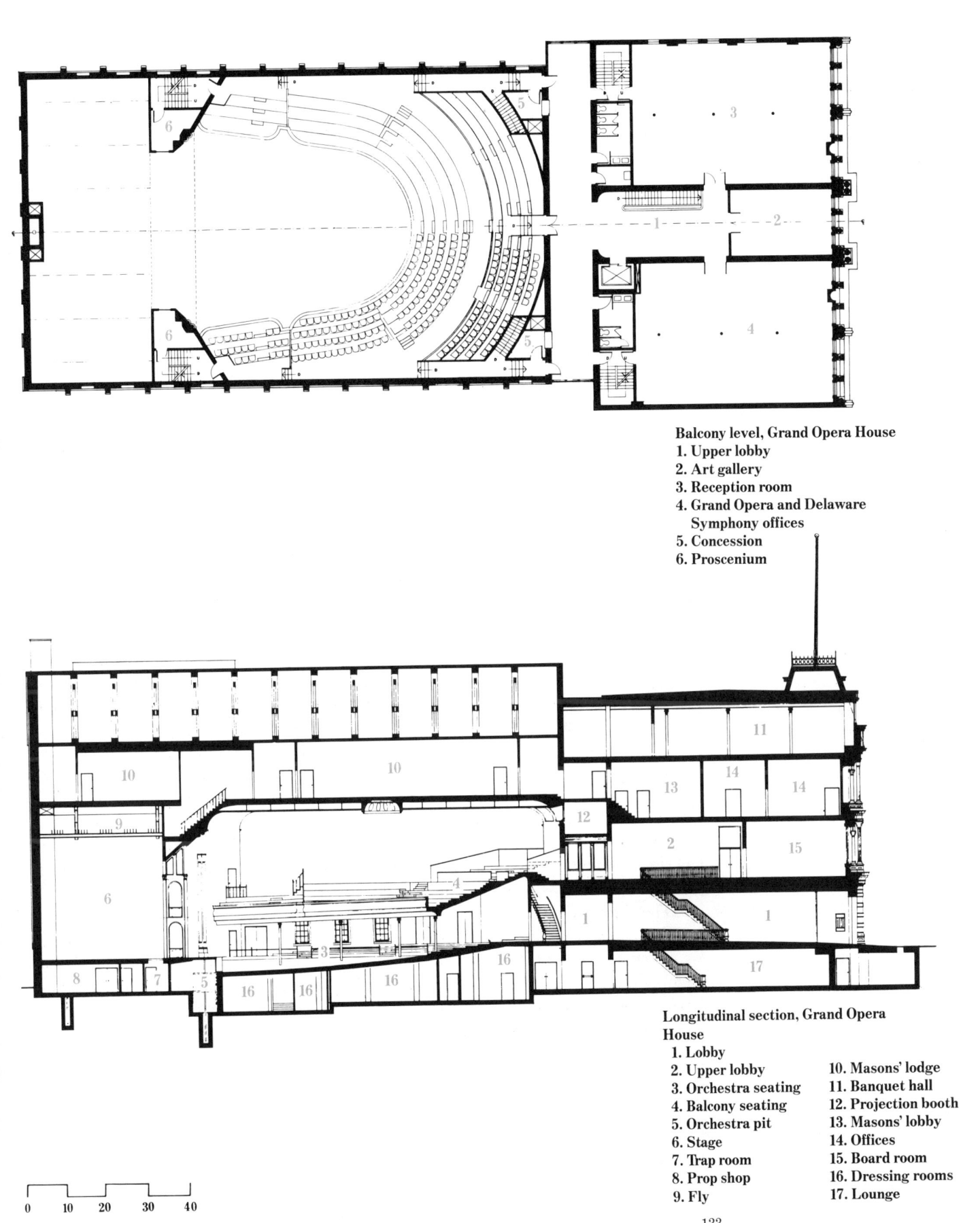

Balcony level, Grand Opera House
1. Upper lobby
2. Art gallery
3. Reception room
4. Grand Opera and Delaware Symphony offices
5. Concession
6. Proscenium

Longitudinal section, Grand Opera House
1. Lobby
2. Upper lobby
3. Orchestra seating
4. Balcony seating
5. Orchestra pit
6. Stage
7. Trap room
8. Prop shop
9. Fly
10. Masons' lodge
11. Banquet hall
12. Projection booth
13. Masons' lobby
14. Offices
15. Board room
16. Dressing rooms
17. Lounge

Open-air dance at The Yard, Chilmark, Massachusetts.

FILENE CENTER, WOLF TRAP FARM PARK
Vienna, Virginia

Open-air theatres pose unique problems for dance. In spring, the stage floor can take weeks to warm up—or to defrost. At the peak of summer, a stage floor exposed to a day's ration of sun may be too hot to dance on at night. And, at theatres where both stage and seating are open to the sky, performers as well as patrons hope for rainless evenings.

Until it burned to the ground in 1982, the Filene Center, at Wolf Trap Farm Park for the Performing Arts, was an unusually successful open-air theatre for dance. Virginia's summer climate—reliably hot and humid—and the architects' careful planning, each contributed to the theatre's worthiness.

The original architects, John MacFadyen, Edward Knowles, and Alfred DeVido, faced more than the usual number of challenges posed by outdoor theatres. Filene Center had to blend with the site, on 130 wooded acres outside Washington, D.C., yet provide good acoustics and visual contact in the house and across the surrounding lawn. The facility, the first National Park dedicated to the performing arts, was expected to accommodate an audience of more than six thousand, and to be built with a budget of $3.5 million.

The architects' analysis of acoustic and physical requirements led to a design that reduced construction to a minimum. Filene Center's wooden roof, spanning 159 feet and set on wood-clad, queen post trusses, was shaped to project balanced sound from the stage to the vast audience (the house seated thirty-five hundred patrons under roof; three thousand more people sat on the sloping lawn beyond). The stagehouse was built on two levels, with dressing rooms and offices beneath the stage itself. Clad entirely in Oregon red cedar, Filene Center merged with the landscape by day. At night, brilliantly lit, it became a glowing invitation to visitors.

Six months after Filene Center's destruction by fire, the United States Congress passed legislation authorizing a $9-million grant to help rebuild the theatre. That money, plus a matching sum to be raised by the Wolf Trap Foundation, is expected to see the project through, with Filene Center II scheduled to open in mid-1984. Design improvements will include a comprehensive fire-protection system, an additional two hundred seats, and updated lighting and sound equipment.

From the audience's perspective, Filene Center II will look much like Filene Center I (architects for Filene Center II are Dewberry & Davis; John MacFadyen is consulting architect). But major changes are being made from the proscenium on back, including better access to dressing rooms, construction of a new rehearsal space slightly larger than the stage, and expanded storage and office space. While the width of the proscenium will remain at 71 feet, the height of the opening will increase from 35 feet to 45 feet. Wing space will increase at stage left and stage right.

The Filene Center's original basket-weave stage floor was constructed almost entirely of wood. According to Dewberry & Davis, the new stage will start with a substructure of steel beams, followed by a concrete floor. Neoprene pads (each 2½ inches tall and spaced 2 feet on center) will rest on the concrete. Atop the neoprene pads there will be a wooden grid of 2 x 4's and, finally, a 2-inch thick dance floor of Douglas fir nailed to the sleepers.

The Filene Center, an open-air theatre in Vienna, Virginia, was built to project sound to more than six thousand patrons—thirty-five hundred in the building and three thousand on the lawn outside. Below, an evening performance draws a full house.

Orchestra and support level,
Filene Center
1. Orchestra pit
2. Orchestra waiting room
3. Instrument storage
4. Office
5. Wardrobe
6. Waiting areas
7. Dressing rooms
8. Toilets
9. Green room
10. Dimmer room and company switch
11. Storage

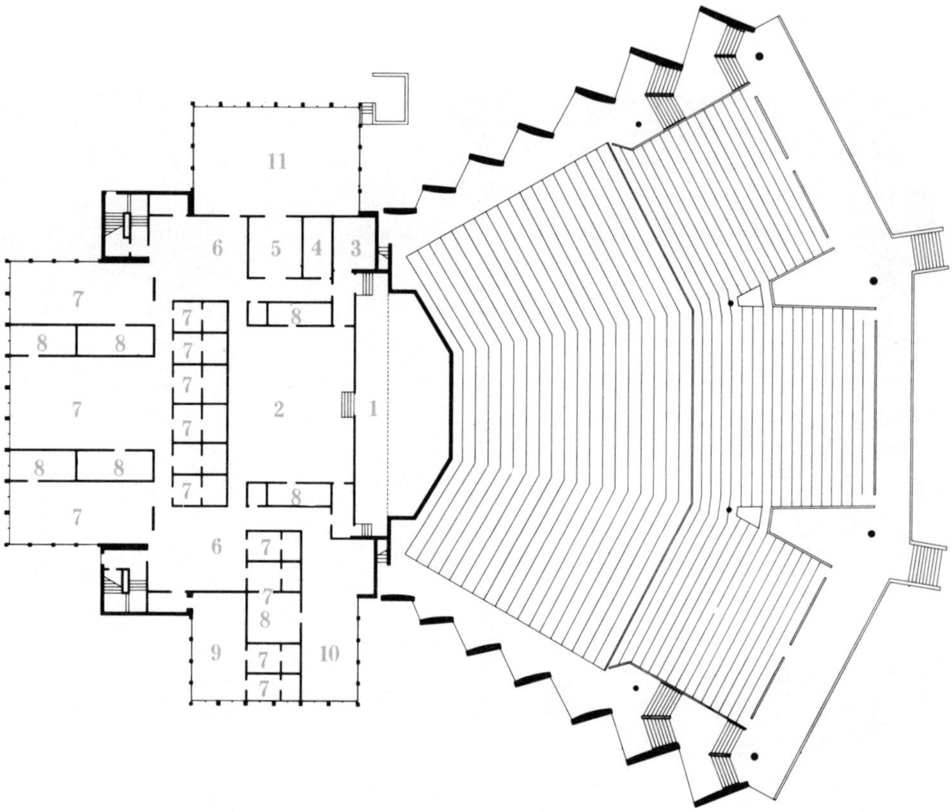

Balcony, Filene Center
1. Stage
2. Pin rail
3. Set storage
4. Loading-in
5. Ramps to grass seating

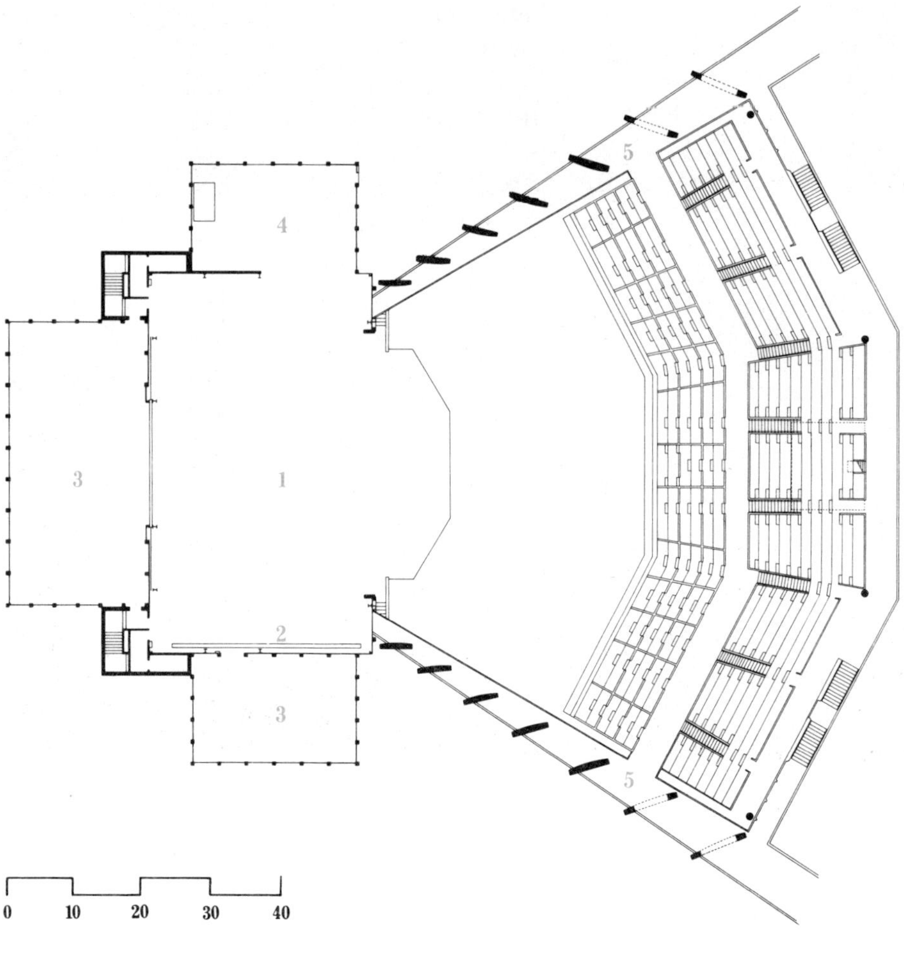

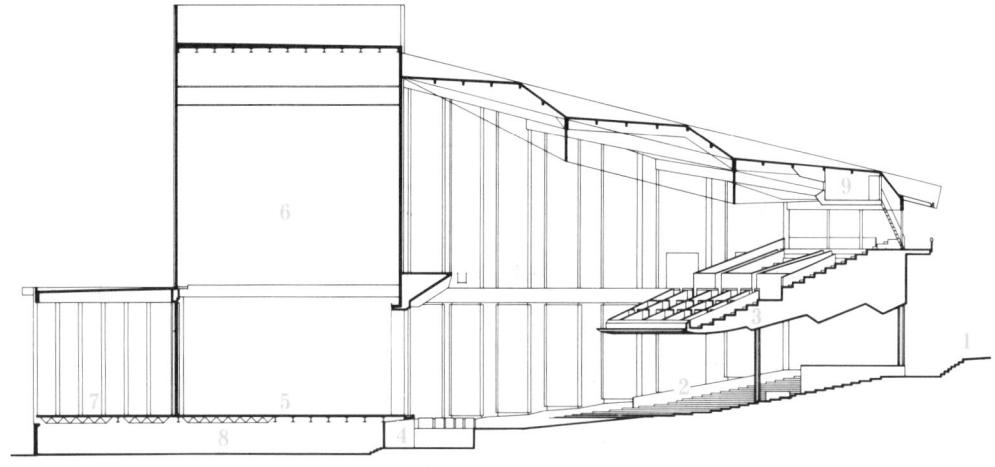

Longitudinal section, Filene Center
1. Grass seating
2. Orchestra seating
3. Balcony seating
4. Orchestra pit
5. Stage
6. Fly tower
7. Set storage
8. Dressing rooms
9. Follow spot and sound control booth

A view of the Filene Center from the rear of the house. Built of Oregon red cedar, the first center burned to the ground in 1982. Filene Center II, now under construction, will look much the same.

9
CASE STUDIES: ALTERNATE SPACES

America's "dance explosion" has produced an astonishing number of small dance companies, many of them clustered in the New York area, where they arouse the enthusiasm of critics and of steadily expanding audiences. Whether referred to as avant-garde or simply vanguard, these experimental troupes—called "this seedbed of independents" by choreographer Agnes de Mille—tend to operate on tight budgets in small alternate spaces.

541 BROADWAY

In New York, one building alone houses four small companies headed, respectively, by choreographer-dancers Trisha Brown, David Gordon, Douglas Dunn, and Lucinda Childs. As one dance buff quipped, "If that building went up in smoke, America's most innovative dance talent would suddenly be left homeless!" The building at 541 Broadway is in the center of SoHo, once the focus of New York's mercantile and dry-goods trade. In the mid-sixties, when real estate prices soared throughout Manhattan, artists, art dealers, and dancers looking for low rents and more space discovered the loft buildings and warehouses of SoHo, the 26-block area that begins south of Houston Street.

An early SoHo settler was Trisha Brown, who formed her own dance company in 1970. For several years she lived in apartments and rented studio space for her dancers. But apartment rentals zoomed, as did the cost of studio space, which rents today for about $15 to $20 an hour. Brown had moved to SoHo in 1965 and had renovated two lofts for her own living space. By the early seventies, she perceived that one large loft—a studio *and* living space—would be the wisest, most economical answer to her needs. After carefully exploring SoHo with a sympathetic real estate agent, she further decided that the soundest investment would be the purchase of a building that could be turned into an artists' cooperative. The problem was finding one that did not have huge pillars intruding in what would be her dance space. In 1974 she discovered such a building—an old sweatshop, she recalls, with hundreds of sewing machines on five floors. Brown then telephoned various choreographers and artists, telling them about 541 Broadway. Within 18 hours, she had initial tenants for the co-op—the green light she needed to purchase the building.

Choreographer David Gordon, in the fortunate position of being able to buy an available unit of 3,000 square feet about a year-and-a-half later, paid $18,000 for his space at 541 Broadway. Monthly maintenance, then $230, has now risen to $650 (mostly due to the increase in oil prices). But no one is quibbling. Today, with "uptown" doctors and lawyers descending on "downtown" SoHo, 3,000 square feet would probably sell for around $250,000.

"Once you're committed to the arts, you're committed to taking risks," says Trisha Brown. "I knew that if I could not buy my own dance space in New York, I'd lose my place in the city." Even so, she points out, it took every nickel from the proverbial piggy bank to install the basics for her dance space—never mind her living quarters.

The priorities for her 35-by-50 foot studio were a new floor, proper heating, and track lighting. After the sewing machines bolted to the wooden floor had been carted away, wooden 2 x 4's with rubber padding were installed atop the original splintery surface. A new maple floor was then nailed to the cushioned 2 x 4's. With its padding, not unlike the zesty filling between layers of a cake, the floor is extremely resilient. Brown says she first had the professional floorers build a small section, so she could "jump around on it," thereby determining how hard or soft a dance surface she wanted. "I burst into tears," she admits, "when I heard the cost." In 1976 Brown's sprung floor cost about $4,000. Today the price would be close to $10,000.

541 Broadway. Studios occupy the four-window slot above the sign. Below, the interior of Trisha Brown's studio at 541 Broadway.

"Once you're committed to the arts, you're committed to taking risks," says Trisha Brown, opposite, first choreographer/dancer to establish a company at 541 Broadway.

St. Mark's Church in the Bowery, New York, above, was the scene of revolutionary dance performances by Isadora Duncan, Ruth St. Denis, Martha Graham, and Charles Weidman in the 20's and 30's. When the sanctuary, center, was gutted by fire in 1978, it was rebuilt to meet the specific needs of dance. Bottom, Lucinda Childs performs "Cross Words" in the sanctuary in 1976, before the fire.

Brown's resilient floor is her prized possession, and studio visitors either remove their shoes or walk along the edges, hugging the wall. "We dance barefoot," she says. "Too much dirt and glass can be brought into the studio on the soles of your shoes."

Although the building at 541 Broadway is warmed by steam heat—and the boiler has come in for its share of repairs—Brown has added an auxiliary gas blower that heats up the air on days when icy gusts rock the panes of her three twelve-foot high windows (David Gordon thrusts old mattresses against his windows. Douglas Dunn covers his with plastic). There is no air conditioning. During muggy New York summers, on days when the humidity becomes unbearable, says Trisha Brown, "We just stop, call it off—and go to the beach."

She wanted track lighting—the third of her studio priorities—because she videotapes rehearsals, works-in-progress, and all her choreography; it was essential that the studio, which has windows only at one end, be well-lit with adjustable lights.

Brown's studio, like Gordon's and Dunn's, is separated from her living quarters by a wall built as part of her initial remodeling. One toilet accommodates Brown's dancers—and herself. "We're a small enough group—five women and two men—so this presents no problem." She has no dressing rooms for her company, and there are none in the studios of Lucinda Childs or David Gordon, who says matter-of-factly, "We dancers just take our bodies for granted. It would be pretty silly to start acting peculiar about a bare limb. The other truth is that we can't afford dressing rooms and you cannot open your half of the loft to dancers for changing clothes. The personal and the professional *must* be separated." Trisha Brown would like her dancers to have their own lockers, but they would take up coveted studio space.

Brown's studio has neither barres nor mirrors. She doesn't need a barre, she explains, because she isn't a "ballet dancer." Of mirrors she says, "If I watch my movement in front of a mirror, I get distracted. My dancers feel the same way. I have developed a way of understanding my movement without mirrors."

David Gordon also dislikes mirrors and there are none in the studio where he rehearses his company of four men and four women. As for a barre, if his dancers need to warm up with a plié or demi-plié, they grab hold of a pipe or a ladder.

An influential figure in new dance, Gordon generally creates his "performance art" without music: he doesn't want music to dominate his creative decisions. But when music is required, Gordon, like the other tenants at 541 Broadway, uses a tape-cassette player. There are no pianos in the building; pianos are expensive, require someone to play them who must be paid, and take up valuable studio space. All in all, Gordon spent about $80,000 renovating his dance and living space. He put track lighting in the studio, installed a $3,000 oak floor, improved the plumbing facilities, and had an office area constructed for himself as well as walls for two bedrooms in his living area, which also required a kitchen.

Plasterers left his new studio wall a blobby grey with rectangular whites. Painting the entire studio—30 feet wide by about 50 feet long—would have been costly. Gordon asked a close friend, artist Power Boothe, who has also done off-Broadway sets, to "finish off" the other walls with matching rectangular "shapes," which now "imbue the space with verve and personality, on a shoestring budget."

When Gordon holds performances, ninety rented folding chairs on risers and a front row of cushions (loge seats for those who don't mind sitting on the floor) are arranged at one end of the studio against the windows. Studio performances, he notes, are logistical challenges, with dance patrons having to be shunted up and down stairs and through a hallway. A makeshift ticket booth has to go someplace noticeable without causing inconvenience. Gordon says good-naturedly, "We get along here, but we don't wish to remain static. We want to grow artistically and that naturally means operating expansion."

Lucinda Childs' dance company rehearses "Congeries on Edges for 20 Obliques" at her studio at 541 Broadway.

His neighbor Douglas Dunn, who danced with Merce Cunningham and whose own company numbers four women and two men, once did a series of eighteen consecutive performances in his studio; the concert piece was taped for public television. For performances, Dunn's studio accommodates sixty people on folding chairs. Dunn asks that everyone remove shoes. His floor is oak ("not an ideal wood; oak can splinter and dry out in a steam-heated building—maple is definitely best") and he is extremely protective of it. In fact, Dunn allows no shoes in the studio at any time, and a huge shoe rack is positioned in the hall. The studio is almost constantly occupied as Dunn also holds classes for as many as thirty dancers at a time. The six-foot high mirrors lined along one wall (mirrors are necessary for class) cost $600, not counting installation.

Dunn has rigged up two curtained changing rooms for his student-dancers, who also have access to a sink and a single toilet. The only stick of furniture in Dunn's studio is a stool, which he perches on.

Trisha Brown stresses that small dance companies, surviving mostly on hope and inspiration, do without amenities (showers, for example, or a comfortable couch to lounge upon) in order to keep dancing. "I'm on the top floor, so if I had a budget I would build a penthouse solarium for the dancers—give them a real place to relax." Asked what she might do differently at 541 Broadway if she were starting over from scratch, Brown says, "I'd hire a good architect and discuss my needs for the next twenty years. I created my own studio and living space *myself*—as did everyone in the building. We had no other choice."

Elsewhere in America's foremost dance city, pioneering choreographers and dancers have carved out studios and small theatres in a variety of found spaces, among them an old tire factory and a former telephone company auditorium.

DANCE THEATRE WORKSHOP

In the mid-1960s dancers Jeff Duncan, Art Bauman, and Jack Moore began the Dance Theatre Workshop, better known as DTW, to help sustain themselves and their work. They leased a small loft on Twentieth Street, where they held classes, rehearsed, and performed. Later, dancer and dance producer David White, a former DTW scholarship student, was asked to manage the facility. Under his direction, DTW began subleting space in 1975 at the American Theatre Laboratory, which had been founded by choreographer Jerome Robbins on the second floor of a former tire factory. The new space, at 219 West Nineteenth Street, was a step up for DTW, which now holds the lease for the building's two studios, offices, workshop, and two dressing rooms.

The larger studio, measuring 48 feet by 54 feet and painted matte black, is DTW's performing space. The performing area itself measures 32 feet from wing to wing, and 26 feet deep from light line to scrim. Behind the scrim there is a crossover and small workshop. The studio's resilient dance floor, says White, consists of "black battleship linoleum" laid over plywood; beneath the plywood there is a wood basket weave. An overhead pipe grid stretches across the entire space and portable chairs for 100 patrons are arranged on stepped platforms fixed to the floor. Depending on the production, from 40 to 50 more people can be seated on cushions.

White, whose title at DTW is executive director and producer, describes the performance space as a "formal, frontal, black-box theatre." The wings are created by "hard legs"—self-supporting and portable wood frames covered with black flameproof cloth. A major American showcase for new dance works, DTW's only apparent drawback is its low, 14-foot ceiling. "This is a found space," says White. "Ceiling height is always a problem."

The Bessie Schonberg Theatre at the Dance Theatre Workshop.

Dance Theatre Workshop is located above a tire shop and garage in Manhattan's lower west side.

Technical elements in the house include a carefully designed sound system, with a tapedeck, mixer, and 400-watt amplifier—all located in the light booth—and with two upstage speakers hung from the ceiling. The two-scene preset light board controls 36 2.4 kilowatt dimmers. There are four lighting booms on each side of the stage. The Dance Theatre Workshop also has a smaller rehearsal studio with a hardwood floor.

Under White's management, DTW has come up with a number of ways to ease choreographers' business headaches. "We have a service program for 500 member artists," he says. "We are a computerized direct-mail service for artists. We are an advertising agency for artists, with allied design services." The DTW staff will temporarily take over production for a dance company, handling its promotion and publicity, running the box office, and helping out with lights, sound, and stage equipment. "We have two full-time lighting designers, on salary, year-round," points out White. "In addition, we are beginning to help commission work, so we can help with pre-production costs."

Some 270 performances a year are produced at the Dance Theatre Workshop. Along with evenings of dance, there are music and theatre productions, poetry readings, and other events. In addition to its major dance production seasons—the Fall Events and Winter Events—DTW presents emerging, unknown dancers in its Choreographers Showcase, and boosts new companies from around the country in its Out-of-Towners Series. Eventually, David White hopes to establish a network of organizations such as DTW to book small dance companies on whistle-stop tours across the United States. "We're going to reinforce the ability of theatres like us across the country to bring in artists they choose to bring in, and reinforce the economic ability of those alternate spaces to move artists around the country." Meanwhile, the demand for DTW's support and for its performance space far exceeds availability.

Rehearsal studio at the Dance Theatre Workshop.

Plan of Dance Theatre Workshop
 1. Lobby
 2. Box office
 3. Offices
 4. Rehearsal room
 5. Performance space
 6. Crossover
 7. Dressing rooms
 8. Technical shop and office
 9. Control booth
10. Storage

MERCE CUNNINGHAM STUDIO

The Merce Cunningham Studio spreads across the top floor of the Westbeth artists' community in the West Village. The main studio was once an auditorium for Bell Telephone, the building's original owner. The rest of the space (built onto the roof of Westbeth) holds two dressing rooms, showers, offices, a projection/light booth, and one more studio. Here, Cunningham runs his dance school, a year-round facility with open classes for some 300 students, plus a professional training program for another 60 students.

Cunningham uses the ex-auditorium for rehearsals by his own company, and regularly rents the space to visiting performers. "We try to book it night to night pretty much the whole year," says Sylvia DeAngelis, the studio's assistant administrator. She adds that the space is also used for video-taping dance, and is sometimes rented to enterprises filming television commercials. The entire Cunningham Studio is used almost daily, from eight or nine in the morning until well past midnight.

A rectangle with a high, slightly vaulted ceiling, the main studio is flooded with natural light. Large windows along two walls look out over the Hudson River and the rooftops of Greenwich Village. A resilient, raised wooden dance floor, 44 feet by 52 feet, has been laid across the entire room except for narrow aisles along the west and south walls. The studio's polished maple floor, white walls, and tall windows contribute to a sense of expansive space. A cyclorama can be pulled around three sides of the dance floor, creating a frontal-presentation format. The studio's lighting grid, with 70 circuits, contributes to the space's total flexibility.

Entrance and mirrored wall in the Merce Cunningham Dance Studio.

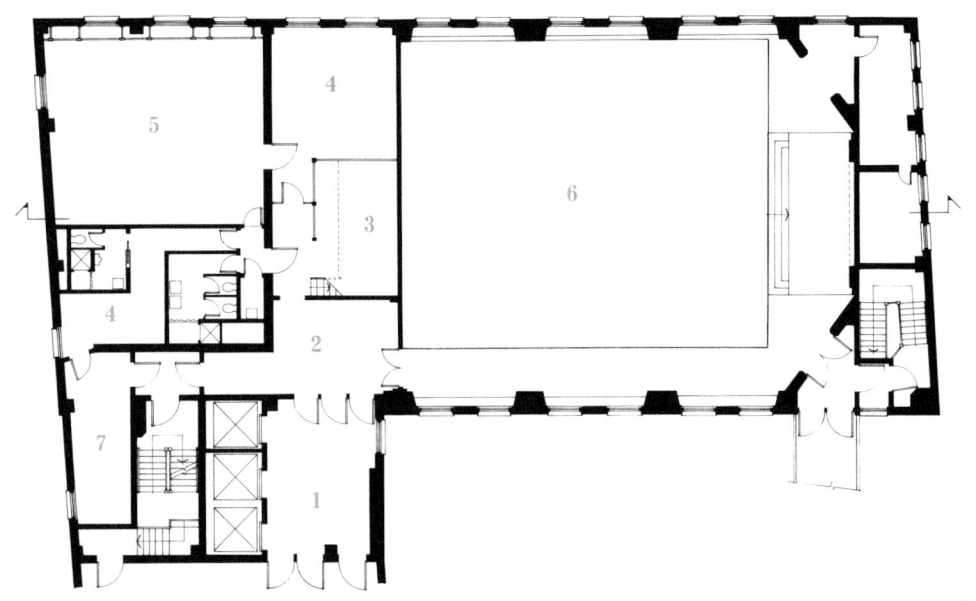

Plan of the Merce Cunningham Studio
1. Outer lobby
2. Inner lobby and ticket sales
3. Storage
4. Dressing room
5. Rehearsal studio
6. Performance space
7. Offices

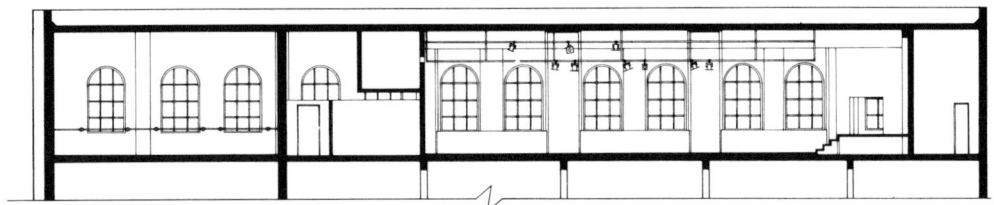

Longitudinal section, Merce Cunningham Studio
1. Rehearsal studio
2. Storage
3. Control booth
4. Performance space
5. Stage
6. Office
7. Apartments below

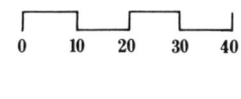

THE NEW PERFORMANCE GALLERY

Three thousand miles west of Greenwich Village, the San Francisco alternate dance space that draws pleased critics and crowds is the New Performance Gallery. Located in the city's Mission district, The New Performance Gallery is booked most of the year, says executive director Matthew Cohen, presenting "the new dance, new music, performance art, mixed-media events, and conferences on dance criticism." West Coast "home" for the Margaret Jenkins Dance Company and the Oberlin Dance Collective, each of which give about two three-week dance seasons there a year, The Gallery also has a dance school.

The New Performance Gallery is a direct outgrowth of the Oberlin Dance Collective. In 1976, five years after that group had been formed at the Ohio college, a batch of adventurous members struck west to pursue postmodern and experimental dance in San Francisco. However, the collective's expansion into what is now called The New Performance Gallery resulted from adversity. Evicted from their original loft, also in the Mission district, and not wishing to remain at the mercy of landlords or the whim of real estate developers, members of the collective bought a one-story building— formerly a warehouse— for $200,000 in 1979. Like Trisha Brown at 541 Broadway, the Oberlin dancers had realized that only property ownership would keep them from losing their toehold in the city.

The building gave them a performing space 50 feet wide and 75 feet long, somewhat reduced when 200 folding chairs on risers are set up for patrons. Dancers also rehearse here, on a resilient maple floor. But there were problems; one restroom for performers as well as patrons; tiny dressing rooms; no showers. Administrative offices, including the box office, were lumped together in a cramped room just off the lobby. The control booth could be reached only by climbing a built-in ladder of four or five rungs.

The lobby at San Francisco's New Performance Gallery, home of the Oberlin Dance Collective and the Margaret Jenkins Dance Company.

The new addition to the gallery was designed by Peter Van Dine.

Then in 1982, a two-story annex costing $260,000 was built adjacent to the original building, solving many of those practical problems. At the same time, Margaret Jenkins, whose company occupied a loft elsewhere, acquired a fifty-percent share of the New Performance Gallery, a move that provided her with more performing and audience space. The Gallery "management," under Matthew Cohen, handles certain administrative details and publicity for both Jenkins (six dancers, staff of two) and the Oberlin Collective (twelve dancers, staff of three) relieving them of many day-to-day operational headaches. Cohen's office is also in charge of The Gallery's school (securing teachers for tap, ballet, mime, modern dance and so on) and acts as a booking agency for other small dance companies.

The annex contains a 25 by 50 foot rehearsal-performance space that accommodates 75 patrons on folding chairs. Movable barres made of wood and metal can be installed for class and removed during performance. Floors in both the new rehearsal-performance space and in a 20 by 20 foot warm-up room are sprung, but with linoleum, rather than maple, laid over plywood. The warm-up room has dressing tables with mirrors, and full-length mirrors along one wall. There are also two annex dressing rooms with lockers and one shower. With the extra space, the Gallery now also has two restrooms for dancers and two for patrons.

With construction of the annex, the tiny dressing rooms and administrative office in the original building were simply knocked down. The lobby was enlarged and The Gallery now has a decent-sized box office and larger office space in the annex. The new building also has an archival room with dance magazines and books, a kitchen, and a 15 by 50 foot "company room" with a lounge reserved for Oberlin-Jenkins dancers. Matthew Cohen points out, "You have to go up some steps to reach the control booth in the annex, but at least there's no ladder."

"I wish we had more backstage space," he says. "As a theatre grows, so do your needs—for more offices and tech space, because your personnel increases. But we're proud of The New Performance Gallery. It is an inspiring environment for the creation and performance of dance."

Dance students take class in the performing space.

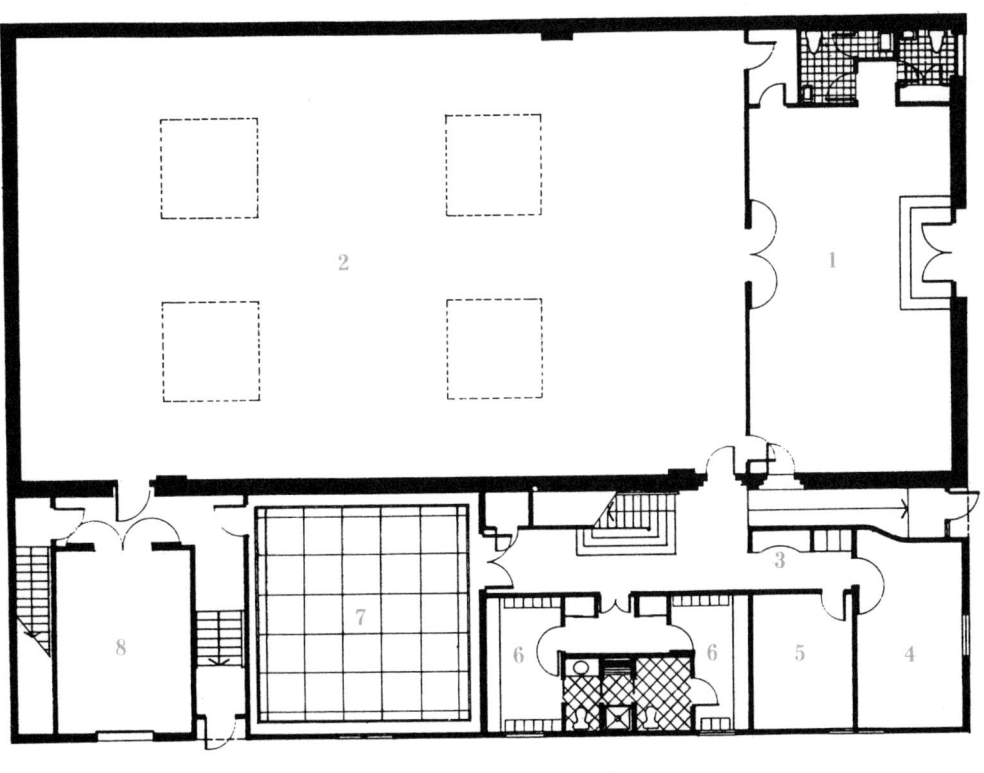

Ground floor plan, New Performance Gallery
1. Lobby
2. Main theatre
3. Box office
4. Executive director's office
5. School/gallery office
6. Dressing rooms
7. Backstage/rehearsal-studio
8. Set/costume storage

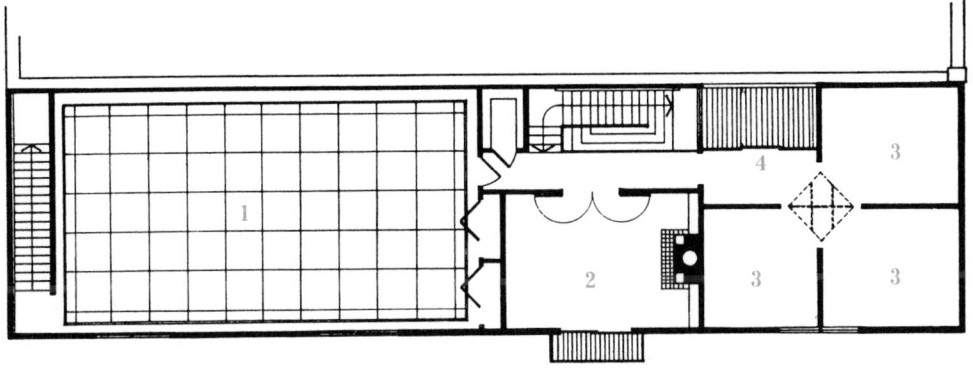

Second floor plan, New Performance Gallery
1. Rehearsal/ballet studio
2. Green room/audiovisual room/ performing arts library
3. Offices
4. Deck

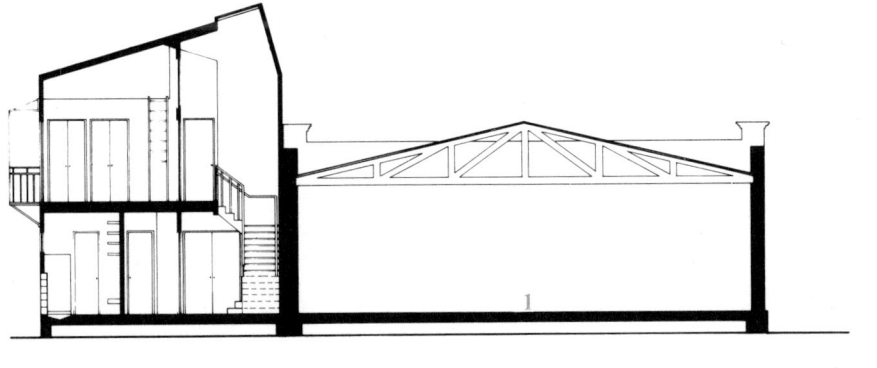

Transverse section, New Performance Gallery
1. Main studio/theatre
2. Dressing rooms

CRITICAL FACTS ON PROSCENIUM THEATRES

A

JOYCE THEATER, NEW YORK CITY

Owner	Original Ballets Foundation, Inc.
Principal tenant	Joyce Theater Foundation, Inc.
Type of construction	Renovation/rehabilitation
Approximate cost	$2.5 million
Design team	
Architect	Hardy Holzman Pfeiffer Associates
Theatre consultant	Jules Fisher Associates
Acoustical consultant	Peter George Associates
Structural engineer	Stanly Goldstein
Mechanical engineer	A.I.M. Collaborative
General contractor	Yorke Construction Co.
Seating capacity	474
Lobbies	Main lobby downstairs, entry foyer upstairs
Handicapped facilities	Unisex WC; front row right can be removed for wheelchairs
Restrooms	1 for men, 1 for women
Productions booked	Dance — roadhouse
Weeks per year theatre used by principal tenant	10-12 weeks
Weeks per year theatre booked for dance	30 weeks
Stage dimensions	40' by 36' Wings 13' 6" SR and SL
Proscenium dimensions	43' 1" H standard opening 49' 1" H maximum opening 18' 1" H to main curtain
Grid height and rigging system	22' H, 8 single-purchase winches, 6 single-purchase counterweight
Floor construction and surface	Linoleum dance floor on ¾" plywood on 3 layers of 2" x 3" sleepers
Traps	1 in wings SR, 10' x 10'
Lighting and electrical	
Power source	Six 150-amp, SL.
Dimmer board	252 at 2.4 kw and 18 at 6 kw; 2 Century Light Palettes (with printout) located in booth.
Patch panel	None (one circuit per dimmer)
Front-of-house hanging positions	2 catwalks
Projection	Equipment provided by visiting companies
Sound system	10 microphones, 4 UPA speakers in front-of-house cluster, 1 subwoofer speaker, 2 UPA speakers on stage; 3 amps for speaker cluster, 1 amp for subwoofer, 1 amp on stage; 1 1/3 octave equalizer, digital delay, 2 reel-to-reel tape decks, 1 8-channel mixer.
Communication system	Minicom cuing system with 14 stations throughout house and stage
Dressing rooms	1 DR for 2, 2 DR for 4, 1 DR for 8, 1 DR for 12, 1 DR for 15
Lounge, canteen, greenroom	Greenroom
Rehearsal room	17' by 25' with sprung linoleum floor, for warm up
Wardrobe facilities	Wardrobe room with washer, dryer, iron, ironing board
Prop and scene shop	None (tools for repair only)
Loading dock	
Door dimensions	10' by 10'
Relationship to street	5' 8" above sidewalk

CAPITOL THEATRE — SALT LAKE CITY, UTAH

Owner	Salt Lake County
Principal tenant/user	Ballet West
Other major users	Repertory Dance Theatre, Utah Opera Company, Ririe-Woodbury Dance Company
Theatre administrative director	Steven Horton
Type of construction	Renovation/rehabilitation
Approximate cost	$4,600,000
Design team	
Architect	Steven T. Baird Associates
Theatre consultant	Roger Morgan Studio, Inc.
Acoustical consultant	Acoustical Engineers, Inc.
Structural engineer	Aposhian Consulting Engineer, Inc.
Mechanical engineer	Trend Engineering, Inc.
General contractor	John Price Associates (construction manager)
Seating capacity	1,943
Lobbies	Main, mezzanine, and balcony lobbies
Handicapped facilities	6 wheelchair spaces, 2 WC's
Restrooms	3 for men, 3 for women
Concessions	Food and drink in main lobby
Productions booked	Dance, opera, Broadway plays and musicals
Weeks per year theatre	
Booked for dance	20-25 weeks
Crew required to man theatre	As needed per production
Stage dimensions	45' W by 40' D. Wings 32' SL, 15' SR
Proscenium dimensions	29' H by 45' W
Grid height and rigging system	75' H, single-purchase counterweight
Floor construction and surface	1¼" tongue-and-groove edge-grain on 5 layers of 1" by 4" sleepers on concrete slabs
Traps	None
Orchestra pit	
Dimensions	50' W by 16' D.
Capacity	50 musicians
Lighting and electrical	
Power source	Three 400-amp, SL-3 phase.
Dimmer board	70 6-kw and 30 12-kw dimmers with infinite memory.
Patch panel	386 20-amp and 14 50-amp circuits, SL
Front-of-house hanging positions	Balcony rail, 4 box booms, overhead cove
Projection	35mm — xenon
Sound system	11 microphones, 18 Altec speakers in main cluster, 1/3 octave filters, digital time delay, 2 tape decks, 9 100-watt amp in 15' by 10' sound booth in left rear of house.
Communication system	Cuing system, stage monitor to dressing rooms with page override.
Dressing rooms	5 DR for 2, 1 DR for 6, 1 DR for 7, 2 DR for 25, and 1 DR for conductor, all below stage level; 18 showers
Lounge, canteen, greenroom	Canteen under SL
Rehearsal rooms	47' by 31' by 9' H, wood floor; 50' by 60' by 12' H, wood floor
Wardrobe facilities	Wardrobe room, washer, dryer
Prop and scene shop	Owned separately by Ballet West
Loading dock	
Door dimensions	9' W by 11' H.
Relationship to street	Loading door on alley

CIVIC CENTER OF ONONDAGA COUNTY — SYRACUSE, N.Y.

Owner	Onondaga County
Principal tenant/user	Cultural Resources Council of Syracuse and Onondaga County
Other major users	Syracuse Symphony, Opera Theatre of Syracuse
Theatre executive director	Joseph Golden
Type of construction	New
Approximate cost	$25 million
Design team	
Architects	Arcop Associates (Lebensold, Affleck & Nichol), Montreal
	McAfee, Malo, Fayetteville, NY
Theatre consultant	Robert Brannigan
Acoustical consultant	Russell Johnson
Structural engineers	Nicolet, Dressel, Mercille, Ltd., Montreal
	Snyder Burns Associates, Syracuse, NY.
Mechanical engineers	Langlois, Crossey, Bertrant, Montreal
	Robson-Woese, Syracuse, NY.
Architectural lighting	Robson-Woese
General contractor	Pahl-Turner
Performing spaces	Crouse-Hinds Concert Theatre
	Proscenium
	2,117 seats
	Carrier Theatre
	Platform/proscenium
	463 seats
	BeVard Community Room
	Black box
	200 seats
Lobbies	Main lobby on street level; lobby for each theatre
Handicapped facilities	1 percent seating capacity, 6 WC's
Restrooms	5 for men, 5 for women
Concessions	1 drink concession
Productions booked	Music, dance, theatre, mime, seminars, lectures, films
Weeks per year theatre booked for dance	2-3 weeks
Crew required to man theatre	Union

Crouse-Hinds Concert Theatre

Stage dimensions	60' W by 46' 4" D.
	Wings 26' SL, 21' SR
Proscenium dimensions	40' H
Grid height and rigging system	78' 6" H, 80 counterweight sets
Floor construction and surface	4' x 8' Masonite surface on 2 layers of ⅝" plywood (laid perpendicularly) on 3 layers of 1" x 4" sleepers (laid perpendicularly) on 18" centers (18" on center) on fiberglass blocks (12" on center); bottom layer of sleepers bolted in compression over fiberglass blocks.
Traps	Exist but not used
Orchestra pit	
Dimensions	Upstage 12' 6" by 50'.
	Downstage 9' 6" by 60'.
Capacity	100 musicians; upstage, lift can convert to 75 seats; downstage, lift can convert to 92 seats.

Lighting and electrical	
Power source	Two 400-amp, 4 200-amp company board connections SL
Dimmer board	Siltron Van Buren Compu-Set 2000, 100 control channels by 250 presets, computer disc memory, 345 2.4-kw dimmers, 15 5-kw dimmers.
Patch panel	40 circuit, in front of house
Front-of-house hanging positions	Front-of-house catwalk, SR and SL tormentors, 1st and 2nd balcony rails, projection booth, fly gallery, wall pockets, trap room, no footlights.
Projection	
Screen dimensions	17' H by 40' W
Booth dimensions	15' W by 10' D
Location	Rear of auditorium
Equipment	Eiki 16mm projector, Kodak slide projector
Sound system	20' W by 12' D sound booth in rear of orchestra, Ward-Beck mixing console in rear, 10 Crown 300-watt amps, 3 Altec speaker clusters on bridge in front of proscenium, 4 tapes, 33 mikes, 16 portable speakers, turntable.
Communication system	Intercom, paging and monitoring to all rooms and areas
Dressing rooms	Stage level: 1 DR for star, 2 DR for 2, 2 DR for 4
	One floor below: 3 DR for 4, 2 DR for 16, 2 DR for 24, 3 locker rooms
	Two floors below: 3 DR for 4
	All with showers and WC's
Lounge, canteen, greenroom	Vending machines, no greenroom
Rehearsal rooms	BeVard Community Room, plus 40' by 24' by 18' H space with floor construction identical to stage
Wardrobe facilities	Wardrobe room with washer, dryer, iron and board, sewing machine
Prop and scene shop	None
Loading dock	Inside, closed, heated; truck-height limit 13' 4"
Door dimensions	10' W by 9' H
Distance from stage	75' from SL

Carrier Theatre

Stage dimensions	57' W by 25' D
Proscenium dimensions	Front curtain gives 38' W by 18' H opening
Grid height and rigging system	25' 6" H, 10 sets electric winches
Floor construction and surface	Same as Crouse-Hinds
Traps	Forestage—5 at 4' by 8' for total opening of 20' W by 8' D
Orchestra pit	Forestage traps.
Dimensions	20' W by 8' D.
Capacity	15-20 musicians; can convert to 25 seats
Lighting and electrical	
Power source	Two 400-amp company board connection SL.
Dimmer board	Siltron Van Buren Compu-Set 2000, 48 control channels by 250 presets, computer disc memory, 120 2.4-kw dimmers.
Patch panel	26 circuit, front of house
Front-of-house hanging positions	Catwalks, SL and SR tormentor, USL and USR wall sockets, no footlights

Projection	
Screen dimensions	20' by 20'.
Booth dimensions	15' W by 8' D.
Location	Front of house.
Equipment	Eiki 16mm projector, 2 Kodak slide projectors
Sound system	Fairchild console with panning-fader, equalization, reverb, etc., in sound booth at rear of audience; ceiling-hung castered Altec speakers, 12 mikes, 2 tapes, 1 turntable, 5 Crown 60-watt amps.
Communication system	Intercom, paging and monitoring systems to all areas
Backstage facilities	Shared with Crouse-Hinds and BeVard
Loading dock	Same as Crouse-Hinds, but stage is 2 levels below dock; access is by elevator, 8' 6" by 8' 6" by 9' H

BeVard Community Room

	Multipurpose room, 60' by 40' by 34' H, with own entrance and lobby
Grid height and rigging system	Chain-link tension grid, 33' W by 24' D by 23' H
Floor construction and surface	Same as Crouse-Hinds
Traps	None
Orchestra pit	None
Lighting and electrical	
Dimmer board	12 3-kw dimmers with 2-scene control board located on upper catwalk
Projection	
Screen	Portable
Equipment	Eiki 16mm projector, Kodak slide projector
Communication system	Same as Crouse-Hinds
Backstage facilities	Shared with Crouse-Hinds and Carrier

PERFORMING ARTS CENTER—SUNY, PURCHASE, N.Y.

Owner	State University Construction Fund
Principal Tenant/User	SUNY students
Other major users	Dance, music, and drama groups
Theatre director	Joan Vinton
Type of Construction	New
Design Team	
Architects	Edward Larrabee Barnes Associates; Arthur Baker & Bruce Fowles Associates
Theatre Consultants	Ming Cho Lee, Martin Aronstein, Bernard Weiss
Acoustical Consultant	Bolt, Beranek & Newman
Structural Engineer	Weiskopf & Pickworth
Mechanical Engineer	Segner & Dalton
General Contractor	Polera Building Corporation
Performing Spaces	Theatre A—Opera House Proscenium 1,372 seats
	Theatre B—Drama Theatre Proscenium/apron 738 seats

	Theatre C—Recital Theatre Proscenium 476 seats
	Theatre D Black box 250-550 portable seats
Lobbies	One large central lobby serving all theatres and one small lobby for each theatre
Handicapped facilities	1 percent of seating capacity, 2 WC's
Restrooms	1 for men for each of 4 theatres. 1 for women for each of 4 theatres
Productions booked	Dance, opera, symphony, chamber music, film, poetry, meetings
Weeks per year theatre booked for dance	25-30 weeks
Crew required to man theatre	Technical director and student crew

Theatre C

Stage dimensions	44' 8½" W by 42' 11" D. Wings 26' 6" SL, 26' 9" SR
Proscenium dimensions	30' H by 44' 8½" W
Grid height and rigging system	76' H, 75 counterweight sets
Floor construction and surface	Yellow pine on basket-weave sleepers
Traps	None
Orchestra pit	
Dimensions	21'11" W by 9' 9" D
Capacity	Converts to 84 seats
Lighting and Electrical	
Dimmer Board	56 dimmer Ward-Leonard with 3 presets
Patch panel	338-circuit patch panel upstage
Front-of-house hanging positions	4 overhead cove, 4 side cove
Projection	No permanent equipment
Sound system	No permanent equipment
Communication system	Backstage console, light-booth stations with headsets, stage monitor to dressing rooms with page override.
Dressing rooms	1 stage-level 2-person DR, 6 2-person, 4 15-person DR's below stage, 15 showers, 15 WC's
Lounge, canteen, greenroom	One greenroom for all theatres, vending machines
Rehearsal rooms	40' by 50' rehearsal room with sprung floor
Wardrobe facilities	Wardrobe room with iron, board, washer, dryer, sewing machine
Prop and scene shop	8,500 sq. ft. shop for college productions
Loading dock	
Door dimensions	8' W by 10' H
Distance from stage	On stage

STATE THEATRE—PLAYHOUSE SQUARE, CLEVELAND, OHIO

Owner	Playhouse Square Foundation
Principal tenant/users	Cleveland Ballet, Cleveland Opera
Other major users	Touring dance, opera, musical theatre
Type of construction	Renovation
Approximate Cost	$8.5 million
Design team	
Architect	Dalton, van Dijk, Johnson & Partners
Theatre consultant	Roger Morgan Studio, Inc.
Acoustical consultant	Jaffe Acoustics, Inc.
Structural engineer	Barber & Hoffman, Inc.
Mechanical and electrical engineer	Byers, Urban, Klug, White & Partners
Seating capacity	3,300
Lobby	Grand lobby, 320' long
Handicapped facilities	Boxes at center of auditorium, just behind cross aisle, can accommodate up to 20 wheelchairs.
Restrooms	1 for each sex at lobby and mezzanine levels; separate rest rooms to accommodate wheelchairs, 1 for each sex, at lobby level.
Productions booked	Large-scale dance, opera, and musical theatre
Performing area dimensions	Approximately 45' by 45'
Grid height and rigging system	80' H, single-purchase, T-Bar counterweight
Floor construction and surface	5-layer basket weave with edge-grain Douglas fir finish flooring over structural concrete floor
Traps	None
Orchestra pit	
Dimensions	Approximately 27' by 49'.
Capacity	90 musicians
Lighting and electrical	
Power source	2000-amps, 3-phase
Dimmer board	Electronic memory with CRT display, 476 dimmer capacity.
Patch panel	None (dimmer-per-circuit system)
Front-of-house hanging positions	Balcony rail, 2 box booms on each side
Followspots	3 in followspot booth at rear of auditorium, 2 on ceiling perches at left and right sides
Projection	None
Dressing rooms	4 men's and women's chorus DR's on basement level (capacity 30M, 16M, 30F, 16F), 7 stage-level DR's (capacity 1-3 persons each)
Lounge, canteen, greenroom	Performers' lounge and canteen at basement level, musicians' room at basement level, crew room at stage level, backstage lobby at stage level with call board.
Rehearsal rooms	Full complex including 2 studios, each approximately 53' by 43', office, changing rooms, and storage room; access to freight elevator.
Wardrobe facilities	Wardrobe room, separate hair/wig and shoe rooms with special ventilation.
Prop and scene storage	Resident companies store stock props and scenery elsewhere; running prop room provided; upstage storage area permits scenery storage for visiting company.
Loading dock and receiving area	Stage-level loading dock has 3 loading doors for trucks and 1 personnel door; truck access via private driveway; receiving area approximately 43' x 43'.

GRAND OPERA HOUSE

Owner	Grand Opera House, Inc.
Principal tenant/user	Grand Opera House, Inc.
Other major users	Delaware Symphony, Wilmington Opera Society
Theatre executive director	David Fleming
Type of construction	Renovation/restoration
Approximate cost	$6.5 million
Design team	
Architect	Grieves Armstrong Childs
Historical consultant	Steven T. Baird Associates
Theatre consultant	Roger Morgan Studio, Inc.
Acoustical consultant	Klepper Marshall King Associates, Ltd.
Structural engineer	Skarda and Rickert, Inc.
Mechanical engineer	Palmer and Clark, Inc.
Murals, frescoes, and permanent scenic elements	Dale Amlund
Architectural lighting	Carroll Cline
General contractor	John E. Healy & Sons, Inc. (construction manager)
Seating capacity	674 orchestra, 436 balcony
Lobbies	Narrow, T-shaped on each of 2 levels
Handicapped facilities	11 percent capacity for wheelchairs
Restrooms	4 for men, 4 for women, 1 for handicapped in each of 2 ground-floor rest rooms
Concessions	5 liquor and soda bars
Productions booked	Classical music, dance, chamber music, travelogues, films, operas
Weeks per year theatre used by principal tenant	89 events per year
Crew required to man theatre	3-man house crew, nonunion
Stage dimensions	38' W by 31' D Wings 11' SL, 12' SR
Grid height and rigging system	30'H, 34-set mechanical winch system driven by 2 movable electric motors
Floor construction and surface	Vinyl on wood dance surface; finish floor 2½" x 1¼" tongue-and-groove softwood on 5 layers of crisscrossed 1" x 3" sleepers on 16" centers; basket weave.
Traps	None
Orchestra pit	
Dimensions	38' W by 20' D.
Capacity	40 musicians; can be converted to 53 extra seats or extended stage apron; screw-jack pit lift gives access to basement storage room.
Lighting and electrical	
Power source	Three 400-amp, 3-phase switches at stage level for touring switchboards; house dimmer rack in basement.
Dimmer board	80 dimmers with memory console.
Patch panel	Slider Patch, 350 circuits at 20 and 50 amps.
Front-of-house hanging positions	Balcony booms, ceiling slot
Projection	
Screen dimension	30' x 30'
Type	Roll-drop
Booth dimensions	40' W by 12' D
Location	Rear of house, above balcony
Equipment	Kneisley Knitron film projector, Kodak slide projector
Sound system	Crown 800 tape deck, 16-channel Auditronics 110-4 mixer, 14 electro-voice microphones, 6 JBL speakers.
Communication system	16 David Clark stations with headsets
Dressing rooms	2 large chorus DR, 1 small DR, 2 star DR (100 performers total)
Lounge, canteen, greenroom	Greenroom in DR's, 12 showers, 15 WC's, soda machine
Rehearsal rooms	Main stage plus "Grand Parlor" on occasional basis
Wardrobe facilities	Wardrobe room, iron, ironing board
Prop and scene shop	Minimal
Loading dock	Sidewalk only, 6' below stage floor; loading is done by 8' x 10' or 38' x 10' lift.
Door dimensions	8' W by 24' H.
Distance from stage	None

FILENE CENTER II

Owner	U.S. Department of the Interior, National Park Service
Principal tenant/user	Wolf Trap Foundation responsible for all Filene Center II bookings
Theatre manager	Ralph A. Hoffmann
Type of construction	New
Approximate cost	$20 million
Design team	
Architects	Dewberry & Davis
	John MacFadyen (consulting architect)
Theatre consultant	Jules Fisher associates
Acoustical consultants	Bolt, Beranek & Newman
	Farrel M. Becker (Wolf Trap)
Structural engineer	Dewberry & Davis
Mechanical engineer	The Office of Lee Kendrick
General contractor	G & C Construction Co.
Seating capacity	2,641 orchestra, 1,145 balcony and loge, 3,100 lawn
Lobbies	Plaza entrance (uncovered)
Handicapped facilities	Special assistance available
Restrooms	Numerous locations
Concessions	Full-course dinners to popcorn and sodas
Productions booked	Opera, symphony, dance, pop acts, festivals, musicals, jazz
Weeks per year theatre booked for dance:	2-4 weeks
Crew required to man theatre:	14 (carpentry, electrical, flys, props, sound)
Stage dimensions:	80' 4" W by 65' 1" D.
	Wings 58' SL, 27' SR
Proscenium dimensions:	44' 8" H by 71' W
Grid height and rigging system	102' H, single-purchase counterweight
Floor construction and surface:	2" x 6" tongue-and-groove Douglas fir resting on flexible elastomeric-membrane isolation pads
Traps:	None
Orchestra pit	
Dimensions:	55' W by 24' D (1,260 sq. ft. of usable space).
Capacity:	90 musicians at 14 sq. ft. per musician; 1 pit lift
Lighting and electrical	
Power source	Two 400-amp SR.
Dimmer board	Strand Color Light Palette.
Patch panel	Soft Patch, dimmer per circuit.
Front-of-house hanging positions	Balcony rail, box boom, overhead canopy, portable side trees, bridge, followspot bridge rail
Projections	None
Sound system	Sound console at right rear of front orchestra, state-of-the-art sound reinforcement.
Communication system	Intercom with matrix for production communication, program monitor with page override for dressing rooms, and offstage areas.
Dressing rooms	Stage level, 2 quickchange with 1 WC each.
	Below stage, 16 principal for 1-4, each with shower and WC, 3 chorus rooms for 50 each, with 6 showers and 6 WC's each
Lounge, canteen, greenroom	Greenroom SR basement, canteen, 2 lounge areas in basement SL, SR
Rehearsal rooms	Main stage and 57' by 96' rehearsal hall
Wardrobe facilities	Wardrobe with washer, dryer, iron, board, sewing machine, steamers, etc.
Prop and scene shop	No shop per se, but full assortment of tools and equipment for scenery assembly and rigging
Loading dock	
Door dimensions	10'11" by 10'6", 3'6" above roadway; auxiliary loading door 2'6" from roadway.
Distance from stage	108'

BARRIER-FREE ACCESS TO DANCE

B

Rendering cultural facilities accessible to people who are physically handicapped calls for more than an occasional wheelchair ramp. Handicapped theatre visitors include those who are partially or totally blind or deaf, as well as patrons with disabled limbs. And because there are handicapped theatre technicians, administrators, and even performers, accessibility must extend beyond public spaces and into backstage areas. Entrances for disabled persons, whether they lead backstage or to lobbies, should be as inviting and convenient as those designed for nondisabled theatre visitors. "Access in itself is not enough," says violinist Itzhak Perlman, a childhood victim of polio. "There must be access with dignity."

Section 504 of the Rehabilitation Act of 1973 is the most important national legislation concerning accessibility to federally funded cultural facilities. The pamphlet "504 and the Performing Arts" (available from state arts councils and from the National Endowment for the Arts' Office for Special Constituencies) states that the federal law does not "require access to every area of a performing arts facility—balconies, for instance ... Instead, portions of programs and facilities will suffice provided that handicapped people have an equal opportunity to the organization's program offerings when viewed in their entirety ..."

Section 504 provides no design criteria. Instead, it refers architects to relevant local laws, building codes, or design guidelines. Those codes vary from state to state. Most architects and theatre builders will want to do more than just comply with local codes. Up-to-date information as well as specifications on barrier-free design are available from the following sources:

- National Center for a Barrier Free Environment
  Suite 700, 1015 15th Street, NW
  Washington, D.C. 20005
  202-466-6896
- Architecture Transportation Barriers Compliance Board
  Room 1010, 330 C Street, SW
  Washington, D.C. 20202
  202-245-1591
- AIA/Codes and Standards Division
  3rd Floor, 1735 New York Avenue, NW
  Washington, D.C. 20006
  202-626-7300

Disabled persons can often suggest effective and inexpensive ways to design for accessibility. Thus, it is worthwhile to form an advisory committee composed of persons with various kinds of disabilities, to evaluate program plans.

FROM THE OUTSIDE IN

Many handicapped patrons arrive at performing arts facilities en masse in special buses, or are driven to the door in taxis or private cars. In addition to ample space for cars and buses to unload passengers, there should be an outdoor covered waiting area, slightly to one side of the theatre's regular public entrance. There, disabled individuals and groups can organize themselves before entering the theatre, without being jostled by the flow of nondisabled patrons.

Some handicapped visitors will drive to the theatre in their own cars. Special parking places must be provided—and designated—for their use. Generally, two percent of the facility's parking spaces, or a minimum of two spaces, should be set

Specially-sized parking places must be provided and designated for handicapped patrons arriving by bus or car.

Wheelchair lifts are an alternative to ramps.

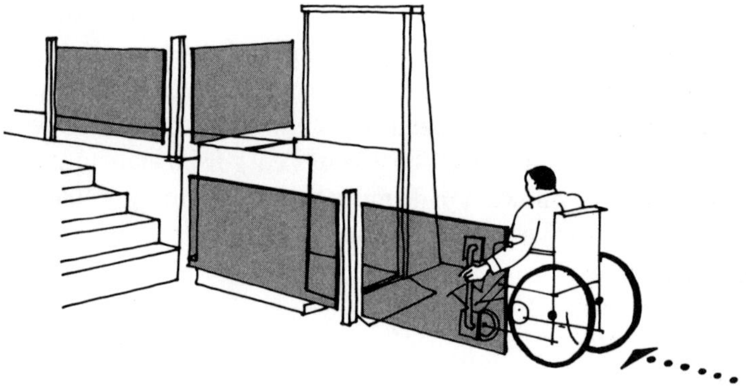

Doorways must be wide enough to permit wheelchairs easy entrance.

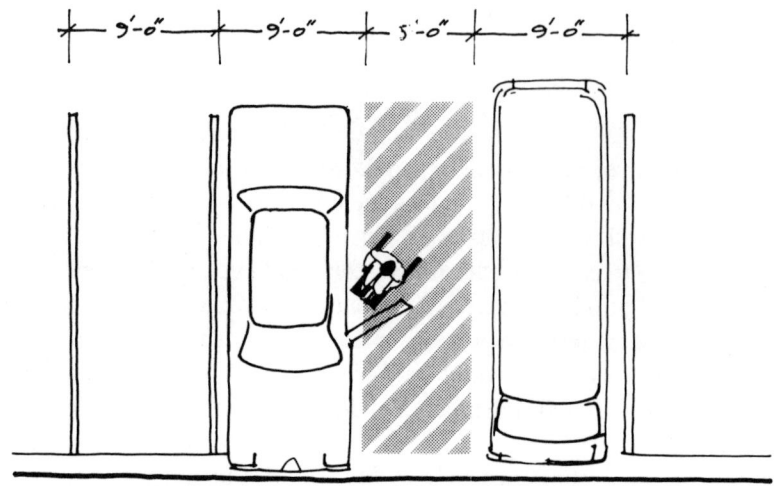

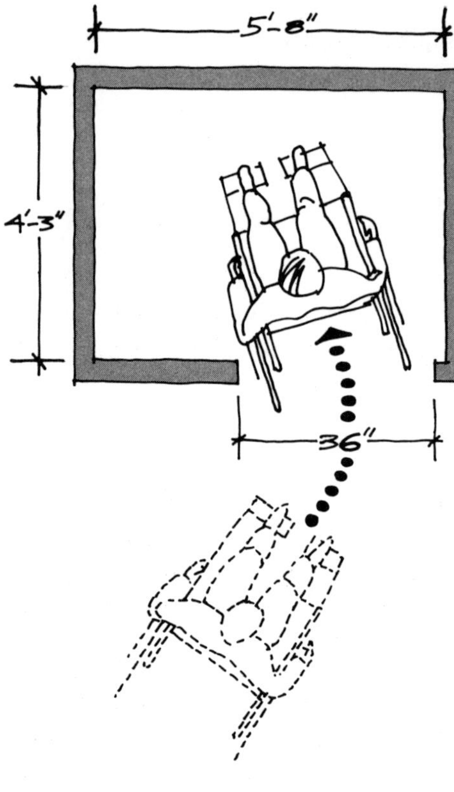

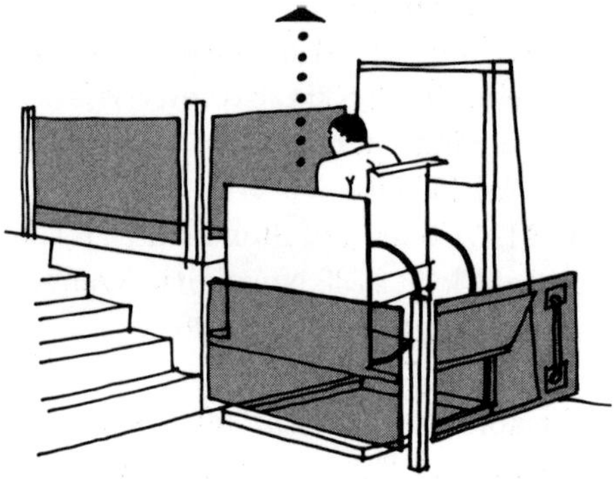

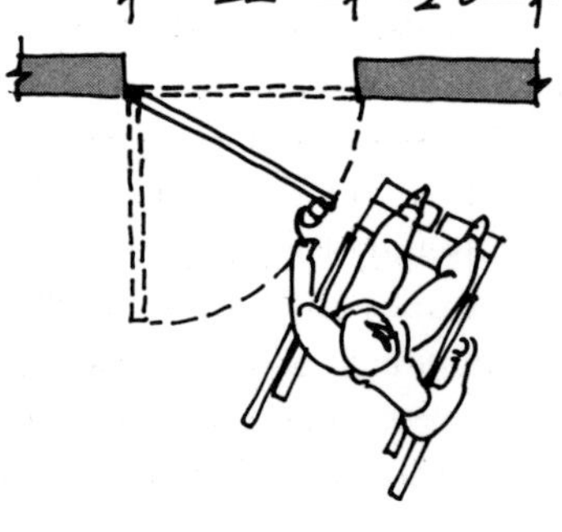

aside for handicapped drivers. Aisles between those spaces should be 5 feet wide, to allow people in wheelchairs room to exit from their cars and to maneuver. Parking spaces for handicapped patrons should be as near as possible to the theatre lobby. Additional handicapped parking should be provided near the stage entrance for disabled performers, crew members, and theatre staff.

Steps and curbs between unloading areas or parking spaces and the theatre doors are an impossible hurdle for wheelchair users. Access ramps must be built. If parking and unloading areas are not indoors, then ramps should be roofed to protect users from rain or snow. The slope of indoor ramps should be no steeper than 1 inch of rise per 12 inches of run. A rise of 1:20 is the suggested maximum slope for outdoor ramps. Access ramps should be at least 36 inches wide, and there should be a 5-foot-long level for every 30 feet of sloping run.

THE LOBBY

When a short run of indoor steps does not allow space for a ramp of the proper slope or length, a small mechanical lift can be installed to carry wheelchair users from one level to the next.

Wheelchairs for adults vary in width from 24 to 29 inches. Thus, all theatre doors—including doors to toilet stalls—should offer a clear width of at least 32 inches, which includes 1½ inches of knuckle space on each side. Floors at doorways should provide a 5-foot level platform (where wheelchair users will negotiate opening the door and passing through the doorway), and thresholds should be no higher than half an inch.

A public-address system is one option for accommodating visually impaired theatre-goers. The system can be used to announce a performance, the end of an intermission, or to provide emergency instructions. Deaf and non-speaking visitors require clear visual cues to help them interpret their environment. For their safety, the theatre's fire and emergency warning systems should be clearly visible throughout the building. Emergency telephones that operate without a spoken message should be installed in elevators, again for the safety of hearing-impaired persons.

THEATRE SEATING

The number of wheelchair spaces required in theatres varies from state to state. The pamphlet "504 and the Performing Arts" cites the Illinois code's requirement of two wheelchair spaces in places of assembly that seat up to fifty persons, four spaces in theatres seating up to four hundred, and—in larger houses—an even number amounting to no less than one percent of seating capacity. Beyond calling for a sufficient number of seats for handicapped patrons, Section 504 itself recommends that "performing arts centers develop a price range of seats accommodating physically disabled people that corresponds to the choices offered the general public."

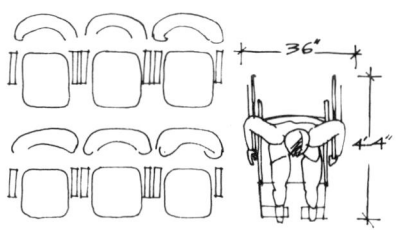

Adequate space must be allowed for integrating wheelchair seating with conventional fixed seating.

Wheelchair spaces may be provided along aisles (but not blocking them) or in back and front rows. Wheelchairs require a level area 32 inches wide by 42 inches long. Given the need to rake house seating to produce proper sightlines, front and back row wheelchair locations may work best. Removing three seats usually leaves space for two wheelchairs. There must be at least 18 inches of clear space behind or in front of the row, to allow for the depth of wheelchairs. If house wheelchair spaces are not sold, portable seating with quick-connecting mounts can be substituted.

In addition to a theatre's wheelchair positions, a sound system for hearing-impaired persons should be installed in one section of seats. Eugene Bergman's "Arts Accessibility for the Deaf" (available from the NEA's Office for Special Constituencies)

Toilet facilities must be easily accessible for handicapped patrons of the theatre.

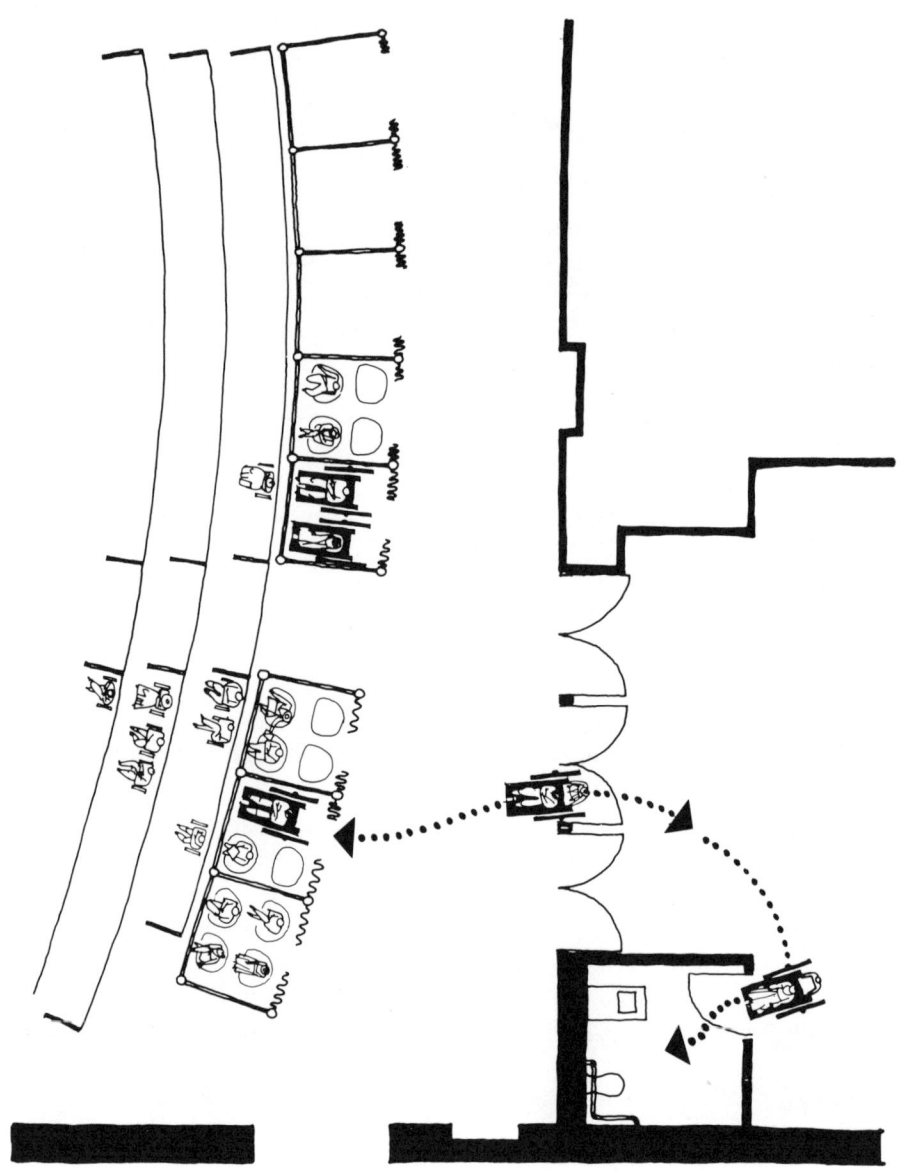

At the State Theatre in Cleveland, boxes at the rear of the auditorium have been designated for wheelchair users. Handicapped patrons are often accompanied by friends, and the arrangement makes it easy for them to sit together. The boxes can also be fitted with movable chairs and used by non-handicapped persons.

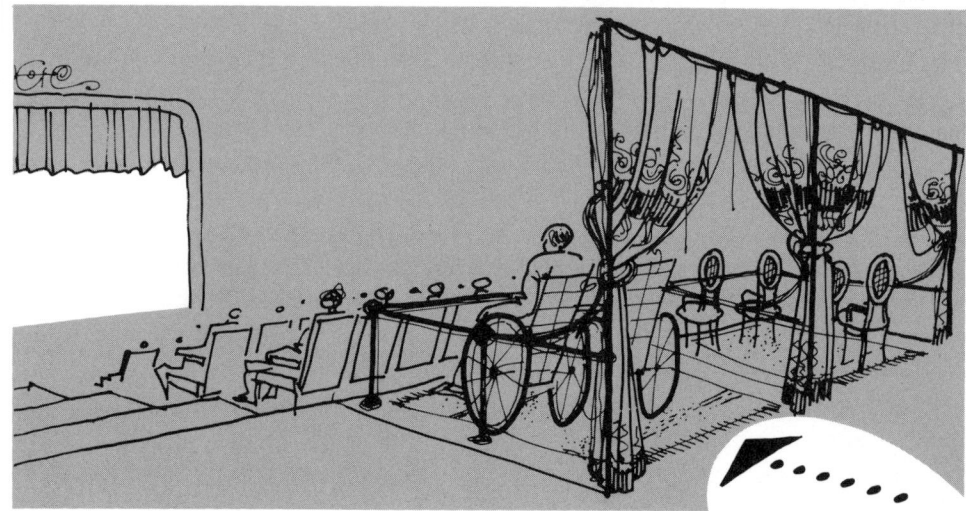

describes wireless listening systems, audio loops, and other specialized amplification systems, and provides sources for design information.

AMENITIES

Telephones and water fountains that can be reached by wheelchair users, as well as by small children, should be installed near public restrooms. The highest buttons on the phones should be no more than 4 feet above the floor. Water fountains should be no higher than 2 feet 6 inches, and must have controls that are easily operated with a closed fist. Beneath phones and water fountains there should be knee space for persons in wheelchairs.

In public toilets, the standard stall for mobility-impaired persons measures 3 feet wide by 6 feet deep. Each such toilet stall should have a 32-inch-wide door that opens out, and should be equipped with grab bars on both interior walls. For maneuvering a wheelchair, there must be a 48-by-54-inch unobstructed space outside the stall entrance. A stall measuring 5 feet square, and with corner grab bars, also works well. Although it claims more space, the larger stall matches the 5-foot depth of conventional stalls, and thus may be easily integrated into the overall restroom design.

ON STAGE AND BACKSTAGE

With the exception of those with hearing impairments, there are few physically disabled dancers. There are, however, disabled dance teachers, such as New York City's Tanaquil Le Clercq and London's Elizabeth Twistington Higgins—both distinguished ballet dancers before they became victims of polio. These and other handicapped teachers of dance need access to stages where their students perform and to studios where they rehearse. Stages and backstage areas should also be rendered barrier-free to accommodate disabled musicians, actors, singers, designers, technicians, and students.

In any theatre-building project, the right of all disabled persons to enjoy access with dignity should be considered well before architectural drawings are developed. As with other everyday needs of dancers, theatre employees, and patrons, the requirements of handicapped persons can be met with ease and grace, provided design solutions are the product of forethought, rather than hindsight.

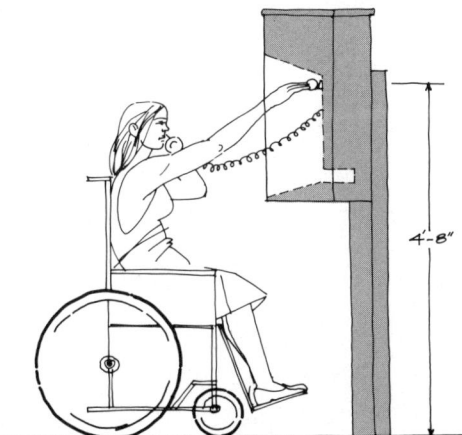
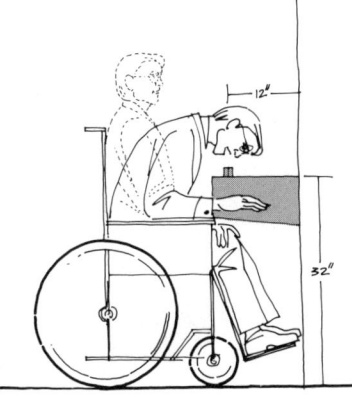

Pay telephones and drinking fountains must be designed to be within easy reach of handicapped persons.

C

A PLANNING WORKBOOK

The materials in this appendix were originally printed in *Building for the Arts: A Guidebook for the Planning and Design of Cultural Facilities,* by Catherine R. Brown, William B. Fleissig, and William R. Morrish, published by the Western States Arts Foundation 1984. The authors appreciate the courtesy of the Western States Arts Foundation in granting permission to reprint these excerpts.

TAKE STOCK OF WHAT YOU'VE GOT

One of the first activities of your committee should be to clearly define your purpose. If you can describe who you are and what you need, you are that much closer to getting funding that will help test your ideas within the community.

AN INVENTORY

Once your committee is able to answer the questions below, your group will be in a solid position to continue the project. In the process, you will create the basis of a prospectus you can use as a fundraising tool. The answers to these questions will, in fact, be a compilation of all the facts, figures, trends and philosophies involved in your decision to create a new facility. By forcing yourselves to document your reasons for becoming involved in the project, you may come up with information you didn't know you had—and you will be ready to answer the toughest question a potential funder can ask.

First, take stock of your organization and community.

1. What is your organization's philosophy in regard to:
    - Arts programming
    - Artistic direction
2. Describe your organization's:
    - Audience composition and attendance
    - Community image and support
    - Strength of management/governing structure
    - Current level of activities
3. Describe your organization's assets and liabilities currently and for the past three years
    - Expenses
        - ☐ personnel
        - ☐ administrative (other)
        - ☐ facility rental/utilities
        - ☐ debt service/taxes
    - Revenues (include sources)
        - ☐ earned
        - ☐ grants from public sources
        - ☐ private grants
        - ☐ other
        - ☐ possible future sources of revenue
4. Describe other arts facilities in the community and their locations. Why are these facilities not acceptable for your use?
5. What other building fund drives are currently under way?
6. Describe the current facility your organization is using in terms of:
    - overall condition
    - level of technical equipment for your needs
    - physical location (assets and liabilities)
    - community image
    - biggest asset

- biggest liability
- budget deficits
- suitability for your needs

Now clarify the kinds of changes you have in mind and the assistance you can draw upon in making these changes.

1. Do you want to make changes at this time in your organization's:
   - programming (level or kind of change)
   - management
   - community image/support
   - funding base
2. What type of facility changes do you want to make?
   - new facility
   - major renovation (be specific)
   - minor addition(s) or interior alterations
   - technical improvements
   - correction of a previous "improvement"
3. What are the space needs of your organization and any other organizations involved?
4. Are there other local arts or community organizations in need of space who might be potential users/renters? What are their needs and use requirements?
5. Will the facility changes require alterations in your:
   - programming
   - management structure
   - community support
   - financing
   - operating costs
6. Who will benefit from the new facility?
   - arts lovers (the already-committed)
   - the local community in general (how?)
   - a 100-mile radius (how?)
   - the region (how?)
   - business—retail, hotel, restaurant
   - industry (by attracting new employees)
7. What kind and degree of support (broken down into capital construction funds, operating funds and political assistance) can you expect from:
   - city/county departments (building/school/planning) and local officials
   - community organizations/neighborhood groups
   - other arts groups
   - corporate and financial leaders in the community, including local merchants
8. Why do you believe this support is forthcoming?

EVALUATING YOUR ANSWERS

Think about your findings, and ask yourselves some tough questions:
- Will your present committee be able to handle the task ahead? (If this seems like a great deal of work so early in the game, remember that potential funders—private individuals as well as foundations—will be asking you the same questions.)
- Who are your supporters? (Include the backgrounds of the committee and key community people who are enthusiastic about your project and can offer concrete assistance.)
- Is your committee sufficiently equipped and broadranging enough to deal with the arts facility issue?

- Do the audiences/artistic resources/community needs justify the changes you are advocating? What evidence substantiates this?
- Do you need to commission a feasibility study at this time to better answer the questions above?
- Do you feel ready to establish yourselves as a public group, publicize your plan in a formal way, and incorporate yourselves into an ongoing committee? In order to do this in a professional way, you need to know exactly what you are advocating—not just that you want to build a museum, but precisely what kind of museum it will be. You must be able to articulate what you want and justify it to consultants, potential funders, people in control of local politics, and community leaders. The real test is to be able to talk someone into spending money on your project—and to do that, you have to make it sound like a winner.

THE THREE COMPONENTS OF A FEASIBILITY STUDY

Financial Feasibility Study

Analysis of all costs for facility operations, planning, and construction. The operating budget includes projects for:

- earned income (admissions, sales, rentals, memberships, etc.)
- contributed income (private and public)
- operating expenses (salaries, overhead, maintenance, etc.)
- special programming costs

Capital Construction estimates for facility planning and construction include:

- consultant fees
- site acquisition and development
- construction costs
- equipment and furnishings
- project financing

Capital Financing Study includes:

- capital dollars available for construction
- financing strategies
- cash flow projections
- economic impact of facility on the community

Arts Program Feasibility Study

Survey of the market to determine what will be on stage and who will be the audience, taking into account:

- intended programming
- needs of organizations in community
- use of existing facilities
- community audience survey
- audience attendance patterns

Site/Building Feasibility Study

Analysis of possible sites and buildings for their ability to accommodate desired arts programming within available budget. Alternative sites are analyzed in terms of:

- fulfilling artistic programming needs
- location
- support available from surrounding area to meet needs of patrons, production, and touring companies
- accessibility
- image
- operations and management implications

- land costs, availability, and financing
- project phasing and implementation

ORGANIZING YOUR BUILDING PROGRAM

General information about the facility, your group, and its plans should include:

1. History of your institution and plans for the future
2. Nature of your current arts programming and changes you foresee
3. Image of the facility
4. Reasons why you have decided to build/renovate now

A description of your site requirements might include, among other considerations peculiar to your project:

1. Parking and pedestrian access
2. Outdoor functional areas (e.g., courtyards)
3. Service entry location (e.g., loading dock)
4. Future expansion needs as you now envision them

If you are planning an addition to your present facility or are renovating a building, you will have to provide:

1. General description of the existing building
2. Functions and sizes of each room or area
3. Floor plans, if available

Finally, include any other information relevant to the project:

1. Budget data
2. Feasibility studies
3. Other consultant reports you might have commissioned

The bulk of your preliminary building program will consist of descriptions of the various spaces needed to house your arts programming. These should include:

1. What exactly will be happening in this space?
2. What is the proposed size of the space? How many people must it accommodate? (State square footage if you can make a reasonable estimate.)
3. What aesthetic qualities should the space have?
4. What spaces must be adjacent to each other? Which should be located near each other?
5. Special needs:
   - Equipment
   - Environmental standards (acoustical/heating and air conditioning/relative humidity)
   - Storage space
   - Number of doors required, where they lead, and how big they need to be
   - Security requirements

PRODUCTS AND DECISIONS FOR DESIGN IMPLEMENTATION

	Building Program Study	**Schematic Design**	**Design Development**	**Working Drawings & Construction**
Committee Responsibilities	Facilitate the program process: advice from users & committee	Review, guide and select alternatives of building design and site organization	Review design of spaces for location, size, and form	Review Work Answer Questions Select Contractor
Decisions To Be Made	Image, type, size quantity, and quality of building spaces	Select design alternative/ direction	Approve design production Approve equipment selection	Review work Questions on construction or design changes Select contractor Approve finished building

Consultants	Specialists as needed. (Arts generalist, architect, etc)	Architect
		Arts Consultants
		  Theater
		  Museum
		  Acoustic
		Building Engineers:
		  Mechanical
		  Structural
		  Electrical
			Same as Schematic Design
			
			Construction Manager
				Same as Design Development
				
				Clerk of the Works

Outside Approvals	Check with the government agencies for building requirements	Review of schematic design by government agencies	Preliminary permit review Insurance broker Lending institutions Energy expert	Building permits Occupancy permit
Time Line	Small project 2 months Large project 3-6 months	Small project 2 months Large project 3-6 months	Small project 3 months Large project 12-18 months	Small project 10 months Large project 30 months

Interim Products	Memos of program alternatives
	
	Worksheets
		Review direction of alternatives Study:
		  Sketches
		  Plans
		  Models
			Review design decisions made by architect	Review specifications/Working Drawings
				Review payments to contractor

Final Products	Building program workbook	Final schematic:
		  Sketches
		  Plans
		  Models
			Finished design— proceed to production of working drawings	Review of finished building

Cost Estimates	Comparable cost estimates with similar types of projects	Preliminary cost estimates	Project cost estimate *definitive*	Very accurate cost estimate at end of working drawings

GLOSSARY

Acoustics

Characteristics exhibited by sound waves; the quality of sound in a given space.

Adaptive Reuse

Redesigning a building for new purposes.

Apron

In a proscenium theatre, that part of the stage floor projecting forward of the house curtain toward the audience.

Arena Theatre

Theatre-in-the-round, where the audience surrounds the stage.

Backdrop

A suspended canvas or velour panel extending the full width of the performing area and providing the background for a performance.

Backstage

Usually a synonym for offstage, but—in this book—any space outside the stagehouse used by performers or crew members.

Batten

An overhead length of steel pipe to which scenery, drapery, or lighting equipment is attached; part of the stage-rigging system, battens run across the stage parallel to the proscenium.

Bidding

Phase of an architectural project when contractors and subcontractors examine construction documents, determine the cost of executing a given portion of the job, and submit their prices to the owner.

Boom

In stage lighting, a vertical length of pipe on which stage-lighting fixtures are mounted one above the other; used most often for side lighting from the wings (tormentor boom), or for lighting positions along the side walls of the auditorium (box boom).

Borders

Overhead masking that forms the upper edge of the stage picture, and that conceals battens and other hanging equipment from view of the audience.

Building Codes

Local, state, or national statutes regulating building construction.

Building Permit

Legal authorization, granted by local officials, to proceed with construction in accordance with a previously approved set of drawings.

Building Program

A list of every space to be included in a building, with descriptions of the function, size, and location of each space, and sometimes of technical equipment and furnishings each space will contain.

Carbon Arc
Intense light created by an electric arc between two carbon electrodes; carbon arc lamps are used in followspots where long throws are required, and where a strong light is needed to stand out against other stage lighting.

Changeover
Preparing a theatre for a new program by changing or rearranging scenery, props, and lighting equipment.

Circuit
The path an electric current follows from its source, to a lighting fixture, and back to its source.

Circuit Breaker
Device that, upon sensing an electrical overload in a circuit, shuts off the flow of power.

Color Media
Colored glass, plastic, or gelatin filters, fitted in front of a stage-lighting fixture to color the light beam it emits.

Construction Documents
Drawings and specifications prepared by an architect, consulting engineers, and other specialists, describing plans, elevations, sections, details, dimensions, materials, and methods for building construction.

Control Console
Unit used for remote control of the entire stage-lighting system.

Counterweight Arbor/Carriage
Device holding steel or lead weights in stacks, used to counterbalance the load suspended from a rigging batten; moving the carriage up or down along tracks or guide wires causes the batten and its load to move in the opposite direction.

Counterweight-Rigging System
An arrangement in which lines from a rigging batten run up to loftblocks (pulleys) above a grid, and then across the top of the stagehouse to a side wall; the lines are then gathered at a headblock and directed down the side wall to a counterweight arbor.

Crossover
Corridor for performers and crew, hidden behind the backdrop or cyclorama, or running behind the stagehouse, and leading from one side of the stage to the other.

Cue
In performance, a signal for action: for a dancer, a musical phrase may be the cue for an entrance; for the stage-lighting operator, a particular dance movement may be the cue to begin a lighting change (each change in stage lighting is called a cue).

Cyclorama
Neutral background, often made of fabric, at the upstage limit of the performing area.

Deck
Stage floor.

Dimmer

Electrical device that regulates the flow of current to a lighting fixture, controlling the intensity of the lamp.

Dimmer Bank/Dimmer Rack

Array of stage-lighting dimmers and associated wiring and circuit breakers, contained in a cabinet.

Dimmer-per-Circuit System

Dimming system in which each branch circuit in the stage-lighting system is permanently wired to its own dimming device and circuit breaker, eliminating the need for a patch panel.

Downstage

Front of the performing area; that part of the stage nearer the audience.

Electronic Memory Lighting Control

Lighting-control system that stores in computer memory all cues and presets of a given stage-lighting design.

End-Stage Theatre

Theatre without a proscenium arch; the audience sits opposite the raised platform of the stage—as in a proscenium theatre—but, with no intervening arch framing the stage, performers and patrons share the same volume.

Fire Curtain

Asbestos, fire-resistant fabric, or steel curtain that, in a fire, is automatically lowered to isolate the stagehouse from the auditorium.

Flat

Scenery panel, usually canvas stretched over a wooden frame and painted; two-fold flats are freestanding and constructed in hinged sections.

Fly Floor/Fly Gallery

Elevated platform along side wall of the stagehouse, where stagehands stand to operate the rigging system.

Flying

Raising or lowering scenery and equipment above the performing area by means of a rigging system.

Fly Space

Space above the stage into which scenery and lighting equipment are raised beyond view of the audience.

Fold-Back System

Sound system that directs music from the pit orchestra or from prerecorded tapes toward dancers on stage.

Followspot

Movable spotlight that pivots both horizontally and vertically, allowing a stagehand to aim it at any portion of the performing area or to "follow" a performer.

Four-Walls Rental House
Theatre offered for rental without any movable theatrical furnishings, such as stage-lighting fixtures, dimming system, drapery, or related production equipment.

Front-of-House
Any part of the theatre, such as the auditorium or lobby, usually accessible to the public; front-of-house lighting positions are located in the auditorium rather than inside the stagehouse.

Grand Drape
Fixed, decorative drapery hung at the top of the proscenium arch, just in front of the adjustable, horizontal masking border.

Grid
Openwork steel floor and associated structure placed above the stage to support and provide access to the rigging system.

Grid Height
Distance between the stage floor and the upper surface of the grid floor.

Hanging Plan
A plan or series of plan drawings developed by a dance company, specifying the location of all its scenery, masking, and stage-lighting equipment; the rigging system in any theatre the company plays must be able to accommodate the company's hanging plan.

Hardwood
Smooth and even-textured woods from deciduous trees such as maple or oak; often used in rehearsal studios or spaces used exclusively for dance for the finished floor surface.

Headblock
Multigrooved drum, or sandwich of independent pulleys, at which two or more lines of a stage-rigging set are gathered; the lines are directed downward to a counterweight carriage or pin rail where they can be manipulated as a group.

Headblock Beam
Structural-steel beam directly above the counterweight array; the beam supports the headblocks and carries the vertical load of counterweights plus the horizontal load of rigging battens.

House Curtain
Decorative curtain between the auditorium and the performing area; it may draw open horizontally or be flown vertically.

HVAC
Heating, Ventilating, and Air Conditioning.

Hydraulic Stage Lift
Elevator system using fluid pressure to raise and lower the orchestra pit or sections of the stage.

Intercom System
Theatre communication system through which the stage manager maintains voice contact with the production crew during performance or rehearsal.

Jumper Cables
Flexible stage-lighting cables; electrical extension cords.

Lamp
Light bulb.

Legs
Masking curtains hung vertically and parallel to the sides of the proscenium; legs define the sides of the performing area and hide offstage dancers, as well as lighting trees and other equipment, from the audience.

Lighting Instrument/Luminaire
Portable stage-lighting fixture, usually mounted in position with clamps.

Lighting Ladders
Steel frames on which lighting instruments are mounted; suspended in the wings, lighting ladders leave the stage floor unobstructed.

Light Plot
Diagram showing the location of all lighting fixtures and equipment required for a given stage-lighting design.

Loading Bridge
High platform, adjacent to stagehouse wall, used by stagehands adjusting loads in counterweight arbors.

Load-In/Load-Out
Load-in is the process of unloading from trucks, and unpacking and setting up for performance, all scenery, costumes, sound, lighting, and other equipment brought to a theatre by a touring company; load-out is the reverse—packing up the equipment when the company leaves the theatre.

Loftblock
Stage-rigging device, consisting of a single grooved wheel or multigrooved drum attached to the roof steel or grid floor, which transfers one of the lines supporting a rigging batten to the headblock.

Masking
Stage draperies and flats used at the side limits of the performing space to conceal equipment and offstage areas from the audience (see *Borders* and *Legs*).

Offstage
Usually a synonym for backstage, but—in this book—any area beyond the wings and out of sight of the audience but within the stagehouse.

On Center
Measurement taken from the center of one object to the center of the next like object.

On Stage
Within the performing area; in view of the audience.

Orchestra Shell
Portable structure used on stage to surround an orchestra or smaller musical group. Curving behind the orchestra, the shell directs sound toward the audience. In theatres designed solely for music, the shell may be permanent.

Paint Frame

Vertical frame that holds a backdrop in place for painting; paint frames are often able to be moved up and down, so an artist at a fixed elevation can reach every part of the backdrop.

Patch Panel

Electrical switchboard allowing any branch circuit in the stage-lighting system to be assigned to any dimmer.

Performance Monitoring/Paging System

Communication system that carries the sound of a performance to performers and crew backstage and permits the stage manager to make announcements to all backstage locations.

Performing Area

Portion of the stage seen by the audience; the top and sides of the performing area are defined by masking.

Pin Rail

Tubular steel rail fitted with belaying pins; in stage-rigging systems, the free end of a single rope line is tied off at a pin rail.

Plan

Architect's drawing of a space, structure, or object as seen from above.

Portal

Neutral border of wood, stretched canvas, or other material, within the proscenium opening; the portal works like a mat around a painting, providing a visual transition between the choreographer's stage picture and the architectural frame of the proscenium.

Presenting Organization

Local organization that contracts with independent performing-arts groups; the "presenter" usually promotes the attraction, sells tickets, and books the theatre; the visiting group is usually guaranteed a minimum fee for performing and sometimes receives a share of box-office receipts.

Preset

In stage lighting, the ability to set all dimmers at the levels required for a particular cue, in advance of executing the actual lighting change.

Producing Organization

Organization that creates its own work for performance; management typically includes an administrative staff and an artistic staff.

Proscenium Theatre

"Picture-frame" theatre, where auditorium and stagehouse occupy separate volumes; the audience views the performance through the proscenium arch, which frames the opening in the wall between auditorium and stage.

Purchase Line

Manila line pulled by a stagehand operating a counterweight-rigging set; pulling the line (which is tied to a counterweight arbor) moves an attached rigging batten and its load of hanging scenery or other equipment.

Rake
Slope of stage or auditorium and balcony floors; rake may be expressed as an inclined plane, dished surface, or series of stepped platforms; a raked stage floor slopes from the upstage end down towards the stage apron.

Register
Grille or louvered panel at the mouth of a heating or air-conditioning duct; the register directs the flow of air entering a room.

Renovation
Making an old building new again; refurbishing a building to serve the same purpose for which it was originally built.

Repertoire
Dance company's stock of works available for performance; also *repertory*, a performance schedule in which a company offers various programs on an alternating or rotating basis.

Restoration
Returning a damaged, altered, or deteriorated space to its original appearance.

Rigging Set/Line Set
Rigging batten and all lines and associated equipment required for its operation.

Risers
Vertical surfaces between the treads in a stairway, or between stepped platforms.

Riser Diagram
Drawing showing the layout of a building's electrical, plumbing, or ventilating system; an electrical-riser diagram for a theatre shows basic circuitry plus components of the entire electrical system, including stage and house lighting, sound systems, and emergency power.

Road Box
Large crate on wheels, used to ship a touring company's scenery, costumes, equipment, and other paraphernalia.

Roof Steel
Structural-steel framework that supports the stagehouse roof, and to which the grid and loftblocks are often attached.

Running Crew
Stagehands who work during a performance, rather than in backstage construction shops or during load-in and load-out.

Scenery
Built or painted elements of the stage picture, including backdrops, wagons, and flats.

Scrim
Loosely woven curtain, opaque to the audience when lit from the front, yet nearly transparent when only objects behind it are lit.

Section Drawing
Scale representation of a vertical slice through a space or structure.

Sheave

Grooved wheel or pulley over which a rigging line passes when changing direction; part of a loftblock or headblock.

Side Lighting

Lighting aimed at the performing area from the wings, to model dancers' bodies.

Sightlines

Theatre geometry that plots an audience's view of the performing area; by analyzing vertical and horizontal sightlines, a theatre designer predicts the views offered by different seats in the house.

Sleepers

Strips of lumber placed at regular intervals to form the substructure for a resilient finished floor.

Sound-Effects System

Combined equipment that distributes recorded music and sound effects throughout the auditorium.

Sound-Reinforcement System

System that amplifies sound from the stage and distributes it throughout the auditorium.

Spotting a Line

Using individual lines to rig special items—such as a banner or chandelier—for which a full-length batten is too long; loftblocks are placed where needed on the grid floor, and a single hemp line supports the object being "spotted."

Stage

The performing area and those offstage areas in its immediate vicinity, all bounded by the stagehouse walls.

Stagehand

Any stage-crew member who works with scenery, props, sound, or stage lighting.

Stagehouse

In a proscenium theatre, the structure containing the performing area and offstage space. The term is generally reserved for theatres with full-height, counterweight rigging systems or a low-grid rigging system.

Stage Left

To the left of a performer facing the audience (to the right of the audience).

Stage Right

To the right of a performer facing the audience (to the left of the audience).

Straight-Lift (Single-Purchase) Counterweight Rigging

Rigging system in which the vertical run of a counterweight arbor equals the vertical distance traveled by a flying batten.

Strike

To dismantle and load-out a production following a performance run; to remove a piece of stage equipment from its playing position.

Synchronous Winch System

Rigging system in which more than one electric motor is used to raise and lower a single load.

T-Bar System

Counterweight-rigging system employing T-shaped steel tracks; the tracks guide counterweight arbors as they slide up and down the stagehouse wall.

Thrust Theatre

Theatre where the performing area projects into the auditorium and is surrounded by seating on three sides.

Tormentor Boom/Torm

Vertical steel pipe in the wings, to which stage-lighting fixtures are attached for side lighting.

Traps

Removable sections of stage floor, allowing access to the performing area from below (traps are rarely used in dance).

Traveller

Curtain that may be drawn open or closed on horizontal tracks.

Treads

Horizontal surfaces in a set of steps or stepped platforms.

Trim

Height established by a scenic designer, at which a piece of scenery, masking, or other element is intended to hang above the stage floor.

Tripping

Where grid height is too shallow to fly hanging backdrops completely out of view, the use of secondary battens to fly the bottoms of the drops.

Upstage

Rear of the performing area; that part of the stage farther from the audience.

Valance

At the top of a traditional proscenium arch, the fixed, decorative element framing the top of the border and grand drape; the valance hangs just downstage of the border, and may be made of drapery, fabric stretched over a frame, or of some other, more permanent material.

Viewing Room

Enclosed booth at the rear of the auditorium, from which directors, designers, and choreographers may watch a rehearsal or performance.

Vomitory

In a thrust or arena theatre, a ramped or stepped tunnel or passage giving performers access to the stage from beneath the seating area.

Wagon

Wheeled platform on which scenery is assembled and then rolled on and off the stage as a single scenic element.

Wings

In a proscenium or end-stage theatre, transition zones between the performing area and offstage, to the left and right of the stage; dancers make entrances and exits through the wings; legs (vertical masking curtains) define the wings.

BIBLIOGRAPHY

I. GENERAL REFERENCE

ARCHITECTURAL DESIGN AND DESIGN STANDARDS

Armstrong, Leslie, **The Little House.** Collier Books, a division of Macmillan Publishing Co., Inc., New York, 1979.

Barrier-Free Design: The Law. Terence J. Moakley, Editor. Eastern Paralyzed Veterans Association, New York, 1979.

Brown, Catherine, and William B. Fleissig and William R. Morrish, **Building for the Arts: A Guidebook for the Planning & Design of Cultural Facilities.** Western States Arts Foundation, Santa Fe, N.M., 1984.

Harkness, Sarah P., and Groom, James N. Jr. **Building without Barriers for the Disabled.** Whitney Library of Design, Guptill Publications, New York, 1976.

Ramsey/Sleeper. **Architectural Graphic Standards,** Seventh Edition. Robert T. Packard AIA, Editor. John Wiley and Sons, New York, 1981.

Time Saver Standards for Architectural Design Data, Fifth Edition. John Hancock Callender, Editor-in-Chief. McGraw-Hill Book Company, New York, 1974.

DANCE — GENERAL INFORMATION

Anderson, Jack, **Dance.** Newsweek Books, New York, 1979.

Banes, Sally, **Terpsichore in Sneakers.** Houghton Mifflin, Boston, 1980.

The Dance Catalogue, Nancy Reynolds, Editor. Harmony Books, New York, 1979.

The Dance Encyclopedia, Anatole Chujoy and P. W. Manchester, Editors. Touchstone Books, New York, 1978.

Contemporary Dance. Anne Livet, Editor. Abbeville Press, New York, 1978.

Louis, Murray, **Inside Dance.** St. Martin's Press, New York, 1980.

Petitjean, Pierre, **Backstage with the Ballet.** Penguin Books, New York, 1979.

Sparger, Celia. **Anatomy and Ballet,** Fifth Edition. Theatre Arts Books, New York, 1970.

THEATRE AND STAGE MANAGEMENT AND PRODUCTION

Arnott, Brian, **A Program Development Workbook: A Planning Guide for the Development of Programs for the Performing Arts.** Ministry of Culture and Recreation, Toronto, Ontario, 1979.

Association of College, University and Community Arts Administrators, **ACUCAA Handbook: Presenting the Performing Arts.** Association of College, University and Community Arts Administrators, Madison, Wis., 1977.

Baker, Hendrik, **Stage Management and Theatre Craft,** Revised Edition. Theatre Arts Books, New York, 1971.

Barrell, M. Kay, **The Technical Production Handbook: A Guide for Sponsors of Performing Arts Companies on Tour.** Western States Arts Foundation, Santa Fe, N.M., 1977.

Beck, Kirsten, **How to Run a Small Box Office.** Off Off Broadway Alliance. New York, 1980.

Ellfeldt, Lois and Carnes, Edwin, **Dance Production Handbook: Or Later Is Too Late.** Mayfield Publishing Co., Palo Alto, Calif., 1971.

Farber, Donald C., **Producing Theatre: A Comprehensive Legal and Business Guide.** Drama Book Publishers, New York, 1981.

FEDAPT, **Box Office Guidelines,** Revised Edition. The Foundation for the Extension and Development of the American Professional Theatre, New York, 1977.

Gruver, Bert A., **The Stage Manager's Handbook,** Revised Edition by Frank Hamilton. Drama Book Publishers, New York, 1972.

Langley, Stephen, **Theatre Management in America: Principle and Practice: Producing for the Commercial, Stock, Resident, College and Community Theatre,** Revised Edition. Drama Book Publishers, New York, 1980.

Lounsbury, Warren C., **Theatre Backstage from A to Z,** Revised Edition. University of Washington Press, Seattle, 1972.

Wolf, Thomas, **Presenting Performances: A Handbook for Sponsors,** Second Edition. New England Foundation for the Arts, Cambridge, Mass., 1977.

II. PLANNING AND BUILDING FOR DANCE AND RELATED PERFORMING ARTS

LONG-RANGE PLANNING FOR THE PERFORMING ARTS

Arnott, Brian, **A Facility Development Workbook: A Planning Guide for the Development of Buildings to Accommodate Non-profit Arts Activities.** Ministry of Culture and Recreation. Toronto, Ontario, 1978.

Baumol, William J., and Bowen, William G., **Performing Arts: The Economic Dilemma. A Study of Problems Common to Theater, Opera, Music and Dance.** Twentieth Century Fund. New York, 1966.

Building for the Arts. Assembled from **Architectural Record** articles. McGraw-Hill, Inc., New York, 1978.

Educational Facilities Laboratories/Council of Educational Facilities, **Community Planning Assistance Kit.** Council of Educational Facilities Planners International, Columbus, Ohio, 1980.

Golden, Joseph, **Olympus on Main Street: A Process for Planning a Community Arts Facility.** Syracuse University Press, Syracuse, N.Y., 1980.

Mayer, Martin. **Bricks, Mortar and the Performing Arts.** Report of the Twentieth Century Fund Task Force on Performing Arts Centers. The Twentieth Century Fund, New York, 1970.

Urban Innovations Group, directed by Harvey Perloff. **The Arts in the Economic Life of the City.** American Council for the Arts. New York, 1979.

THEATRE DESIGN AND PLANNING

Alberta Culture Facility Development Branch, **The Theatre Handbook: An Introduction to Planning and Design of Performing Arts Facilities.** Alberta Culture Facility Development Branch, Edmonton, Alberta, 1979.

American Theatre Planning Board, **Theatre Check List: A Guide to the Planning and Construction of Proscenium and Open Stage Theatres.** Wesleyan University Press. Middletown, Conn., 1969.

Association of British Theatre Technicians, **Theatre Planning**, Roderick Ham, Editor. University of Toronto, Toronto, Ontario, 1972.

Burris-Meyer, Harold and Cole, Edward C., **Theatres and Auditoriums**, Second Edition. Robert E. Krieger Publishing Co., Inc., Huntington, N.Y., 1975.

Department of the Army, **Design Guide for Music and Drama Centers.** (DG 1110.3.120). Issued by Engineering Division, Military Programs Directorate, Office of the Chief of Engineers, U.S. Army, under contract with Hardy Holzman Pfeiffer Associates, New York, Jules Fisher and Paul Marantz, Inc., New York, and Jaffe Acoustics, Inc., Norwalk, Conn., 1981.

Elder, Eldon, **Will It Make a Theatre? A Guide to Finding, Renovating, Financing, Bringing up-to-Code, the Non-Traditional Performance Space.** Associate writers: Marcia Imhof and Sharon Lee Ryder. The Off Off Broadway Alliance, New York, 1979.

Friedman, Daniel and Valerio, Joseph, **America's Movie Palaces: Renaissance and Reuse.** Educational Facilities Laboratories, New York, 1982.

Izenour, George C., **Theater Design.** McGraw-Hill Book Company, New York, 1977.

Mielziner, Jo, **The Shapes of Our Theatre**, C. Ray Smith, Editor. Clarkson N. Potter Inc. Publisher, New York, 1970.

Stewart, H. Michael, **American Architecture for the Arts.** Handel & Sons Publishing, Inc., Dallas, Tex., 1978.

SOUND SYSTEMS AND ACOUSTICS

Burris-Meyer, Harold; Mallory, Vincent; and Goodfriend, Lewis S., **Sound in Theatre.** Theatre Arts Books, New York, 1979.

Collison, David, **Stage Sound.** Drama Book Publishers, New York, 1976.

Egan, M. David, **Concepts in Architectural Acoustics.** McGraw-Hill Book Company, New York, 1976.

Mankovskii, Viktor S., **Acoustics of Studios and Auditoria.** Christopher Gilford, Editor. Hastings House, New York, 1971.

SCENIC DESIGN AND STAGE TECHNOLOGY

Bellman, Willard F., **Scenography and Stage Technology: An Introduction.** Harper & Row Publishers, New York, 1977.

Burris-Meyer, Harold and Cole, Edward C., **Scenery for the Theatre: The Organization, Process, Materials and Techniques Used to Set the Stage**, Second Revised Edition. Little, Brown & Co., Waltham, Mass., 1972.

Gillette, A. S., and Gillette, J. Michael, **Stage Scenery: Its Construction and Rigging.** Harper & Row Publishers, New York, 1981.

Pecktal, Lynn, **Designing and Painting for the Theatre.** Holt, Reinhart and Winston, Inc., New York, 1975.

Schubert, Hannelore, **The Modern Theatre: Architecture, Stage Design, Lighting.** Praeger Publishers, New York, 1971.

Wilfred, Thomas, **Projected Scenery: A Technical Manual.** Drama Book Publishers, New York, 1965.

STAGE LIGHTING

Bellman, Willard F., **Lighting the Stage: Art and Practice.** Harper and Row Publishers, New York, 1967.

Bentham, Frederick, **The Art of Stage Lighting.** Theatre Arts Books, New York, 1967.

Bongar, Emmet W., **Theatre Student: Practical Stage Lighting.** Rosen Press, New York, 1971.

McCandless, Stanley, **A Syllabus of Stage Lighting.** Drama Book Publishers, New York, 1964.

Pilbrow, Richard, **Stage Lighting,** Revised Edition. Drama Book Publishers, New York, 1979.

Reid, Frances. **The Stage Lighting Handbook.** Theatre Arts Books, New York, 1976.

Rosenthal, Jean and Wertenbaker, Lael. **The Magic of Light.** Little, Brown & Co., Waltham, Mass., 1973.

Sellman, Hunton D., **Essentials of Stage Lighting.** Prentice-Hall, Inc., Englewood Cliffs, N.J., 1972.

Warfel, William B., **Handbook of Stage Lighting Graphics.** Drama Book Publishers, New York, 1974.

Welburg, Albert F. C., **Theatre Lighting: An Illustrated Glossary.** Drama Book Publishers, New York, 1979.

COSTUME DESIGN

Dryden, Deborah M., **Fabric Painting & Dyeing for the Theatre.** Drama Book Publishers, New York, 1981.

Ingram, Rosemary and Covey, Elizabeth, **The Costumer's Handbook.** Prentice Hall, New York, 1980.

Motley, **Designing and Making Stage Costumes.** Prepared by Elizabeth Montgomery, Sophie Devine, Margaret Hains. Watson Guptill Publications, New York, 1964.

Prisk, Bernice, **Stage Costume Handbook.** Greenwood Press, Westport, Conn., 1979.

Russell, Douglas A., **Stage Costume Design—Theory, Technique and Style.** Appleton Century Crofts, New York, 1973.

Troster, Frantisek, **Costume on the Stage.** Artia, Prague, Czechoslovakia, 1962.

Wilcox, R. Turner, **The Dictionary of Costume.** Scribner & Sons, New York, 1969.

INDEX

Aaron Davis Hall, 20
  lobby, 48
Acoustics
  bibliography, 184
  defined, 173
  problems in alternate spaces, 44
Adaptive reuse, defined, 173
Administrative offices, 83
AIA/Codes and Standards Division, 161
Aisle, width, 53
Alternate spaces, 10
  acoustical treatments, 44
  backstage facilities, 71
  basic decisions, 23-24
  building codes, 25
  construction, 27
  control booth, 99
  dimming system, 98
  draperies, 97
  exterior checklist, 25
  heating and ventilation, 44
  house lighting, 99
  inspection by engineer, 24
  interior checklist, 25-26
  masking, 97
  master plan and budget, 26-27
  minimum space requirements, 42, 44
  offstage requirements, 44
  performance lighting, 98
  renting versus owning
    building, 23-24
    sound and lighting equipment, 99
  ripping systems, 97-98
  safety violations, 25-26
  seating arrangements, 55
  site selection, 24
  sound system, 99
  stage floor, 44
  track lighting, 138
  zoning regulations, 25
American Ballet Theatre
  sample light plot, 92
  wardrobe room on tour, 78
American Guild of Musical Artists
  arrival of cases at dressing stations, 51
  on rehearsal floors, 69
  transportation to places of performance or rehearsal clause, 16
American Institute of Architects, summary of architect's and owner's responsibilities during construction, 21
Apron, 11, 29, 32
  dancers taking bows, 29
  defined, 173
Architect
  responsibilities during construction, 21
  selection, 21
Architectural Graphic Standards, 73
Architecture Transportation Barriers Compliance Board, 161
Arena stage, 11
  access, 10
  defined, 173
Armstrong, Leslie, 26
Arts Accessibility for the Deaf, 163
Arts-planning expert, 15
Ashamu Dance Studio, Brown University, color scheme, 57

Backdrop, defined, 173
Backstage
  access of handicapped people, 165
  administrative offices, 83
  alternate spaces, 71
  carpentry department, 75-76
  costume departments, 77-78
  defined, 36, 175
  electrical department, 79, 82
  heating and ventilation, 59
  lighting, 61
  lounge and canteen, 67
  mailing and duplicating rooms, 83
  performer circulation, 37
  physical therapy room, 67
  rehearsal space. *See* Rehearsal studios
  sound insulation, 59, 61
  see also Crossover; Offstage
Balanchine, George, on space, 9
Balcony
  Crouse-Hinds Theatre, 116
  Filene Center, 136
  Grand Opera House, 131-132
  house, 53
  in lobby, 50
  State Theatre, 126
Ballet West
  hanging log sample, 86
  see also Capitol Theatre
Barrell, M. Kay, portable dance flooring, 36
Barres
  portable, Joyce Theater, 103
  rehearsal studio, 70
  warm-up room, 62
Barrier-free design, 161
Basketweave floor, 34
Batten, defined, 173
Battleship linoleum
  permanent flooring, 34
  portable flooring, 36
Bella Lewitzky Dance Company, rehearsal studio, 69
Bergman, Eugene, 163
Bessie Schonberg Theatre.
  See Dance Theatre Workshop
BeVard Community Room, 111
  color scheme, 57
  facts about, 155
  longitudinal section, 117
  plan
    entry level, 115
    street and stage levels, 114
Bidding, 21
  defined, 173
Blues Armory, feasibility studies, 19
Boom, defined, 173
Borders, defined, 173
Box office, 49-50
Brooklyn Academy of Music, Opera House, proscenium, 100
Brown, Carolyn, on choreography and space, 11
Brown, Trisha
  on dressing rooms, 59, 140
  on lack of amenities in small dance companies, 141
  on purchasing 541 Broadway, 139
Brown University, Ashamu Dance Studio, color scheme, 57

Budget, items in, 26
Building codes
  alternate spaces, 25
  defined, 173
  lobbies, 52
  requirement examples, 17
  wiring stage lighting, 94
Building permit, defined, 173
Building program
  decisions for design implementation, 171
  defined, 173
  heating-ventilating-cooling systems, 17
  identification of needs, 17
  operating and maintenance costs, 17
  organization, 170
  preparation, 17
  sample, 18
Building program, 16-17, 21

Cahan, Cora
  on finances of small company, 101
  on fly tower, 102
  on stagehands' union negotiations, 101
Canteen, 67
Capitol Theatre, 107, 152
  facade, 106
  facts about, 152
  lobby, 106
  longitudinal section, 109
  plans
    balcony, 108
    basement, 109
    orchestra and street level, 108
  proscenium arch, 107
Carbon arc, defined, 174
Carpentry department
  house carpenter office, 75
  properties, 76
  scene painting shop, 75-76
  scenery shop, 75
Carpets, offstage and backstage floors, 37
Carrier Theatre, 111, 154
  electrical batten, 86
  facts about, 154-155
  plan, street and stage levels, 114
Catwalk rigging system, 90-91
Changeover, defined, 174
Changing room
  for costume shop, 77
  rehearsal studios, 71
Childs, Lucinda, performing at St. Mark's, 140
Choreography
  dancer's body dimensions as building block, 9
  defined, 9
  placement of dancers and description of space, 10
  for small or alternate spaces, 11
Circuit, defined, 174
Circuit breaker, defined, 174
City College of New York. See Aaron Davis Hall
Civic Center of Onondaga County, 111
  County Office Building plans
    first floor, 115
    terrace, 116
  facts about, 153
  marquee, 110, 153

  sound insulation, 59
  see also BeVard Community Room; Carrier Theatre; Crouse-Hinds Concert Theatre
Cleveland's Music Hall, basketweave portable floor, 36
Client, defining, 15
Coat checkroom, 52
Cohen, Matthew, on New Performance Gallery, 148
Color media, defined, 174
Concessions, 53
Construction, 21
  alternate spaces, 27
  decisions for design implementation, 171
  performed by dancers, 26
Construction documents, 26
  defined, 174
  measuring material quantities, 26
Construction manager, role, 21
Contract documents. See Construction documents
Contractor
  dance group as, 26-27
  responsibilities, 21
Control console, defined, 174
Control room, 79
  alternate spaces, 99
  elevation, 80
  Joyce Theater, 103
  location, 80
  in renovation projects, 80
  Theatre C, 119-120
  windows, 81
Corridors
  backstage, 61
  chamfered corners, 61
  size, 61
  as temporary storage, 61
Cost consultant, 15
Costume departments
  costume shop, 77
  wardrobe room, 78
Costume design bibliography, 185
Counterweight arbor/carriage, defined, 174
Counterweight-rigging system, defined, 174
Crossover
  defined, 37, 173
  floor, 37
  size, 37
Crouse-Hinds Concert Theatre, 111-113, 153
  facts about, 153-154
  longitudinal section, 117
  plan
    balcony level, 116
    entry level, 115
    street and stage levels, 114
  stage, 117
  stage floor construction, 35
Cue, defined, 174
Cunningham, Merce, 11
Cyclorama, defined, 176

Dance companies, comparative table
  personnel types and requirements, 12
  size and touring equipment, 85
Dance Theatre of Harlem, 12
Dance Theatre Workshop, 142-143

  allied services, 142
  light focusing, 142
  longitudinal section, 143
  performance area, 142
  plan, 143
  rehearsal studio, 142
Dancers, demands of work space, 9
De Lavalade, Carmen, 8
Deck, defined, 174
deGroat, Andy, performing at The Kitchen, 24
Design development phase, 21
  decisions for design implementation, 171
  design team, 21
Dimmer, defined, 175
Dimmer bank/rack, defined, 175
Dimmer-per-circuit system, defined, 175
Dimming equipment room, 82
Dimming system, 94
  alternate spaces, 98
Downstage, defined, 29, 175
Draperies, alternate spaces, 97
Dressing rooms, 62, 66-67
  costume storage, 66
  dressing tables, 62, 66
  fixture requirements, 62
  lack of at 541 Broadway, 140
  lighting, 66
  lockers, 64, 66
  plan, State Theatre, 64
  shoe storage, 66-67
  showers, 66-67
  space requirements, 62
  toilets, 66-67
Dressing tables, 62, 66
  size, 62
  two-sided, 65
DTW. See Dance Theatre Workshop
Dunn, Douglas, studio, 141
Duplicating rooms, 83

Elder, Eldon, 23, 53
Electrical department
  control room, 79
  dimming equipment room, 82
  film projection booth, 79
  followspot booth, 79, 82
  lighting workshop and storage, 82
  sound requirements, 82
  viewing room, 79
Electrical outlets
  dressing room, 66
  rehearsal studios, 71
Electronic memory lighting control, defined, 175
Elevator
  receiving and loading area, 75
  to grid floor and counterweight-loading platforms, 37
Elgin Theatre, renovation, 101
Emmons, Beverly
  minimum height for proper lighting, 42
  on nontraditional space, 11
End-stage theatre, 10-11
  defined, 175
Feasibility study, 15-16
  arts program study, 169
  financial study, 169
  renovation, 16
    Blues Armory conversion, 19

187

State Theatre, 120
site/building study, 169
Feld Ballet. *See* Joyce Theater
Feld, Eliot
   on fly tower, 101
   tilting rehearsal studio mirrors, 69
Filene Center, 132-133
   house, 136-137
   longitudinal section, 137
   plan
      balcony, 136
      orchestra and support level, 136
   stage floor, 134
   stage set, 135
Filene Center II, 134, 159
   facts about, 159
Film projection booth, 79
Fire curtain, defined, 175
Fitting room, for costume shop, 77
541 Broadway, 139-141
   David Gordon's studio, 140
   Douglas Dunn's studio, 141
   lack of dressing rooms, 140
   Trisha Brown's studio, 139-140
504 and the Performing Arts, 173
Flat, defined, 175
Floor
   rehearsal studio, 69-70
   stage. *See* Stage floor
   Trisha Brown's studio, 137-138
Fly floors, 87, 175
Fly gallery, defined, 175
Fly space, defined, 38, 175
Flying, defined, 38, 175
Fold-back system, 95
   defined, 177
Followspot, 93-94
   defined, 177
Followspot booth, 79, 82, 93-94
   size, 81
Found space. *See* Alternate space
Four-walls rental house, defined, 176
Front-of-house, defined, 176

Garage. *See* Parking areas
Golden, Joseph, on popularity of Civic Center
   of Onondaga County, 59, 111
Gordon, David
   541 Broadway, 139
   cost of renovation, 140
   on lack of dressing rooms, 140
Graham, Martha, performing, 28
Grand drape, defined, 176
Grand Opera House, 129-130, 157
   before renovation, 129
   box office, 50-51
   catwalk, 130
   ceiling cove, 23
   facts about, 157-158
   foyer for box office, 50
   fresco designs, 127
   front-of-house lighting, 127-128
   lobby, 51
   longitudinal section, 133
   low-grid rigging system, 127
   orchestra shell, 130
   plan
      balcony, 132
      orchestra and street level, 132
   proscenium boxes, 22
   renovation, 131
   rigging system and pinrail, 84
   seating risers formwork, 23
   specifications for floor construction, 45-47
   stage, 131
      floor construction, 35, 45-47
      layout, 22
Grid, defined, 176
Grid floor, 89
Grid height, defined, 176
*Guide in the Planning of Theatres and
   Public Building Auditoriums*, 93

Hammond, William, on site selection, 15
Handicapped people
   arrival at theatre, 161, 162, 163
   barrier-free design, 161
   deaf, 163
   defined, 161
   door clearance, 162
   drinking fountains, 164
   lobby design, 163
   pay telephones, 164
   seating, 163-164
   toilets for, 52, 165
   visually impaired, 163
   wheelchair lifts, 162
Hanging plan
   defined, 176
   sample, Ballet West, 86
Hardwood, defined, 176
Headblock, 89
   defined, 176
Headblock beam, defined, 176
Heating-ventilating-cooling systems
   alternate spaces, 44
   backstage spaces, 53
   costs, 17
   defined, 176
   duct placement, 37
   temperature maintenance, 36-37
Hemsley, Gilbert
   on building design, 21
   on rehearsal space, 67
   on stage space, 31
House, 53, 55
   acoustics, 55
   balconies, 53
   horizontal sightlines, 53-54
   jack for headset connections, 55
   vertical sightlines, 53, 55
House curtain, defined, 176
HVAC. *See* Heating-ventilating-cooling
   systems
Hydraulic stage lift, defined, 176
In Search of Design, 9
Inside Dance, 53
Intercom, 97
   defined, 176
Jacob's Pillow, 12
Joyce Theater, 101-102, 151
   control room, 103
   facade, 102
   facts on, 151
   longitudinal section, 105
   plans
      basement level, 105
      orchestra and street level, 104
      upper level, 104
   portable barres for rehearsal, 103
   renovation of Elgin Theatre, 101
   seating capacity, 13
   stage, 103
Jumper cables, defined, 177
Kitchen Center for Video, Music, Dance
   and Performance, 24
Lamp, defined, 177
Laundry, for costume shop, 77
Le Blond, Richard, on heating and
   ventilation, 59
Legs, 85
   defined, 177
Lighting
   backstage, 61
   dressing rooms, 66
   house, alternate spaces, 99
   rehearsal studios, 71
   stage. *See* Stage lighting
   workshop and storage, 82
Lighting booth, control console, 94-95
Lighting instrument, defined, 177
Lighting ladders, 96
   defined, 177
Light plot
   American Ballet Theatre, 92
   defined, 177
   small modern dance company on tour, 92
Little House, The, 26
Lincoln Center, parking areas, 49
Line set, defined, 179
Loading area. *See* Receiving and loading area
Loading bridges, 89
   defined, 177
Loading dock, height, 73
Load-in/Load-out, defined, 177
Lobby, 50, 52
   Aaron Davis Hall, 48
   balconies and grand stairs, 50
   building codes, 52
   coat checkroom, 52
   concessions, 53
   Grand Opera House, 51
   and the handicapped, 163
   New York City Center, 101
   New York State Theatre, 52
   provision for late-comers, 50, 52
   public toilets, 52
   size, 50
   State Theatre, 123
   State University of New York at
      Purchase, 118
   support spaces, 53
   Zellerbach Hall, 50
Lockers
   in lobby, 52
   room plan, State Theatre, 64
Loftblock, 87
   defined, 177
Louis, Murray, on Zellerbach Hall, 53
Lounge, for dancers, 67
Lucinda Childs Dance
   Company rehearsing, 141
Luminaire, defined, 177

Mailing room, 83
Maintenance costs, 17
Mali Theatre, Leningrad, orchestra pit, 43
Margaret Jenkins Dance Company, 146
Marley, portable flooring, 36
Martin, Elizabeth, on site selection, 16
Masking, 85
    alternate spaces, 97
    catwalk rigging system, 90
    defined, 177
Merce Cunningham Studio, 144-145
    longitudinal section, 145
    plan, 145
Mirrors
    lack of at 541 Broadway, 140
    rehearsal studios, 69-70
Music. *See* Orchestra pit; Sound systems
Music library, 42

National Ballet of Canada, finish floor, 34
National Ballet School, finish floor, 34
National Center for a Barrier-Free
    Environment, 161
New Performance Gallery, 146-148
    annex, 147-148
    lobby, 146
    performance space, 146, 148
    plan
        ground floor, 149
        second floor, 149
        transverse section, 149
New York City Ballet, 12
    painting a drop, 76
    rehearsal schedule, 60
    see also New York State Theatre
New York City building code
    lobbies, 52
    seating in alternate spaces, 55
New York City Center, 101
New York State Theatre, 13-15
    dressing room, 58
    lobby, 52
Nutcracker, The, 32

Oberlin Dance Collective, 146
Offstage
    alternate spaces, 44
    crew and choreographer circulation, 37
    defined, 36, 177
    pass door, 37
    performer circulation, 37
    stage left, 37
    subflooring, 37
    see also Backstage; Crossover
On center, defined, 177
On stage, defined, 177
Opera, working height needs, 39
Orchestra pit, 39, 42
    acoustical requirements, 42
    fully raised, 41
    height, 39, 42
    intermediate position, 41
    lowest position, 41
    Mali Theatre, Leningrad, 43
    support spaces, 42
    undercut, 42
    width, 42
Orchestra shell, defined, 177
Owning. *See* Renting versus owning

Paging system, defined, 178
Paint frame, defined, 178
Parking areas, 49
    for handicapped, 161, 162, 163
Patch panel, defined, 178
Performance monitoring, defined, 178
Performing area
    defined, 178
    see also Stage space
Perlman, Itzhak, on access of handicapped, 161
Physical therapy room, 67
Piano, storage space, 42
Pin rail, defined, 178
Pit. *See* Orchestra pit
Planning
    bibliography, 183-184
    evaluation of inventory, 168-169
    inventory of group's needs and resources,
        167-168
Portal, defined, 178
Power source, for television control truck, 82
Presenting organization, defined, 178
Preset, defined, 158
Producing organization, defined, 178
Properties, 76
Proscenium theatre, 9-11
    arch, 38
    Brooklyn Academy of Music Opera House,
        100
    Capitol Theatre, 107
    defined, 178
    empty, 30
    floor plan of performace area, 31
    in full operation, 20
    height, 38
    proportions for arch, 39
    stagehouse. *See* Stagehouse
    stage masking and stage picture size, 38
    Theatre C, 116
    width, 38
Purchase line, defined, 178

Rake, defined, 179
Ramps
    for handicapped, 163
    receiving and loading area, 75
Receiving and loading area, 73, 75
    direct line with stage, 73
    elevator, 73
    loading dock, 72-74
    number of bays, 75
    ramps, 75
    sorting space, 75
Register, defined, 179
Rehearsal schedule, New York City Ballet, 60
Rehearsal studio, 67-69
    barres, 70
    changing rooms, 71
    choreographer's niche, 69
    draperies, 70
    floor, 69
    lighting, 71
    mirrors, 69-70
    New York School of Ballet, 69
    number needed, 71
    observers, space, 69
    size, 68-69
    stage monitor and paging override, 71

    storage area for sound equipment, 69
    typical dimensions, 70
    Vagarova School of the Kirov Ballet, 58
Renovation
    Capitol Theatre, 105-107
    defined, 181
    Grand Opera House, 129
    New York City Center, 101
    State Theatre, 123
    see also Feasibility study, renovation
Renting versus owning
    building, 23-24
    sound and lighting equipment, 99
Repertoire, defined, 179
Resilient pad base, 34
Restoration, defined, 179
Rigging batten, 86
Rigging set, defined, 179
Riser diagram, defined, 179
Risers, defined, 179
Road box, defined, 179
Roof steel
    beam spacing, 87
    defined, 179
Rueger, Charles
    on barres, 70
    on finish floor, 34
Running crew, defined, 179

Safety violations, alternate spaces, 25-26
St. Mark's Church, the Bowery, 140
San Francisco Ballet Building, 21
    administrative offices, 83
    construction, 23
    rehearsal studio, 21
Scene painting shop, 75-76
Scenery, 85
    defined, 179
Scenery shop, 75
Schematic design phase, 21
    decisions for design implementation, 171
School of American Ballet, finish floor, 34
Scrim, defined, 179
Seating
    alternate spaces, 56
    capacity and expressivity, 11
    continental, 53, 55
    David Gordon's studio, 140
    and the handicapped, 163-164
    radial aisle, 55
    rights of patrons, 49
    widths, 53
Section drawing, defined, 179
Sewing area, for costume shop, 77
Sheave, defined, 180
Showers
    dressing room, 55-57
    plan, State Theatre, 64
Side lighting, defined, 180
Sightlines, defined, 180
Single-purchase counterweight rigging,
    defined, 180
Site selection, 15
    alternate spaces, 24
    dancers' needs, 16
Sleepers, defined, 180
Sound effects, 95
    defined, 182
Sound insulation, 59, 61

cross-sections, 63
plan and vertical section, 63
Sound reinforcement, 95
defined, 182
Sound systems, 39, 95, 97
alternate spaces, 99
bibliography, 183
consultant, 55
control booth, 82
Dance Theatre Workshop, 142
fold-back, 95
intercom, 97
performance monitoring and paging, 71, 95, 97
Sound Transmission Coefficient rated construction, 61, 63
Space, George Balanchine on, 9
Speakers, locations, 55
Spotting a line, defined, 180
Spraying room, for shoes and slippers, 78
Spring box base, 34
Stage
access of handicapped people, 165
Carrier Theatre, 111
Crouse-Hinds Theatre, 117
defined, 180
Joyce Theater, 103
Theatre C, 119
Stage entrance, 73
Stage floor, 31
alternate spaces, 44
battleship linoleum, 34, 36
bearing pressure of dancers, 32-33
Capitol Theatre, 106
causing stress, 32
color, 35
Dance Theatre Workshop, 142
Filene Center, 134
maintenance, 32
portable flooring, 36
substructure
coil springs, 34
fiberglass blocks in compression, 35
rubber pads, 34, 139
substructure, 32, 34-35
Theatre C, 118
traps, 35
types, 34
Stagehand, defined, 180
Stagehouse
defined, 180
defined, 38
fly space, 38
grid height. *See* Stagehouse, working height
height, 40
low-grid, rigging system and pinrail, 84
State Theatre, 123
working height, 38-39
Stage left, defined, 180
Stage lighting, 90, 93-95
alternate spaces, 98
bibliography, 183-185
dimming systems, 94, 98
equipment mounting, 93
541 Broadway, 140
followspots. *See* Followspots
front-of-house, 91, 93

Grand Opera House, 127
light plot
for American Ballet Theatre on tour, 92
small modern dance company on tour, 92
lighting control console, 94-95
lighting ladders, 95
wiring devices, 94
Stage rigging, 86-89
alternate spaces, 97-98
backdrop during load-in, 89
catwalk rigging system, 90-91
dead hung pipe grid, 98
double-purchase rigging system, 90
hanging log sample, 86
high-grid stagehouse, 86-87, 90
Joyce Theater, 102
low-grid stagehouse, 84, 90, 127
motorized winches, 89, 90
single-purchase rigging system, 90
Stage right, defined, 180
Stage space, 29-32
alternate spaces, 42, 44
apron, 29 32
dimensions, 31
exit needs, 31
Stairs, in lobby, 50
State Theatre, 123, 127, 156
dressing room, locker room, toilet and showers, 64
facts about, 156-157
loading dock, 74
lobby, 122, 124-125
longitudinal section, 127
plan
balcony level, 126
basement level, 124
orchestra and state level, 125
seating for handicapped, 164
State University of New York at Purchase
central lobby, 118
site plan, 118
see also Theatre C
Storage room, adjacent to orchestra pit, 42
Straight-lift counterweight rigging, defined, 180
Strike, defined, 180
SUNY Purchase, *see* State University of New York at Purchase
Synchronous winch system, defined, 180

T-bar counterweight rigging, 86-88
defined, 181
Technical Production Handbook, The, 35
Telephones, for handicapped, 165
Television taping
clean feed, 82-83
control truck power source, 82
Temperature, performance and rehearsal spaces, 36
Ter-Arutunian, Reuben on space, 9
Theatre
size, 11
types, 9-10
Theatre C, 118, 155
control room, 119
facts on, 155-156
finish floor, 34
longitudinal section, 121

plan
box level, 120
entry and control room level, 120
main support and state level, 120
rear of house and side boxes, 119
stage, 119
stagehouse, 118
see also State University of New York at Purchase
Theatre-design expert, 15-16
Thrust theatre, 10
defined, 181
see also Apron
Time-Saver Standards for Architectural Design Data, 73
Toilets
dressing room, 66-67
plan, State Theatre, 64
public, 52
for handicapped people, 52, 167
number and sex, 52
Torm, defined, 181
Tormentor boom, defined, 181
Trap, 35
defined, 181
Traveller, defined, 181
Treads, defined, 181
Trim, defined, 181
Tripping, defined, 181

University of California at Berkeley. *See* Zellerbach Hall
Upstage, defined, 181

Valance, defined, 181
Viewing room, 79
defined, 181
Villella, Edward
on showers, 66
on use of dressing rooms, 62
Vomitory, defined, 181

Wagon, defined, 181
Wardrobe room, 78
Warm-up room, 61-62
Water fountains, for handicapped, 165
Wax, 37
Wheelchairs, space requirements, 163
White, David, on performance space at DTW, 142
Will It Make a Theatre?, 23, 53
Wings, 32
defined, 183
Wolf Trap Farm Park. *See* Filene Center II
Working drawings, decisions for design implementation, 171
Working height, 38-39

The Yard, Chilmark, Mass., 134

Zellerbach Hall, 17
lobby, 50
relationship between audience and stage, 53
Zoning regulations, alternate spaces, 25

CREDITS

Page		Photographer
Cover		Lois Greenfield
3		Martha Swope
4	below	Paula Court
5	above, right	Martha Swope
5	below	Jack Mitchell
8		Philip Leonian
12	top	Martha Swope
	bottom left	Martha Swope
	bottom right	Stephen Driscoll
14		Esto/Ezra Stoller
15	above	Esto/Ezra Stoller
15	below	Esto/Ezra Stoller
16	above	Esto/Ezra Stoller
16	below	Esto/Ezra Stoller
17	above	Morley Baer
20	above	Esto/Ezra Stoller
20	below	Richard Sexton
21	above	Tony Plewick
21	below	Tony Plewick
22	above	Grand Opera House
22	below	Grand Opera House
23		Richard Sexton
24		Paula Court
24		Paula Court
25		David Richardson
28		Martha Swope
36		Tim Buchman
43		Leslie Armstrong
48		Esto/Ezra Stoller
50		Vernon DeMars
52		Esto/Ezra Stoller
53		Vernon DeMars
57		Michael Boyer
62		Martha Swope
66		Martha Swope
67		Martha Swope
69		Martha Swope
71		David Richardson
72		Martha Swope
73		Martha Swope
75		Martha Swope
76		Martha Swope
78	above, right	Martha Swope
78	below, left	Martha Swope
83		Richard Sexton
84		Alan Buchsbaum
86		Cultural Resources Council of Syracuse and Onondaga County
87		Martha Swope
96		Martha Swope
100		Brooklyn Academy of Music
101		David Richardson
102		David Richardson
103	above, left	David Anderson
103	above, right	David Richardson
103	below	David Anderson
106		Roger Morgan Studio, Inc.
107	left	Salt Lake Convention and Visitors' Bureau
107	right	Salt Lake Convention and Visitors' Bureau
110		Cultural Resources Council of Syracuse and Onondaga County, Inc.
111		Cultural Resources Council of Syracuse and Onondaga County, Inc.
112		Cultural Resources Council of Syracuse and Onondaga County, Inc.
113		Cultural Resources Council of Syracuse and Onondaga County, Inc.
117		Cultural Resources Council of Syracuse and Onondaga County, Inc.
118	above	Norman McGrath
118	below	Norman McGrath
119	above	Norman McGrath
119	below	Norman McGrath
122		Foto Arts, Inc./William Gesten
124		Foto Arts, Inc./William Gesten
125		Foto Arts, Inc./William Gesten
127		Roger Morgan Studio, Inc.
128		Ron Solomon
129		Grand Opera House
130		Ron Solomon
131	above	Ron Solomon
131	below	Alan Buchsbaum
134		Michael Zide
135	above	Bill Maris
135	below	Bill Maris
137		Bill Maris
138		R. Alexander
139	above	David Richardson
139	below	David Richardson
140	above	David Richardson
140	middle	David Richardson
140	below	Babette Mangotte
141		Babette Mangotte
142	above	David Richardson
142	below	David Richardson
143		David Richardson
144		David Richardson
145		David Richardson
146		Tanner and Van Dine Architects
147	above	Tanner and Van Dine Architects
147	below	Tanner and Van Dine Architects
148		Tanner and Van Dine Architects
151		David Anderson
152		Salt Lake Convention and Visitors' Bureau
153	above	Salt Lake Convention and Visitors' Bureau
153	below	Cultural Resources Council of Syracuse and Onondaga County, Inc.
154		Cultural Resources Council of Syracuse and Onondaga County, Inc.
155		Norman McGrath
157		Roger Morgan Studio, Inc.
158		Ron Solomon
159		Bill Maris

725.822   Armstrong, L.
A736s   Space for dance